Unbaptized God

The Basic
Flaw in
Ecumenical
Theology

ROBERT W. JENSON

FORTRESS PRESS   MINNEAPOLIS

FOR CARL

UNBAPTIZED GOD
The Basic Flaw in Ecumenical Theology

Copyright © 1992 Augsburg Fortress. All rights reserved. Except for brief quotations in critical articles or reviews, no part of this book may be reproduced in any manner without prior written permission from the publisher. Write to: Permissions, Augsburg Fortress, 426 S. Fifth St., Box 1209, Minneapolis, MN 55440.

Scripture quotations unless otherwise noted are from the New Revised Standard Version Bible, copyright © 1989 by the Division of Christian Education of the National Council of the Churches of Christ in the United States.

Cover and interior design: Pollock Design Group

Library of Congress Cataloging-in-Publication Data

Jenson, Robert W.
    Unbaptized God : the basic flaw in ecumenical theology / Robert W. Jenson.
        p.   cm.
    Includes bibliographical references and index.
    ISBN 0-8006-2607-9 (alk. paper)
    1. Christian union.   2. Theology, Doctrinal.   I. Title.
BX8.2.J46   1992
262'.001'1—dc20   92-7930
                                                                    CIP

The paper used in this publication meets the minimum requirements of American National Standard for Information Sciences—Permanence of Paper for Printed Library Materials, ANSI Z329.48-1984.   ∞™

Manufactured in the U.S.A.   AF 1-2607

96   95   94   93   92   1   2   3   4   5   6   7   8   9   10

Contents

Acknowledgments

A decisive part of the research behind this book was made possible by the Lutheran Theological Seminary in Gettysburg, which granted me sabbatical leave to do it, and by the Aid Association for Lutherans, which supported the work with a Franklin Clark Fry fellowship. It is a considerable loss to scholarship that these excellent fellowships are no longer given.

Much of that sabbatical was spent at the Institute for Ecumenical Research at Strasbourg. Because of the close connection between the project of this book and the institute's major study of "Basic Differences" between the separated churches, Blanche Jenson and I were granted the exceptional privilege of living in the institute and setting up workspace in its library. We are most grateful for the support of all connected with the institute, which went far beyond the call of duty. Particularly we must thank Professor Harding Meyer, then director of the institute, and Professor André Birmelé for making these arrangements and for essential guidance and discussion. These two friends were and remain reference points for all my reflections on ecumenics.

In every one of my books I have thanked Blanche Jenson. It is time, I think, to say more. In my judgment, both our names should appear as coauthors on most of those books. She, however, does not agree. The best I can do, therefore, is state the reasons for my view. Through the course of my theological work, I have had few thoughts or insights that she has not suggested or occasioned. We have carried on a theological discussion and debate daily over thirty-eight years, which is one year more than we have been married. Her research, moreover, has provided an indispensable part of my knowledge. Thus in Strasbourg we sat each at our desk space from nine to five, reading each our stack of documents and essays, for discussion over supper at one of Strasbourg's splendid restaurants. So it has gone.

Introduction
The Frustration of Dialogue

I

The occasion of this book is the specific current frustration of ecumenical dialogue. For three decades the contemporary form of dialogue has been conducted with passion and great learning, in multilateral and bilateral formats and at all levels and in all corners of the ecumene. It has become a labor of intensive scholarship to keep even roughly informed. The dialogues' achievements, moreover, have been arresting.

In dialogue between the main churches divided by the Reformation, the old questions are either insofar resolved as no longer plausibly to be church-divisive or are believed by responsible participants to be capable of such resolution. A typical report came early from international dialogue between the Roman Catholic Church and the Anglican communion. Having listed the chief items of historical controversy, the commission wrote, "Although we are not yet in full communion, what the Commission has done has convinced us that substantial agreement on (all) divisive issues is now possible."[1] Nor has dialogue between East and West failed to produce once undreamed-of concord.[2] In the train of the dialogues it is thus regularly affirmed at the highest churchly levels "that the division which then took place did not strike to the heart of the common root and that our common belief goes essentially deeper and reaches further than what divides us."[3]

Yet the restoration of unity at Christ's table has been achieved only between groups whose separation there was never fixed. Across the actual great divides true churchly fellowship has come no nearer.

The frustration is not simple disappointment that encompassing fellowship has not been so speedily restored as ecumenical enthusiasm must wish. If some did once entertain overly naive hopes, no particular disasters were needed to disabuse of them, only calmer reflection. But also reasonably founded hope is now disappointed by the repeated experience that successful ecumenical labor does not ameliorate separation. Nor can we quietly accept this disappointment. For the

1. Anglican-Roman Catholic International Commission, *Final Report,* Introduction, 2.
2. For a typically remarkable case, Finnish Orthodox-Lutheran dialogue unveiled the doctrines of deification and justification as versions of the same truth! Honnu T. Kamppuri, ed., *Dialogue between Neighbors* (Helsinki: Luther-Agricola Society, 1986).
3. Jan Cardinal Willebrands, "Confessio Augustana: A Form of Encounter," *Lutheran-Roman Catholic Discussion on the Augsburg Confession: Documents 1977–1981,* ed. Harding Meyer (Geneva: Lutheran World Federation, 1982), 56. Or we may cite the pastoral letter of the German Roman Catholic bishops on the same occasion. "We are happy to discover not simply a partial consensus on some truths but rather a full accord on fundamental and central truths" ("Thy Kingdom Come," ibid., 55).

conviction that fueled initial passion remains true. "To have the right to live in separated churches, one must know with exactitude that this is unambiguously demanded for the sake of the gospel. It does not suffice, only to lament that we are perhaps after all not quite unanimous. . . . Church-divisive differences must be demonstrated and not merely presupposed."[4] That believers are one body because we eat of one loaf, belongs to the substance of our believing; where we cannot share the Eucharist, our very faith is in question.

The experience of frustration has at least three modes, only one of which will occupy this book. One is posed by the problem of reception, of traversing the distance between agreement achieved in ecumenical commissions and the knowledge and will of the churches themselves.[5] A second frustration is that of churchly authorities who have received the dialogue results, but who can envisage no actual sacramental or institutional moves toward reunion that would not make matters worse instead of better.

A sheer temporal immobility of the churches may well be the chief ecumenical problem. Nor should this immobility be attributed merely to sin or sociologically explicable lethargy, though there is plenty of both to deplore. Churchly stability is itself a deep and interesting theological question, closely related to those this book will discuss.

Nevertheless, a third mode of frustration will provide my thread: an experience of the dialogues themselves. The dialogues, whether multilateral or bilateral, have necessarily begun their work with the heritage of division: with the occasions and products of the schism between East and West and of the condemnations of the Reformation. That is, their work has begun with an assigned program of doctrinal and spiritual conflicts. It has been the supposition of the dialogues that as these conflicts were worked through, the divisions of the eleventh and sixteenth centuries could begin to heal. Moreover, as the dialogues have progressed from item to item of traditional controversy, each one taken up has, in its own terms, in fact proved insofar ameliorable as no longer to appear in itself church-divisive, at least to most participants in the discussions.

Within the West, the key items of the program have been those that once actually did accomplish the division of the churches, namely, those over which in the sixteenth century the parties formally condemned one another. These Reformation-era anathemas have been worked through with insight and painstaking scholarship,

---

4. Walter Kasper, "Zur Frage der Anerkennung der Ämter in den lutherischen Kirchen," *Evangelium—Welt—Kirche*, ed. Harding Meyer (Frankfurt: Otto Lembeck, 1975), 409.
5. The distance between the positions reached in ecumenical dialogue and what is acceptable by the churches can now conveniently and depressingly be measured by perusing the official churchly responses to the one great report of multilateral dialogue, *Baptism, Eucharist and Ministry*, as these are gathered in *Churches Respond to BEM*, ed. Max Thurian, 6 vols. (Geneva: World Council of Churches, 1986–88). Reading vols. 2 and 6 will suffice; vol. 6 contains the response of the Roman Catholic Church and vol. 2 has somehow accumulated the responses of a high percentage of major Protestant bodies. With most of the latter, it is hard to know whether one should be more dismayed by the obliviousness with which they maintain traditional denominational positions, or by their sheer theological lack of imagination. See, for example, the responses of such by no means negligible bodies as the (Lutheran) Church of Norway or the United Church of Canada, both in vol. 2.

and at the highest theological level, by a specific dialogue devoted to them, by an appointed commission of leading Evangelical and Catholic German ecumenists. Here I need cite only the comprehensive recommendation. "Even in the situation of that time," the old condemnations did not result from "fully clarified material understanding on both sides"; and "in any case" they "do not touch the opposite party as it now is. . . . The Joint Ecumenical Commission therefore urges the governing bodies of the respective churches to declare officially that the condemnations of the 16th century do not touch the opposite party of today, in that neither party's teaching is now determined by the errors which the condemnations sought to ward off."[6]

II

Just so, however, the strange frustration has occurred. As the dialogues have worked down the program of controversies, and as each traditional controversy has in the event been mitigated, its divisive power has seemed merely to rise from it and settle elsewhere; nor is the process terminated by completing the program, since the process seemingly proves circular. On each traditionally disputed item, the dialogues have sought what has come to be called convergence, a narrowing of the distance between differing positions to the point where a particular dispute can no longer be incompatible with fellowship inside one churchly communion. And such convergence has, with almost monotonous consistency, been regularly achieved. But from each remaining small and apparently tolerable divergence, an urgent reference has emerged to some other topic on the agenda, causing a newly virulent division within that topic. And with that topic it has gone the same way, and so on, finally back to the beginning.

Thus the chief more advanced dialogues between Roman Catholicism and churches of the Reformation (the international and North American dialogues with Lutherans, the international dialogue with the Anglican communion, and the unofficial French Roman Catholic-Protestant dialogue of the Groupe des Dombes) have followed a remarkably similar course.[7] All began by ascertaining, explicitly or implicitly, that the great Reformation disagreement about justification by faith had been reduced to manageable proportions. As the initial report in 1972 of international Lutheran-Roman Catholic dialogue put it, "At this point the traditional polemical disagreements were especially sharply defined. Today, however, a far-reaching consensus is developing in the interpretation of justification."[8]

6. Ökumenischer Arbeitskreis evangelischer und katholischer Theologen, *Lehrverurteilungen—kirchentrennend?*, ed. Karl Lehmann and Wolfhart Pannenberg (Freiburg: Herder, 1886), 1:195.

7. See André Birmelé, *Le salut en Jésus Christ dans les dialogues oecuméniques* (Paris: Cerf, 1986), 321–88. Of all these, the work of the Groupe des Dombes has often been pioneering of solutions later ecumenically adopted; see Birmelé, *Le salut*, 326 and below. The international official dialogue between Roman Catholicism and the Reformed tradition, whose two reports, *The Presence of Christ in Church and World* (1977) and *Towards a Common Understanding of the Church* (1990), do not present formal accords, has in general retraced the course of the Lutheran-Roman Catholic dialogues; see Birmelé, *Le salut*, 322–27. It must also be said that their results are by comparison meager and platitudinous.

8. Joint Lutheran-Roman Catholic Study Commission, *The Gospel and the Church* (1972), 26.

If the separation once produced by differing understandings of justification has produced still-effective occasions of division, these must, it appeared, be located in other doctrines; and such were suspected in the doctrines of Christ's presence in the Eucharist and of the Eucharist's sacrificial character. So the dialogues turned to these questions and achieved remarkable agreements about them, only to discover that just these agreements made disagreements about the doctrine of ministry newly menacing. And, as traditional differences on this matter were amazingly diminished, the struggle about justification was rekindled at a new, ecclesiological level— as what, it now appears, remaining differences really contain.[9]

If any two of the great confessions should reach satisfactory agreement about *all* the items on their list of traditional disputes, the very discussion that achieved this would generate some new question, in order to continue the division. The dialogues' initial supposition, that it is their task to engender convergences, to move the two sides of each old dispute so toward one another that the remaining distance can be born within one fellowship—is itself now called into question. No set of convergences ever seems to be enough, once the separations are there. Dissensus that would not have sufficed to divide the united church is, evidently, sufficient to perpetuate existing division, and seemingly not only illegitimately.

The structure of achieved convergence and remaining difference has been re-markably uniform throughout the dialogues. On each topic taken up, a statement of agreed understanding is eventually offered, which is to be sufficient or basic or something of similar import. For example, the North American Lutheran-Catholic report on justification reads: "Our entire hope of justification and salvation rests on Christ Jesus and on the gospel whereby the good news of God's merciful action in Christ is made known; we do not place our ultimate trust in anything other than God's promise and saving work in Christ. This excludes ultimate reliance on our faith, virtues, or merits, even though we acknowledge God working in them."[10]

Then doctrinal differences, it is said, remain. Looking at the same case, the Catholic doctrine of justification is said to describe the transformation of the believer by Christ's grace,[11] while the Reformation doctrine is about the essential

---

9. A Roman Catholic who has contributed greatly to the achieved consensus-statements summed up the situation. "Il nous semble que . . . la question de la justification continue de se poser, mais cette fois sous une forme nouvelle. Il ne s'agit plus du sola fide . . . mais bien plutôt du role de l'Église dans l'acte de justification. . . . L'Église est-elle extérieure à la justification? L'étude des discussions théologiques appuyant les dialogues oecuméniques en cours, même au plus haut niveau, montre qu'ici deux visions s'affrontent, et qu'elles touchent au point précis ou naissent nos divisions." In deliberately crass formulation: "L'opus gratiae (la justification) vient-elle à Deo solo ou est-elle à Deo et ab ecclesiae?" (J. M. R. Tillard, "Vers une nouvelle problématique de la 'Justification'?" *Irenikon* 55(1982): 1856–87. It is no wonder that, in a review of this same history, Otto Herman Pesch, an advanceman and founder of the early consensus on justification, asked: "Ist die ökumenisch-theologische Arbeit an dem Thema (justification), mit dem vor spätestens drei Jahrzehnten das ökumenisch-theologische Gespräch in seine hoffnungsvollste Phase einzutreten schien, inzwishen zur hoffnungslose Sysiphus-Arbeit geworden?" ("Rechtfertigung und Kirche," *Ökumenische Rundschau* 37[1988]: 22–23).

10. *Justification by Faith*, vol. 7 of *Lutheran and Catholics in Dialogue*, ed. H. George Anderson, T. Austin Murphy, and Joseph Burgess (Minneapolis: Augsburg, 1985), 4.

11. Ibid., 20.

character of the saving gospel itself.[12] Over against the stated agreement, however, the differing theologies are judged mutually tolerable,[13] and not to impede the judgment that a fundamental consensus has been reached.[14]

But in between, pages are devoted to worries about what the theology of the other side may lead to. A leading participant's summary of this dialogue says that Roman Catholics fear Lutheran teaching "can lead to a lack of concern for holy living," while Lutherans fear believers in Catholic doctrine may be "tempted to turn . . . inward in search of evidence that God has infused grace, and thus . . . subvert the affirmation that they should ultimately rely only on God's promises in Christ."[15] This typical characteristic of the dialogues is a matter to which I wish to attend. What at each point of convergence remains between the confessions are the fears that each side has about the temptations to which the teaching of the other may be exposed. And this is regularly made explicit, especially in accounts that responsible participants give of the dialogues' course and result.

We may take Harding Meyer's authoritative descriptions of the more general consensus about justification as paradigmatic in their reference to *fears*. The Catholic and the Reformation positions are "two . . . lines" that are "determined by specific concerns and corresponding fears"; achieved consensus consists in discovering that these lines nevertheless "cross over, meet, and mutually support each other."[16] In the case of the doctrine of justification, mutual suspicions have to do with a main point of the reformers' doctrine, its place over against other formulations, and topics of Christian truth. "Even though Catholics could say that the doctrine of justification presents an appropriate explication of the gospel's center, which cannot simply be exchanged for other theological models . . . there has nevertheless not finally been any unanimity about the systematic place of the doctrine."[17] But in summary: "The certainly present differences do not reach so far that the one doctrinal position overlooks, to say nothing of denying, what the other emphasizes; or intends, to say nothing of proposing, what the other fears."[18] In these very precise formulations, note that the convergence is satisfactory while the fears remain. But why, if each position is acknowledged appropriate to the gospel, should there be fears? Where do they come from?

For an example of authoritative use of the category of *temptation* to describe remaining divergence, we may cite Bernard Sesboüé in the national dialogue between French Catholicism and French Protestantism. "If the Catholic Church

---

12. Ibid., 95.
13. Ibid.
14. Ibid.
15. George Lindbeck, "Justification by Faith: An Analysis of the 1983 Report of the U.S. Lutheran-Roman Catholic Dialogue," *Partners* 6, no. 6 (1985): 10. For a clear general account of the matter generally, see pp. 9-12 of this article.
16. Harding Meyer, *Lutherische Rundschau* 19:478–79.
17. Ibid.
18. Harding Meyer, "Rechtfertigung im ökumenischen Dialog: Eine Einführung," *Rechtfertigung im Ökumenischen Dialog,* ed. Harding Meyer and Günther Gassmann (Frankfurt: Otto Lembeck, 1987), 44.

is naturally tempted to overemphasize its bond of unity with Christ . . . are not the churches of the Reformation tempted to hold the Church at a distance from its founding event, for the sake of an immediate and purely 'spiritual' bond with the Holy Spirit?"[19] But why, if each position is satisfactory to its holders, should they regard its solicitations as temptations?

The 1986 report of this French dialogue can provide a remarkable paradigm for the entire present situation of dialogue. Locating, as has itself become usual, their continuing discomfort with one another in the understanding and experience of the church, French Catholics and French Protestants pose a desperate question. "How does it happen that common confession of the same symbols of faith . . . including their third articles on the Spirit and the church, and the fundamental agreement now achieved on justification by grace through faith, does not issue in a fundamentally common ecclesiological conception and practice?"[20] How indeed?

Our situation has not proved to be like that of the old councils. For these dealt with *threatened* separations, and as often as not themselves created separation by defining heresy and imposing the anathema. The evil against which the modern dialogues have to formulate common confession is, very differently, existing separation itself. What can be the form and object of the confession that such dialogue is to achieve? Amelioration of the clash between existing opposed positions can only be a necessary preliminary, which must at some stage be broken off for reflection or action at another level. The achieving of convergences is vital but proving to be endless; the decisive step must apparently be the achieving of a quite different sort of common understanding and confession. We need, it appears, mutual understanding that transcends the old conflicts and does not merely ameliorate them.

III

Such experience, often repeated, recently led some ecumenists to revive an old supposition:[21] that there is, between each pair of separated confessions, a "basic difference,"[22] or "basic decision,"[23] underlying the apparent occasions and manifestations of division. It has come to seem that the traditional conflicts between any two of the great confessions must be only symptoms and manifestations of

---

19. Bernard Sesboüé, "Nos différences ecclésiales: leur enjeu dans la recherche de l'unité: Analyse catholique," Comité mixte catholique-protestant en France, *Consensus oecuménique et différence fondamentale* (Paris: le Centurion, 1987), 62.

20. Comité mixte catholique-protestant en France, *Consensus oecuménique et différence fondamentale* (1986), 7.

21. For a useful quick summary of the history, see Birmelé, *Le salut,* 276–87.

22. Again the French: "Actuellement on se demande de plus en plus de divers côtés si ces contentieux nesont pas sous-tendus par un clivage plus profond, que l'on appelle souvent 'différence fondamentale' " (Bernard Sesboüé, "Nos différences ecclésiales," 45).

23. Joseph Cardinal Ratzinger has both in one sentence. He lists, on request, the usual menu of disputes, and then continues, "Eine solche Aufzählung kontroverser Lehrstücke löst aber nur die Frage nach dem Gruntscheid aus: Beruht dies alles auf einer Grunddifferenz, und wenn, lässt sie sich benennen?" ("Luther und die Einheit der kirchen: Fragen an Joseph Kardinal Ratzinger," *Communio* 12[1983]: 572–73).

difference hidden at some conceptual level deeper than that occupied by the traditional matters of controversy. Walter Kasper, an early Roman Catholic ecumenist, was also early in saying: "One cannot understand any of the churches . . . by listing specific doctrines. One must understand each by its total conception of the faith. . . It is quite possible that only now, after having eliminated mountains of misunderstanding and having begun to resolve many if not most particular problems, we will discover the true fundamental difference. One cannot say in advance if the ecumenical question will thereby become easier or harder."[24]

The French can again be paradigmatic. Although they agree not only in large tracts of formerly controversial theology but also in identifying any basic remaining area of difference, they then acknowledge that they cannot even give the same priority to the various elements of that area; what seems church-divisive to the one party does not seem so to the other.[25] The same phenomenon has been observed in other dialogues.[26] The French conclude from this: "We follow different patterns of thought and comprehension."[27]

A very considerable effort of scholarship and analysis was recently directed to search for such basic differences.[28] At the time of writing, the discussion seems to be dying down, but we may be certain that it will flare up again, probably under some other slogan, until consensus is achieved at the level to which the search for basic differences (by whatever title) leads. I hope to contribute to that effort in this book, but with two somewhat idiosyncratic expectations.

First, the suggestion that something like a basic difference must exist is often made in an ecumenically pessimistic, or even malicious, fashion. Exactly to the contrary, it is a hypothesis of my work that precisely the most fundamental flaws, if they can be clearly delineated, will prove not divisive of churchly fellowship.[29] This does not by itself mean that *no* differences are actually or legitimately church-divisive, only that the problems at the source of our conflicts—the basic problems— are not. Indeed, it is my hypothesis that clearly stating the basic flaws will itself help remedy our divisions. I cannot argue this hypothesis now; the success or failure of the whole book must be the argument.

24. Walter Kasper, "Das Petrusamt in ökumenischer Perspektive," *In der Nachfolge Christi* (Freibourg, 1980), 103–4.

25. Comité mixte catholique-protestant en France, *Consensus,* 13: "Nous ne donnons pas la même valeur aux différents éléments de cette différence, au point que ce qui apparait primordial et séperateur pour les uns, semble compatible avec la communion pour les autres, et réciproquement."

26. E.g., International Reformed-Roman Catholic Dialogue, *Towards a Common Understanding of the Church* (1990), 92: "We find, among other things, that we disagree about what issues are serious enough to be church-dividing."

27. Ibid , 15.

28. Perhaps most intensively by the Institute for Ecumenical Research at Strasbourg, under Lutheran auspices.

29. André Birmelé has made the same point, though perhaps with somewhat less enthusiasm; *Le salut,* 308–20. The danger is that which Birmelé warns against: "L'analyse de la différence fondamentale pour devenir un certain 'culte' de celle-ci et fonctionner comme une securité" (Sesboüé, "Nos différences ecclesiales," 47). The hope that the basic differences will not prove church-divisive is, of course, the motive behind the Strasbourg institute's study.

Second, I do not anticipate that the basic problems will in fact turn out to be *differences*. There is indeed something amiss in the basement that constantly generates occasions of division. But this need not be a difference; it can just as well be a disastrous unanimity.

While I cannot at this point fully present or argue the proposal I intend to make, readers should have some advance indication of it. Within a grasp of reality shaped by the Bible, the concepts by which we interpret reality generally (the basic concepts) are determined by the apprehension of God. I will argue that Christendom cannot now help but be riven by interpretive cross-purposes, because we have together stopped halfway with the faith's great spiritual-intellectual challenge, the new interpretation of God by the specific Christian message of the gospel. Our common apprehension of God is only partly Christian, and this generates dialectics in the church's history that must constantly compel choice between false alternatives. Thus the underlying reason of our compulsions to disagree is that we are together in deficit before a common task. And nothing prevents us from taking this up anew and with each other.

IV

The limits of such reflection I propose to undertake should already be clear. As Jan Cardinal Willebrands, who has given his life to ecumenism, has said, clearly we will never arrive at the point where "one more dialogue" will reunite the churches.[30] Nor can a book aimed to serve dialogue be the breakthrough. Indeed, those most responsible for the unity of Christ's church often think we have arrived at a wall through which we cannot break at all, that a new specific act of God's grace is needed. Joseph Cardinal Ratzinger, prefect of the Roman Congregation for the Faith, has said that only from "a new depth of faith"[31] can the churches overcome their separation; and it can surely be ecumenically agreed that faith is not in our power.

God may just now be teaching us what we can truly do about the church's unity: We can wait for it. That is, we can pray for it, and we can as churches live in and by the expectation of God's act to grant it.[32] Such counsel is not a recommendation of inactivity, however. If we thoughtfully, specifically, and continuously prayed for the church's unity, each party would find itself praying for specific changes in its own life. These might well be granted. And were we to set out to order our separated churchly lives by the concrete expectation of restored unity, all parties would have more than enough reforming to occupy a generation or two. To name only one matter for my own Lutheran confessional group: If we really

30. As well as on other occasions, in conversation with the author, Rome, 22 April 1988.

31. Joseph Cardinal Ratzinger, in conversation, Rome, 19 April 1988. It is not arbitrary that I cite him; we may see ecumenism's frustration personified in this prefect of the Roman Congregation for the Faith. He was a pioneering ecumenist and architect of Vatican II, and his continuing ecumenical longing and hope should not be questioned. Indeed, precisely in the exercise of his office he has been accused of closet Lutheranism. Yet by virtue of his duties in his present position of responsibility for the unity of Roman Catholicism, he is widely seen as a roadblock to ecumenism.

32. Ibid.

expected some day to be reunited with Orthodoxy or Roman Catholicism, how would we now order our episcopacy?

Moreover, *theology* comes just so into its own. For events of grace are not invisible or inaudible. A new event of God's graceful providence and of our faith must be a concrete transformation of the means of grace and of our response; it will be a visible and audible liturgical, homiletical, and church-political revolution. And if we cannot accomplish the event itself until God accomplishes it, we can prepare its theological way; we can reform our understanding and concepts to receive it. It is to that work of preparation that I hope to call the dialogues, and to which I hope by this study to contribute.

V

Where then do the lines run at which basic problems may be expected? To understand the current ecumenical situation and its frustration, we must first grasp that these are only two functioning divides in modern ecumenical dialogue.

The one is between East and West, established by long centuries of divergent development, and accidently become enduringly divisive of sacramental fellowship by the excommunications of 1054. The line is genuinely between East and West. There are, of course, enormous differences between Orthodox attitudes and relations to the Roman Catholic Church and their attitudes and relations to Protestant churches, but the fundamental divide is antecedent to the West's internal divisions. The experience of an early Anglican delegation to the Orthodox is typical. "One phenomenon which the Anglicans encountered and which caused some of them surprise . . . was that the points of theological disagreement did not mostly occur over Protestant or Reformation doctrine. . . . The main difference was between the Western Latin and the Eastern Greek theological traditions. The Anglicans found themselves defending St. Augustine and St. Thomas Aquinas more often than Luther or Calvin or Cranmer."[33]

The other line is the division within the Western church produced by the events of the sixteenth century. Contrary to what one might expect from the proliferation of Western bilateral dialogues, which cross each other organizationally in all directions, and from the mere existence of multilateral dialogues, there is again only one such line. It runs between Catholic and Protestant—between the Roman Catholic Church, together with those Protestants who on any given question support it, and what is on any given question the remainder of the Protestants. No one has longer experience of supposedly multilateral dialogue than Max Thurian, who shepherded the discussions and negotiations leading to *Baptism, Eucharist and Ministry* (*BEM*). Of that process he wrote: "Multilateral dialogue always tends to become bilateral, when specific questions are broached. We had experience of that in Faith and Order, during the discusssion of *BEM*. At first diverse traditions might express themselves around a theme, but as soon as we had to make any specific decision in order to draft a paragraph, the division was not multilateral

33. Bishop Richard Hanson, cited by Kallistos Ware in *Introduction to Anglican-Orthodox Dialogue,* ed. Kallistos Ware and Charles Davey (London: SPCK, 1977), 67–68.

but between two positions only, one more 'catholic' and the other more 'protestant'."[34]

One might antecedently have supposed that proverbially fissiparous Protestantism would manifest divisions in the dialogues that were peculiarly its own, but this has not proven to be the case. Where Protestants divide in ecumenical dialogue, this turns out to be on some line that also divides the one group of Protestants from the Roman Catholic Church and allies the other group of Protestants with it. Part of the reason for this may be that dialogue with sectarian Protestantism has not yet progressed beyond the most superficial level.[35] Perhaps the situation will change somewhat when and if such groups do come seriously to grips; the present situation, in any case, is very little shaped by the magisterial Reformation's old controversies with anabaptists and so-called enthusiasts.

One might at least have expected the old and deeply theological division between Lutheranism and the Reformed tradition to have its own dialogical place apart from the division with Rome, but it has not been so. In Reformed-Roman Catholic dialogue the same problems have appeared, and the same convergences (though far less decisively) been proposed, as in the Lutheran-Roman Catholic dialogues.[36] The one significant Reformed-Lutheran dialogue has been the European continental dialogue that issued in the *Leuenberg Concord* (*LC*), by which sacramental and ministerial fellowship has been ratified between much of the worldwide Reformed

---

34. Max Thurian, "Bapteme-Eucharistie-Ministère: Convergences théologiques, méthode et ecclesiologie," *Les dialogues oecuméniques hier et aujourd'hui*, ed. Centre Orthodoxe du Patriarchat Oecuménique (Chambésy: Centre Orthodoxe, 1985), 378. In illustration of the situation, we may note how in Reformed-Baptist conversations, the Reformed can simply join the Baptists on most ecclesially interesting points, determined by joint opposition to Rome. So the *Report of Theological Conversations sponsored by the World Alliance of Reformed Churches and the Baptist World Alliance* (1977). In bilateral dialogue, the line can sometimes fall bizarrely. Thus in international Methodist-Lutheran dialogue, on justification: "Man verweist . . . auf eine Reihe von Unterschieden, die methodistische Position so beschreiben, dass ihre Nähe zur katholischen Auffassung recht deutlich wird" ("Einführung," *Rechtfertigung im Ökumenischen Dialog*, ed. Harding Meyer and Günther Gassmann [Frankfurt: Otto Lembeck, 1987], 46). It should be noted with Birmelé, *Le salut*, 347, that this rapprochement decidedly does not translate into ecclesiology, as Lutheran-Catholic and Anglican-Catholic divergence apparently does.

35. We may note, for example, the American dialogue between Lutherans and Conservative Evangelicals, whose 1981 summary "Declaration" could on the central ecumenical problems say no more than "We acknowledge that our Lord has called us into his body, the Church. The Church lives by his gifts of grace. We acknowledge the importance of baptism, the Lord's Supper, and the exercise of spiritual discipline in the Church, without having attained a consensus concerning the definition of those ministries and offices" (*The Covenant Quarterly* 41, no. 3 [1983]: 7). Roman Catholicism has been holding dialogue with every group that will, and the reports are appearing. Or we may note the near total vacuity of the common statements on *Divine Initiative and Human Response, Baptism and the Theology of the Child*, and *Church and Ministry* achieved during three years of American Baptist-Lutheran dialogue (*American Baptist Quarterly* I[1982]: 103–13). Or again, five years of international Roman Catholic-Baptist dialogue have now reported, with what is in many ways a splendid expression of Christian unity, but which arrives at no convergences whatever (*Summons to Witness to Christ in Today's World* [1988]).

36. The "analogy between the Reformed-Catholic dialogues and the Lutheran-Catholic dialogues is remarkable" (Birmelé, *Le salut*, 326).

communion and German-speaking Lutheranism.[37] In retracing the history of this dialogue, it is impossible to avoid the impression that its agreements in large part came to pass as the posit of a common front against Rome.[38] And a remarkable phenomenon appeared around this dialogue, which confirms the judgments just made. I will display the phenomenon on one critical issue.

The chief ancient quarrel between Reformed and Lutheran Christianity has been, of course, about Christ's presence in the Eucharist. Throughout the negotiations that led to Leuenberg and in the concord itself, the key move that enabled the seeming termination of this quarrel was that the "real presence" was no longer to be "grasped in a static or physical manner; 'body' and 'blood' designate the *person* of Jesus Christ. . . . The accord is not established by agreement in any certain mode of Christ's presence by the bread and wine but in an understanding of what happens during the celebration of the Supper. The real presence is grasped in a *dynamic* and *actualist* fashion."[39] (emphasis added) The goal and result were "a rejection of element- and consecration-piety," in that the "myth of locality" is overcome, whether this is the Lutheran "localisation of the sacramental gifts in the elements" or the Calvinist localization of Christ's body in heaven.[40]

But this pattern of thought, while it may have reconciled some Lutherans with their Calvinist partners, divided those Lutherans from other Lutherans. From a large set of possibilities, I may instance an early official document. "Is 'the person of Christ' really the same as 'body and blood of Christ' . . . ? Should not precisely a biblical understanding of the Lord's Supper counteract a complete dissolution of ontological elements into personalist expressions?"[41]

The point in our present connection is that precisely this same line of criticism was that taken also by Roman Catholic observers of the Leuenberg Agreement.[42]

---

37. Other European continental dialogue has simply approved the Leuenberg Agreement. The American dialogue, whose reports are contained in *An Invitation to Action*, ed. James E. Andrews and Joseph A. Burgess (Philadelphia: Fortress, 1984), is distinguished by impressive superficiality; and for justification of its recommendations it simply refers to Leuenberg.

38. Leuenberg's chief drafter, Marc Lienhard, had to remark, "Trotzdem haftet den Gesprächen so etwas wie ein anti-katholischer Zug an, als ob de Reformatorische Einheit am besten im Gegensatz zu Rom bezeugt würde" (*Lutherisch-Reformierte Kirchengemeinschaft Heute* [Frankfurt: Otto Lembeck, 1972], 71).

39. Birmelé, *Le salut*, 410–11.

40. Hans Grass, "Diskussionseinleitung," *Wort und Abendmahl*, ed. R. R. Williams (Stuttgart: Evangelische Missionsverlag, 1967), 22.

41. A circular letter of the Bavarian Lutheran Church, in *Lehrgespräch über das heilige Abendmahl*, ed. Gottfried Niemeyer (München: Chr. Kaiser, 1961), 24. The personal statement of a deeply committed Lutheran ecumenist states the problem; Albrecht Peters, "Unionistisches Mittelmass," *Von der wahren Einheit der Kirche* (Berlin: Die Spur, 1973), 153. "Doubtless it was at first a . . . clarification, that we learned better to articulate the personalist . . . relations of faith. . . . But now . . . the quarrel of the Reformation has reappeared on this new level of understanding. . . . A spiritualising variety of this personalism has appeared, which . . . in the dimension of the coram Deo flees from bodily-communicative concretion. . . . We are barely willing to celebrate the Supper, and here we venture even so far as to take seriously the acts of eating and drinking, but from the earthly elements that are eaten and drunk we keep Christ's presence as distant as possible; we will barely allow 'with,' but not 'in' or 'under,' and surely nothing like a 'praedicatio identica' between the risen Lord and a created gift."

42. E.g., Albert Brandenburg, "Der Leuenberger Konkordienentwurf in der Sicht eines katholischen

And it is this same criticism that is made of Lutheran-Roman Catholic agreements about real presence, by Roman Catholic critics who regard these as insufficient.[43]

In general, when Lutherans have criticized Leuenberg, their criticisms have been the same as those which Catholics make of Protestantism on the same issues; and where Reformed churchmen have responded to Lutheran critique, their criticisms of these adverse Lutheran positions have been the same as those which they make of Catholicism on the same issues. The self-consciously Lutheran position has not been a thing of its own; in dialogue, Lutheranism has simply been more Catholic than most other Protestants and more Protestant than are normal Catholics.[44] A similar phenomenon has appeared in other communions. Thus in Roman Catholic international dialogue with Anglicans, the Roman Catholics found themselves allied with particular Anglican parties on each specific question; the actual dialogue on each such question was then conducted between these catholic allies and Anglicans of a more "evangelical" sort.[45]

VI

The final purposes of this book, as of the study that prepared for it, are discovering the fundamental causes of Christian division, and using that diagnosis to open new theological paths for ecumenical dialogue. To make my diagnosis plausible, I must, of course, be able to construe the penultimate dissenses that have frustrated the dialogues. To that goal, the following seven chapters will examine the convergences and divergences that have emerged as the dialogues worked down the inherited program of disputes. The examination must, lest it all together burst the bounds of my subject, still be summary in the extreme. But we can at least follow a simple outline without undue distortion, since, as André Birmelé has exhaustively established, "The same focal points appear in all the dialogues."[46]

Theologens," *Leuenberg: Konkordie oder Diskordie?* ed. Ulrich Assendorf and Walter Künneth (Berlin: Die Spur, 1974), 167. "It must be said with all decisiveness: in the . . . question of the real presence, we can quickly come to an understanding with Luther, but not with what is here presented. So long as Luther is scolded for his doctrine of 'oral eating' . . . so long will *we* defend *Luther's* position."

43. Thus a semiofficial Roman response to the international document, Cipriani Vagaggani, "Observations au sujet du document de 1978 de la commission mixte catholique-luthérienne sur l'eucharistie," *Documentation Catholique* 1979:34, takes up points where Catholic sensibility "interrogates" Lutherans. First and foremost is "a strong sensibility for the real presence under the elements: for the fact that such a presence is the foundation which determines all the rest of the eucharistic reality. . . . One can see in the document how this sensibility probes the Lutheran confession. One has the impression that the document is overly timid in expressing the Lutheran position."

44. Often enough, Lutherans are explicit about this. E.g., the generally inept and malaprop official response of the American Lutheran Church to *Baptism, Eucharist and Ministry*, "General Observations," nr. 4: "True ecumenical advance will require careful attention to both 'Catholic' and 'evangelical' concerns. 'Baptism, Eucharist and Ministry' reflects a conceptual framework that is dominated by Catholic understandings and appears to slight evangelical understandings."

45. See the dissertation by Ravi S. Kamath, "Convergence on the Eucharist" (Diss. Gregoriana, Rome, 1977), 19–41, 83–84. In general, of course, every ecumenical division runs through the Anglican communion. The point need not be belabored; one delicious citation will suffice, from the official response of the Anglican Church of Canada to *Baptism, Eucharist and Ministry*, nr. 8: "According to the particular theological background and orientation of the individual, some Anglicans find either too much, or too little, said . . . about the presence of Christ in the elements."

46. Birmelé, *Le salut*, 470.

Because of limited time and space, I will deal directly only with the intra-Western dialogues between Catholic and Protestant in this volume. The very interesting and potentially salvific dialogues between East and West will appear only as I draw on Orthodox critique of Western alternatives and on the possibilities that Orthodoxy often poses for the overcoming of Western stalemates.

Part 1

THE EARLY ECUMENICAL
CONVERGENCES

1

Justification

I

As already noted, the problem of justification was thought no longer divisive at the beginning stage when one might have expected it to be a major concern; only at the end of the sequence of agreements on other matters has remaining divergence been found still virulent. It will nevertheless be appropriate to put my explicit discussion of justification at the beginning. That was the original order of the dialogues and it had reason: Between Catholic and Protestant, "every other consensus is built on sand, if an authentic consensus in the doctrine of justification does not support it."[1] Moreover, just such consensus was thought to be present throughout the dialogues devoted to other matters.

We will then move, on the general path of the dialogues, to Christ's eucharistic presence and the Eucharist's character as sacrifice. Then must come ordained ministry, and the ministry's ordered structure, and the magisterium this ministry possesses. Thus we will arrive at the position where the dialogues thought to discover that it is the interpretation of the church that had been dividing us all along. And here, it has appeared, the doctrine of justification again becomes divisive.

II

In this chapter I will consider the doctrine of justification in its original context. The extent of possible Catholic-Protestant agreement appears when Rome at the highest level can say of the international Anglican-Roman Catholic report on the matter: "All in all, it is our conviction, from a Roman Catholic point of view, that one has achieved an 'accord' in what concerns the principle and essential aspects of the theme. . . . What has been so far ascertained in this document clearly does not . . . authorize, with respect to the subject handled, an actual division between the Anglican Communion, so far as it explains itself in the document, and the Roman Catholic Church."[2] Moreover, Harding Meyer is undoubtedly right when he says of the more general dialogical consensus on justification, that "it is time . . . to accredit a 'dialogically definitive status' to the consensus in the doctrine

1. Ökumenischer Arbeitskreis evangelischer und katholischer Theologen, *Lehrverurteilungen—kirchentrennend?* ed. Karl Lehmann and Wolfhart Pannenberg (Freiburg: Herder, 1886), 1:43.1

2. Donato Valentini, "Contribution pour la lecteur du rapport de la Commission Internationale Anglicane-Catholique Romaine 'Le salut et l'église,' " *Service d'Information* 63(1987): 53.

of justification, which should not be always newly put in question by ever more subtle strategies of argument."[3]

As Meyer continues, one can only attribute such solidity to the existing consensus if one recognizes its precise character. We must free ourselves from "an abstract concept of consensus . . . and understand consensus in a . . . churchly sense, as agreement in the confession of faith which founds fellowship. . . . It belongs to the sign of all dialogue about justification . . . that it explicitly acknowledges continuing differences" between lines of concern that can be shown to need and not reject one another.[4]

A summary report by a theological leader of the American Lutheran-Roman Catholic dialogue can represent the consensus achieved. "The central point on which both parties agree involves both an affirmation and a negation. The affirmation is that ultimate trust for salvation is to be placed in the God of Jesus Christ alone. . . . Like all assertions, this one implies an exclusion. Trust in God alone 'excludes ultimate reliance on our faith, virtues or merits, although we acknowledge God working in them by grace alone.' "[5] In this formulation, the affirmation states a position that never was in acknowledged dispute between Christians. One might ask why then it needed to be affirmed. But the answer is plain: Because each side has feared that the other implicitly undermined it.

Thus the first part of the exclusion rejects the error to which the churches of the Reformation have feared Catholic teaching must lead—a recursive reliance of the believing person upon something in him- or herself, on "virtues or merits." Such a recursion of the person on him- or herself must be the negation of faith, since faith is precisely the person's reliant attention to an other than him- or herself; it is this recursion of the believer on what is his or hers that Reformation theology has called justification by works. The exclusion's second part rejects the errors to which Catholics have feared Reformation polemics must lead: an ultimately prideful refusal to acknowledge that God's grace does indeed work real changes in the believer's life, and that the believer may rightly note these changes and praise God for them; and reliance on faith as a subjective quality, to the denigration of reliance on God himself.

Since justification was the matter over which the parties of the sixteenth century anathematized one another, the German study of Reformation-era condemnations examined with extraordinary care the mutual accusations then made under this heading. Throughout this study, rethinking of old controversies was in general enabled by mutual acknowledgment of concerns. With respect to justification they reported:

> Today, the Catholic Church and its theology acknowledge without reservation the personal and irreplaceable character of faith, on which everything rests which happens between God and the human person, and so also all the certainty

3. Harding Meyer and Günther Gassmann, eds., *Rechtfertigung im Ökumenischen Dialog* (Frankfurt: Otto Lembeck, 1987), 55.
4. Ibid.
5. George Lindbeck, "Justification by Faith," *Partners* 6, no. 6 (1985): 8-9.

and joy of Christian existence. Today, the Evangelical Church and its theologians better understand the pastoral alarm of the Reformation's opponents, who feared, from the literal text of reforming teaching about justification, a threat to the seriousness of ethical concern.[6]

Starting from this basis, painstaking analysis of Reformation-era charges and countercharges then leads to the result.

> No one can condemn those . . . who in the experience of the misery of sin, of opposition to God, of their lack of love for God and the neighbor, in faith trust only in the savior God, are sure of his mercy, and in their lives seek to correspond to this faith—even if Christians and theologians who in the track of the Reformers think in this way, may always be asked if they do not, under the earnest of their consciousness of sin, think too little of God's recreating power. And neither can anyone condemn those . . . who, deeply impressed by the measureless power of God, emphasize the glory of God and the victory of his gracious action on us also in the event of justification, and take our failure and half-heartedness over against this gracious action for a matter of the second rank . . . —even if Christians and theologians who in the track of the Council of Trent think in this way, may always be asked if they take the misery of sin with sufficient earnest.[7]

Genuine differences had to be acknowledged, as the very formula of reconciliation just cited shows. Three in particular were seen as more than sheer "misunderstanding" or "difference of expression or linguistic usage."[8] Yet in each case, to the question "Do we really stand here before an opposition that negates consensus and compels mutual condemnation?" analysis of the nature of remaining difference led to the answer readers have doubtless already learned to expect, that neither party "overlooks" what the other "emphasizes" or "affirms" what the other "fears."[9]

One difference is that Reformation theology "defines the essence of grace . . . as a reality on God's side, 'outside us,' " and Catholics define it as "a reality in the human soul, as a 'quality' that 'inheres' in the soul."[10] Yet biblical exegesis has made both sides see the "indissoluble connection" between "those realities that in the Catholic tradition are called 'uncreated' and 'created' grace . . . and in Reformation theology are called 'forensic' and 'effective' justification."[11] Study of the theological history has made it plain that the accusations each side has made against the understanding of the other do not touch that understanding in its own intention or necessary result.[12]

Again, Catholicism and Reformation theology "have had different uses of the word 'faith,' which in the time of the Reformation made the one party stand on

6. Ökumenischer Arbeitskreis evangelischer und katholischer Theologen, *Lehrverurteilungen*, 45.
7. Ibid., 46–47.
8. Ibid., 53.
9. Ibid., 54–55.
10. Ibid., 53.
11. Ibid., 54.
12. Ibid., 54–55.

the formula 'faith, hope and love,' and the other on the formula 'faith alone.' "[13] Yet now it can be said, "What is decisive in the Reformation's understanding" of that faith by which alone we are said to be justified, "unconditional trust in the merciful God now and in the final Judgment, is for present-day Catholic theology no longer a problem."[14]

Finally, Luther asserted that the believer is "certain" of salvation and Trent flatly denied it.[15] Yet here Trent's condemnation was indeed a misunderstanding, in that the fathers of Trent supposed Luther taught one of the very positions he intended by his doctrine to attack: that the believer should take his or her own introspectively ascertained faith as evidence of God's will for him or her.[16] When such misunderstanding is cleared away, both parties can agree. "It can surely occur, that someone loses or abandons faith, that is, the giving over of him/herself to God and God's word of promise. But no one can in this last sense believe and simultaneously hold God in his word of promise for unreliable. In this sense, Luther's dictum holds . . . : faith is certainty of salvation."[17]

Yet after all this, different doctrinal modes remain, although it is denied that this divergence can now be legitimately church-divisive.[18] The German group refers to the American dialogue for specification of "a sort of basic difference . . . between two understandings of justification," which are "characterised (as) 'transformational' . . . and 'proclamatory.' "[19]

No doubt there is indeed such a difference. It is the *message* of the church, whether in audible or visible words, with which the Reformation's doctrine was concerned; and it was the work of grace in the lives of believers with which Trent and subsequent Catholic theology have been concerned. Yet surely there is an obvious pairing of these two concerns. Indeed, the Anglican-Roman Catholic dialogue has stated it. "Justification and sanctification are two aspects of the same divine act. . . . This does not mean that justification is a reward for faith or works: rather, when God promises the removal of our condemnation and gives us a new standing before him, this justification is indissolubly linked with his sanctifying recreation of us in grace. . . . God's grace effects what he declares; his creative word imparts what it imputes. By pronouncing us righteous, God also makes us

---

13. Ibid., 56. Harding Meyer has accurately stated the point. "Glaube . . .war für die Reformation nicht, wie die katholische Kritik auf dem Hintergrund mittelalterlichen Sprachgebrauchs es hörte, 'Zustimmung des Verstandes.' . . . Vielmehr verstanden die Reformatoren 'den Glauben als die durch das Verheissungswort selbst gewirkte Vergebung und Gemeinschaft mit Christus'. . . . Dieser Glaube macht den Menschen 'notwendig neu . . . und ist . . . darum nicht . . . ohne Liebe. . . .' Dennoch . . . sind es nicht die Liebe . . . sondern 'allein' der die Verheissung Gottes ergreifende Glaube, der rechtfertigt. Die Zusammengehörigkeit von Glaube und Liebe wird also lutherischerseits nicht weniger eng, sie wird aber wohl anders gesehen als auf katholischer Seite" (Meyer and Gassmann, *Rechtfertigung*, 5).

14. Ibid., 57.
15. Ibid., 59–62.
16. Ibid., 61–62.
17. Ibid., 62.
18. *Lehrverurteilungen*, 46, 75.
19. Ibid., 55.

righteous. He imparts a righteousness which is his and becomes ours."[20] A teaching in which the proclamation works the transformation looks like it should achieve convergence indeed. Yet both sides remain uneasy.

III

There is a second continuing unease. Especially Lutheran-Roman Catholic dialogues have been distressed by the inability to find agreed statements about, as the heading has come to be, "the theological-systematic weight"[21] of the doctrine of justification. The problem, already formulated by the very first round of international dialogue, has two prongs.[22]

On the one line, it could be agreed from the first that the doctrine of justification is an *indispensable* "interpretation of the center of the gospel." But Catholics have insisted that "the event of salvation to which the gospel testifies can also be expressed comprehensively in other representations derived from the New Testament, such as reconciliation, freedom, redemption, new life and new creation."[23] Nor, of course, could Lutherans deny this. Yet they have insisted that precisely the theme of justification has a peculiar "theological-systematic weight" that other soteriological themes lack. And there the question remained through years of dialogue.[24]

On the other line, it could from the first be agreed that the doctrine of justification has "implications for the life and teaching of the church" that are specific to it. But it had to be asked whether "both sides similarly evaluate" these implications. For it was the great reforming insistence of the Reformation that "all traditions and institutions of the church" must be judged by the criterion of justification, that a teaching or practice that might in any way "obscure the unconditional character of the gift of salvation" is illegitimate in the life of the church.[25] Again, that this is true in itself could be agreed from the start. But Catholics from first to last of the dialogues have pointed out that *all* doctrines have a like critical function; and have not agreed that the doctrine of justification is somehow unique in this respect.[26]

---

20. Anglican-Roman Catholic International Conversation, *Justification*, 15.
21. Lutheran-Roman Catholic Conversations, "The Malta Report," *Das Evangelium und die Kirche* (1972), 28: *"Welcher theologische Stellenwert kommt (der Rechtfertigungslehre) zu?"* The published English text reads "theological importance" for *theologische Stellenwert*, which misses entirely the point of the originally German formula.
22. Harding Meyer, "Report" (on the first session of the current round of the international Lutheran-Roman Catholic dialogue), *Lutherische Rundschau* 19:478–79: "Wenn auch von den Katholiken gesagt werden konnte, dass die Rechtfertigungslehre eine geeignete Explikation der Mitte des Evangeliums darstelle, die nicht einfach durch andere theologische Modelle austauschbar sei und die darum in der Kirche bleibende Geltung habe, and wenn auch . . . von den Lutheranern anerkannt wurde, dass der Rechtferigungslehre—schon im Neuen Testament—eine gewisse Situationsbedingtheit anhafte und es durchaus andere mögliche Explikationen des Christusgeschehens . . . gibt . . . , so gab es dennoch in der Frage nach dem Stellenwert der Rechtfergigungslehre letztlich keine Einmütigkeit."
23. Lutheran-Roman Catholic Conversations; *Das Evangelium und die Kirche*, 27.
24. For the history stated comprehensively and authoritatively, see Meyer, "Report," 60–79.
25. Lutheran-Roman Catholic Conversations; *Das Evangelium und die Kirche*, 28–29.
26. E.g., Otto Herman Pesch, "Rechtfertigung und Kirche," *Ökumenische Rundschau* 37(1988):

IV

To penetrate to the level of analysis which is the purpose of this book, illusory dissensus will need to be repeatedly cleared away by proposing ecumenical solutions at levels preliminary to that of a basic difference. Regarding justification, an elementary, persistently overlooked, and vital point exists. Indeed, nearly all remaining difficulties about justification result, in my judgment, from a mere confusion. The stubborn persistence of this confusion is itself, of course, of great interest.

Regularly in the dialogues on justification it is noted that different forms of doctrine or modes of teaching are in play. But these are nevertheless forms of teaching within the same *locus* of theology, that is, they are different answers to or different ways of answering the same question. This assumption, however, is surely false; and its hidden persistence accounts, in my judgment, for most, if not all, remaining difficulty with justification in its original context.

In the historic discourse of the church, the phrase "the doctrine of justification" is severely multivocal. The phrase's formulaic use, however, has regularly led into the unstated supposition that it must be univocal, that justification is the caption for some one problem together with its proposed solutions. This is not the case. At least three different questions with their own sets of proposed answers have, at various times, gone under the one title "justification." Confusion would not have ensued if the three questions had been merely unrelated.

As a first *locus* of doctrine labeled justification, we have the apostle Paul's question "How does God establish his righteousness among us?" together with his and others' labor to answer it. For a second *locus* labeled "justification" we have Western Augustinianism's several efforts to describe the *process* of individual salvation, to lay out the factors and steps of the soul's movement from the state of sin to the state of justice. A third *locus* under the same label—the specifically *reforming* doctrine of justification—includes the body of teaching that the American Lutheran-Roman Catholic dialogue called "hermeneutic" or "metatheological" or "proclamatory."[27] This doctrine *describes* nothing at all, neither God's justice nor the process of our becoming just. It is instead an *instruction* to those who would audibly or visibly speak the gospel, a rule for preachers, teachers, liturgists, and confessors. This instruction may be formulated: So speak of Christ and of hearers' actual and promised righteousness, whether in audible or visible words,

---

23–24: "The basic concept which brought movement into the frozen opposition of evangelical and catholic doctrines of justification, was the idea of a legitimate plurality of thoughtforms and thought-models in dealing with one and the same matter of biblical witness. . . . But one proposition of Reformation teaching about justification cannot be accommodated on this line: Luther's proposition according to which the article of justification is 'the Lord . . . and judge over all other kinds of doctrine. . . .' How so? Is the church supposed to stand or fall with one model . . . within the . . . concert of historical-relative articulations of faith's truth? Is one of them supposed to be the determining criterion over against all available old and conceivable new concepts? Catholic theologians by and large do not concede this."

27. *Justification by Faith*, vol. 7 of *Lutherans and Catholics in Dialogue*, ed. H. George Anderson, T. Austin Murphy, and Joseph A. Burgess (Minneapolis: Augsburg, 1985), 88–93.

whether by discourse or practice, that what you say solicits no lesser response than faith—or offense.

This hermeneutical doctrine can—and in the sixteenth century did—become a reforming doctrine because of its critical function. For such instruction to pastors will necessarily become polemic whenever the church solicits responses less obligating and energetic than faith, in other words, works.

When Paul's question and that of the reformers are straightforwardly set beside each other, they are not quite the same; nor then have Catholicism and the Reformation been directly in dispute over Paul's problematic. Certainly, were it not for the Pauline presence in the canon, the Western church would not have been concerned with those matters that occasioned the Reformation. What Luther and his colleagues were about, until the indulgence controversy interrupted, was a Pauline renewal of Wittenberg's theological curriculum. Nevertheless, the question to which the reforming doctrine of justification responds is not identical with that to which Paul devoted himself.

I do not say that the exegesis of Paul's doctrine of justification is not disputed; the dispute, however, is not between the confessions. Long sections in dialogue documents of Pauline exegesis about justification rarely contribute to the consensus achieved in them, and some apparent but illusory remaining dissensus may even result from their presence.

The historical relation between the second and third *loci* of justification is more complex. If patterns of proclamation or practice judged unacceptable by reforming critique are traceable to specific theological opinions, the critique will also attack those opinions. And in the sixteenth century, the reformers made the standard descriptions of the salvation-process the target of such theological polemic.

Some theologians of the Reformation have directed this sort of polemic only against particular late medieval and Tridentine accounts of the movement from sin to righteousness and have proposed their own replacements. Other theologians of the Reformation do not conceive the work of the gospel in the human soul as a process at all, and have thought that Lutheran and Reformed alternatives to late medieval or Tridentine descriptions of the process were intrinsically no more appropriate than those they replaced. But both sorts of Reformation theology were present from the beginning; and Reformation theologians of the more radical sort have yet to persuade more Augustinian colleagues to abandon their enterprise. Moreover, when Protestants do produce descriptions of the salvation-process, these do not notably differ from those currently approved by Roman Catholic theologians and available, if not dominant, at the time of the Reformation. Therefore, the second doctrine of justification is not itself a doctrine that divides Catholicism and the Reformation.

It remains that of the questions about justification only one has stood between Catholicism and the Reformation: Is the reformers' hermeneutical instruction necessary in the church, and is the critique this instruction will surely generate legitimate and needed? And if this question is kept clearly in view, if its focus is not blurred by subliminal identification with other connected but distinct questions, full consensus is now achieved. For whenever this question has been asked in its own right, Catholic participants in the modern dialogues from first to last have answered yes.

Also the problem of the justification doctrine's special critical weight loses its impact, if we keep it rigorously clear which *locus* on justification we are talking about. Every defined churchly doctrine has general critical force in the church. If, for example, an expression or practice violates Chalcedon's christological definitions, the expression or practice is not tolerable in the church. Catholic theologians have insisted upon this; surely the Reformation may take the point calmly. For the critical priority of the hermeneutical doctrine of justification can indeed not consist in a monopoly of critique, or in some quantitatively greater importance. It consists, first, precisely in the doctrine's specifically hermeneutical character, and second, in the contingently unique impact of the critique generated by the doctrine.

In that the reforming doctrine of justification is hermeneutical, its critical function occurs at a specific location, which it indeed occupies alone. The reforming doctrine of justification does not stipulate subject matters or propositions about subject matters; it stipulates *how* the church must speak, about whatever. Just, and only, so its critical work is unique. The reforming doctrine of justification does not stipulate "say such-and-such about justification." It stipulates, "If your subject is, for example, oppression, so speak of Christ and of your hearers' oppression that the only response opened is faith in Christ, or offense."

It is further undeniable that the hermeneutical doctrine of justification, once formulated, proved uniquely critical in its impact on the church's organizational life. This is, at one level, a historical contingency. The reformers might have formulated their critique under some other rubric altogether and, in their total theological work, often did. Yet it was no mere accident that the language about justification assumed a chief critical role. For a corollary of "not by works" is "the freedom of the Christian"; therefore critique of ecclesial institutions by this doctrine must directly challenge the nearest and dearest temptations of any governing establishment, also in the church. The Reformation's assertion that the doctrine of justification must be the "judge and measure," the critical principle, asserts just this eminence. It does not—or, anyway, plainly ought not—assert that no other critical principles are to be at work in the church.

Recent dialogue has moved toward the positions just taken. Thus the most recent document of the international Lutheran-Roman Catholic dialogue says:

> All our agreements on single points of justification doctrine . . . will be confirmed only if we are agreed on the fact that, and on the modality in which, the doctrine of justification is of critical significance for all of church doctrine, order and practice. But on this agreement is given. For Scripture makes it clear that the message of the justification of the sinner through faith in Jesus Christ is an irrevocable explication of the Gospel, because it witnesses to the radical gratuity of the reception of salvation and correctly describes God's free and gracious action. . . . In doctrine and theology, the special critical function of the doctrine of justification is rightly understood only when

one heeds the integrating significance of the Trinity, creation, the incarnation, and the working of the Holy Spirit.[28]

Yet it will be seen in this very statement how uncertain the writers still are about which doctrine they are discussing. In consequence, it is not evident in the statement that the grounds given for the doctrine of justification being "an irrevocable explication of the Gospel" actually entail this conclusion, or that being "an irrevocable explication of the Gospel" stipulates "the modality in which the doctrine of justification is of critical significance for all of church doctrine, order and practice." Until the underlying equivocations are repaired, such statements may be greeted as signs that the authors are guided by a correct intuition, but not as statements of achieved knowledge.

V

We will return to the subject of justification in chapter 7. For now, it may be taken as ecumenically definitive, despite all confusions and remaining divergences, that individual believers are justified only by their faith. But is the *community* of believers, the church, so justified? Once this question appeared, it was taken by many to mark the Catholic-Protestant basic difference.

---

28. International Lutheran-Roman Catholic Conversations, *Ascertaining the "Far-Reaching Consensus" on Justification.*

2

Real Presence

I

No less gratifying than convergence in the doctrine(s) of justification has been convergence in the ancient disputes about the Eucharist. To avert misunderstanding, let it be reiterated that convergence here is not between Catholic interpretation and what may have come to be thought of as typically Protestant, that is, the originally sectarian position that simply ignores or denies the necessity and efficacy of sacraments. Dialogue with normatively sacramentarian groups has, as previously noted, scarcely begun. It is Rome, Canterbury, Wittenberg, and Geneva, in their normative guises, whose convergences and divergences we can in this matter consider.

The program of inherited controversy is, How do we assert Christ's presence in the Supper? Is the Supper a sacrifice? And if so, how and by whom? This chapter takes up the first item of the menu.

Here again an established consensus exists. It appears even in the multilateral *Baptism, Eucharist and Ministry (BEM)*, though there in such cautious and open-ended fashion as to have obtained assent also from representatives of the older sectarian traditions. "The eucharistic meal is the sacrament of the body and blood of Christ, the sacrament of his real presence. Christ fulfills in a variety of ways his promise to be always with his own. . . . But Christ's mode of presence in the eucharist is unique. Jesus said over the bread and wine of the eucharist: 'This is my body . . . this is my blood. . . .' What Christ declared is true, and this truth is fulfilled every time the eucharist is celebrated. The Church confesses Christ's real, living and active presence in the eucharist."[1]

Here affirmed are: Christ's "real presence" in the Eucharist, as a personal, "living and active" presence; that the meal is the sacrament of this presence; and that being the sacrament "of the body and blood" and being the sacrament of this "real presence" somehow coincide. Note, however, how carefully the coincidence of the person, the body and blood, and the meal elements is left unspecified. As the commentary to the passage says, "Many churches believe that . . . the bread and wine . . . become, in a real though mysterious manner, the body and blood . . . of the living Christ present. . . . Some other churches . . . do not link that presence so definitely with the signs of bread and wine."[2]

---

1. *Baptism, Eucharist and Ministry*, "Eucharist," 13.
2. Ibid., "Eucharist," Commentary, 13. How necessary *BEM*'s caution is here may be seen from

Unfortunately, it is exactly this linkage that has been the ecumenical problem. As friends and foes both noted in connection with the *Leuenberg Concord* (*LC*), there is a specific basis of recent inner-Protestant agreement: a shift of attention from objects to events, from what is just *there* during the celebration of the Supper, to what *happens* in it, so that the real presence is "not grasped in a static or physical manner" but as the "dynamic and actualist" coming of Christ the living person. So far as the positive part of this intention goes, well and good. But the Catholic-Protestant question is, How does Christ's dynamic presence as person relate to the not notably dynamic and decidedly "physical" presence of the objects bread and wine (about which, after all, the promises of "real presence" are made)?

More rigorous agreement has been attained in bilateral dialogue between Roman Catholicism and the Anglican and Lutheran communities. The German anathema study provides a succinct summary of achieved results. "The exalted Lord becomes present in the Supper, in his sacrificed body and blood, with his deity and his humanity, through his word of promise, in the meal-gifts of bread and wine, in the power of the Holy Spirit, for reception by the congregation." The German ecumenists regard these results as adequately protecting the "unique, 'sacramental,' mode of the real presence . . . on the one side from . . . a naturalistic or spatially limited presence of the 'body of the Lord' and on the other side" from a subjective apprehension of the Lord's presence. And they certify that in such consensus, "all the essential elements of faith in the eucharistic presence of Jesus Christ" are stated.[3]

Typical Catholic and Protestant concerns here receive equal attention. International Anglican-Roman Catholic dialogue states this sort of mutual acknowledgment bluntly. On the one hand, classic Catholic doctrine is received. Christ's "true presence (is) effectually signified by the bread and wine which, in this mystery, become his body and blood." Here, no doubt is left but that the bread and wine mediate the personal presence that they signify, and that they do so because they become what they were not before, Christ's body and blood. "Before the Eucharistic Prayer, to the question: 'What is that?', the believer answers: 'It is bread.' After the Eucharistic Prayer, to the same question he answers: 'It is truly the body of Christ.' " And on the other hand, all this must be understood in the context of a comprehensive and manifold personal presence of Christ to his congregation.[4]

---

any number of officially Protestant responses to the document, which regularly find even its doctrine too strong. For example, the Presbyterian Church of Wales: "A real presence that is more than memorialism can be contained within a Reformed eucharistic theology, but the statement . . . 'Christ's mode of presence in the eucharist is unique,' certainly cannot . . . command general assent. . . . Here Reformed suspicions about the false understanding of symbolism and material mediation of the divine are pertinent" ("Eucharist," Q.1(c)).

3. Arbeitsgruppe der deutschen Bischofskonferenz und der Kirchenleitung der Vereinigten Evangelisch-lutherischen Kirche Deutschlands, *Kirchengemeinschaft im Wort und Sakrament* (Paderborn: Bonifatius-Druckerei, 1984), 122.

4. Anglican-Roman Catholic International Commission, *Eucharistic Doctrine* (1971), 6–7; *Elucidations* (1979), 6.

Other aspects of general consensus may also conveniently be noted in the quoted summary. The body and blood of Christ, "in" which he is personally present, are "sacrificed."[5] Here, consensus opens to the question of eucharistic sacrifice, about which it is generally agreed that many traditional positions on all sides are inadequate. The presence as body and blood has a purpose: the congregation's eating and drinking. This is a major Catholic acknowledgment of Protestant concern. The elements are *not* the body and blood for us to use according to our religious needs. Instead, they are the body and blood as means of Christ's specific self-giving, and so to be received in the meal he specified. Nor does *BEM* say, on the other side, that when the elements—indeed for the purpose of eating and drinking—once are the body and blood, *all* other uses than eating and drinking are illegitimate.

Finally, the specific eucharistic presence is "through" the word and "in" the power of the Spirit. This pairing, which has a long liturgical and theological history, is general in the dialogues.[6] For them, it was perhaps made standard by the Groupe des Dombes. "It is in virtue of the creative word of Christ and by the power of the Holy Spirit that the bread and the wine are made the sacrament and therefore the 'communication of the body and blood' of Christ."[7]

In the work of the Groupe des Dombes itself, the "Spirit/word" pairing is a piece of trinitarian doctrine. The group discovered early in its work that progress in the matters that divide Catholics and Protestants depends on robust constructive use of trinitarian doctrine[8]; and the passage cited comes from a general interpretation of the Eucharist that is trinitarian in outline and detail. Within it, the mutual efficacy of "word" and "Spirit" belongs to the perichoresis of the second and third triune hypostases.[9]

Moreover, we may note that precisely such trinitarian interpretation somehow enabled the Groupe des Dombes to reach consensus on the seemingly small point on which other dialogues have not, and which will turn out to put the entire general consensus in doubt. "That which is given as the body and blood of Christ remains given as the body and blood of Christ, and demands to be treated as such."[10]

II

Official Roman Catholic evaluations have consistently had one objection to the results on eucharistic presence of the more official major dialogues with Protestants. To *BEM:* "We have to ask, what it means for the understanding of the real presence and the reality of the transformation, when someone denies the persistence of the real presence after the celebration."[11] To the international Lutheran-Roman Catholic

5. *dahingegeben.*
6. So international Lutheran-Roman Catholic consensus, *The Eucharist* (1978), 22: "In the power of the Holy Spirit the bread and wine become the body and blood of Christ through the creative word." See also the Anglican-Roman Catholic International Commission, *Elucidations, 6b.*
7. Groupe des Dombes, *Vers une même foi eucharistique?* (1971), 19.
8. Ibid., "La doctrine du Saint-Esprit" (1965).
9. Ibid., *Vers une même foi eucharistique?* (1971), 7–16.
10. Ibid., nr. 19.
11. The Secretariat for the Promotion of Christian Unity, with the Congregation for the Faith, *Response to 'Baptism, Eucharist and Ministry'* (1987), III.B.2.

document: Catholic "sensibility . . . interrogates" Lutheran understanding about "the duration of the presence . . . and the necessity of veneration which follows therefrom."[12] And to international Anglican-Roman Catholic consensus: the document "admits the possibility of a divergence not only in the practice of adoration of Christ in the reserved sacrament, but also in the 'theological judgment' relating to it. But the adoration rendered to the blessed sacrament is the object of a dogmatic definition in the Catholic Church."[13]

It is distressing to acknowledge that the question of the temporal *extent* of the eucharistic presence can undo consensus, when that presence itself has been agreed in such seemingly clear language. Yet it turns out so in all dialogues but that of the Groupe des Dombes.

It is sometimes proposed to remove the difficulty by mutual agreement to avoid offensive practices. For the sake of those who believe that the instituted use is the only legitimate use, Catholics are to refrain from uses of the reserved host that are too obviously remote from its instituted purpose, and are to emphasize in preaching and teaching that the originating and fundamental purpose of reservation is communion of the sick. Protestants are to refrain from treating remaining bread and wine in ways offensive to those who see them still as the body and blood of Christ. But the proposals have not satisfied; disagreement about what the elements are after the celebration does in fact turn out to unravel consensus about what they are during it.

On the one side, Catholicism must worry about what someone who denies the persistence of the real presence can possibly mean when he or she asserts its occurrence at all. What sort of identification made of enduring objects, here of the bread and cup with Jesus' body, ceases to be true while the objects are still there?[14] On the other side, André Birmelé summarizes Protestant objections. Mere mutual avoidance of offensive practice "does not resolve the theological problem which resurges here: the posit of a thing-like . . . presence of Christ, separate from the sacramental celebration itself."[15]

But is not Christ's real presence as the consecrated bread and wine after all "thing-like," in that the bread and wine are obviously things? If Christ is never present in a thing-like manner, what exactly is the sense of "as" in the previous sentence? If the proposition that the objects bread and wine are the person of

---

12. Cipriano Vagaggani, "Observations au sujet du document de 1978 de la commission mixte catholique-luthérienne sur l'eucharistie," *Documentation Catholique* 1979:34.

13. Typically and perhaps fundamentally, Congregation for the Faith, "Observations on the ARCIC Final Report," *Origins* 11(1982): 754.

14. Even so enthusiastic a Roman Catholic ecumenist as Joseph Hoffmann must write: "Il nous semble en particulier que certaines façons de traiter les espèces consacrées induisent une compréhension de la présence réelle qui ne fait pas pleinement droit à l'objectivité de la conversio." Joseph Hoffmann, "Le Repas du Seigneur," *Istina* 24(1979): 377.

15. André Birmelé, *Le salut en Jésus Christ dans les dialogues oecuméniques* (Paris: Cerf, 1986), 145. For an example of a stoutly Protestant position, one may ponder the response of the Presbyterian Church of Wales to *BEM*, "Eucharist," Q.3(b): " 'Consecration' signifies the setting apart of the elements for the purpose of communion, with the result that the method of disposal is an irrelevance."

Christ does not imply that Christ is on this occasion personally an object, what is the meaning of "are" in the proposition? Yet, on the other hand, if Christ is present in a thing-like manner, as the things bread and wine, what indeed is to prevent our doing as we like with him, however remote from his intention in this self-giving? And what could such doings be, except the most blatant sort of allegedly salvific works?

Moreover, dissensus on the persistence of Christ's presence as the elements casts doubt on consensus that in the service the elements truly *become* the body and blood of Christ. For an actual *change* must happen at some time or other, so that there will be a before, when the elements were not yet Christ, and an after, when they are. But if it belongs to the eucharistic presence that the elements are Christ after some event of change, how are they not Christ in those moments after that change that also happen to be after some benediction? Does some sort of *de*consecration occur? Perhaps no bread or wine should remain after the communion, but if they do? Due to this problematic, Protestants are skittish about using the notion of change, even when they do join in affirming it.[16]

J. M. R. Tillard, himself greatly responsible for Anglican-Catholic consensus formulas, provides a nicely nuanced statement both of the contemporary Roman Catholic thinking that enables consensus and of the remaining difficulty. "Serious theological thinking has broken with the far too narrow vision that tries to identify the exact utterance after which the presence would be achieved. Today's understanding sees the efficacy of the Spirit and of the Word . . . as extended through the whole of the anaphora."

But, Tillard continues, precisely the dramatic character of the Supper's reality, "the fact that we are within a sacramental world, the laws of which will be obeyed also by the presence, should induce us to distinguish, within the plot of the rites' succession, two sacramental moments linked together in one . . . indivisible dynamism of salvation:" first a moment of consecration and thereafter the moment of reception. It is just "the fundamental fact, dominating the whole mystery of Jesus, that God is prevenient, that his gift is not only prior to human response but intends and enables it," which demands a distinction between these two sacramental moments—a nice irony in a rebuttal of Protestant positions! But between the two moments, there is then necessarily a certain "pause" in the eventful proceedings, during which an *object,* "the broken bread," is indeed "identified with the Body."[17]

Just this pause is what those on the Protestant side of the line—which, we must always remind ourselves, situates some denominational Protestants on the Catholic

---

16. So in the report of international Lutheran-Roman Catholic dialogue, *The Eucharist,* 51: "In this sense (undefined in the text!) Lutherans also could occasionally speak . . . of a 'change'." Of international Anglican-Roman Catholic dialogue, Ravi S. Kamath, "Convergence on the Eucharist" (Diss. Greg., Rome, 1977), 53, 60, observes that "evangelical" Anglicans interpret the dialogue's statement that the elements become the body and blood of Christ to mean that they become the "appointed means" for conveying Christ's body and blood to the worshippers, and rightly asks if there is genuine consensus after all.

17. J. M. R. Tillard, "Catholiques romains et Anglicans: l'Eucharistie," *Nouvelle Revue Théologique* 103(1971): 632.

side—fear. For in it not only is a thing-like presence of Christ given, to offend all who locate salvation exclusively in the spiritual, but this is a palpable presence of what Christ *sacrificed,* and admission of *such* a presence must open the most ferociously contested item on the entire Catholic-Protestant agenda of dissensus. The connection is succinctly stated by Rome's official response to *BEM.* "Jesus did not merely say, 'This is my body . . .; this is my blood. . . .' According to the New Testament he added, '. . . my body, given for you; . . . my blood, poured out for many.' In the Eucharist, Christ himself initially offers himself sacramentally to the Father, in an offering that actualizes the redemption of humankind. When he then gives himself to the faithful as the means of sacramental communion, this is to make it possible for them to unite themselves with his self-offering to the Father. Only because Christ in the offering-act of the church's liturgy gives himself to the Father, do the elements become for the communicant the sacrament of his self-offering."[18] We have arrived at the matter of chapter 3.

III

Despite all, a deep ambiguity at the heart of ecumenical consensus on the eucharistic presence seems unavoidable. As earlier noted, a churchly gremium asked the diagnostic question already about the *LC:* whether the phrase "person of Christ" really means exactly the same as the phrase "body and blood of Christ." Insofar as in consensus formulas "person of Christ"—at least as this phrase is often understood in modern theology—interprets "body and blood," Catholics draw back. And insofar as "body and blood" interprets "person of Christ," Protestants draw back.[19]

There is indeed that certain inner-Protestant consensus. We may be additionally instructed in it by an Anglican scholar and spokesman, declaring his agreement with continental Lutheran and Reformed representatives. "It seems better to accord with the dynamic character of the Sacrament to speak of the real presence that is given in act and meeting. . . . The truly present Christ uses material means for his self-giving, but his self-giving must be understood as a genuine coming, as a dynamic act, and not as a presence to which any other change in the elements pertains than that of use, meaning or value."[20] Or we may be instructed by a characterization of the *LC*'s doctrine, by the concord's chief drafter. "The real presence is understood personalistically. 'In the Lord's Supper, we do not have to do with a something, but with a someone.' "[21] Precisely this doctrine appears

18. The Congregation for the Faith, "Observations," III.B.2.
19. Even, in some cases, from the "memorial/representation" theology (see chapter 3), which from their side enables current consensus. E.g., "the theology of memorial . . . seemingly leads only in one direction, to the real presence of Christ as person, as subject and act, and to lead away from the traditional conception of the presence as object and as gift of the Eucharist" (Theodore Suss, "Dans quelle Mesure la Doctrine de la Présence Eucharistique sépare-t-elle encore les Eglises Luthérienne et Réformée?" *Positions Luthériennes* 18[1970]: 103).
20. Hugh E. W. Turner, "Das Heilige Abendmahl," *Wort und Abendmahl,* ed. R. R. Williams (Stuttgart: Evang. Missionsverlag, 1967), 13.
21. *Leuenberg Concord,* nr. 8.

whenever Protestant critics attack the sort of consensus their denominational colleagues commonly reach in dialogue with Catholicism.[22]

IV

Plainly, the difficulty is about what constitutes a person. Is a "someone" indeed not a "something"? Can a person be present where no *body* is present? And if the necessary embodiment of personhood be granted, can there be a body that is not somehow an object, a something? That is not at all static or thing-like? But if the Lord is indeed present in the Eucharist, and if for a person to be present a body must be present, and if a body must somehow be an object, do not the biblical texts specify the bread and cup as this object? At some point in this paragraph, Protestant hesitation must dissent from the ductus of questioning, or be taken after all to the Catholic position.

The disagreement is over personhood's temporal constitution. Is a personal entity sheerly actual, there for others only in the very act of self-presentation? Or does a personal entity also have persistence, even a certain static givenness? Even if this thing-like entity is perhaps there in order ever and again to be overcome in the liveliness of personal self-transcendence, does it not even so belong intrinsically to that self-transcendence?

My rhetoric will have shown that in this precise matter, I think the Catholic side is right. Protestant hesitation to affirm the thing-like presence of Christ as the objects bread and cup derives from a spiritualizing conception of personhood[23] that might be explicitly disavowed also by those who trade upon it. Protestant thought has dwelt too exclusively on the "I" and the "thou" of personal communion, and has not integrated the "it" that each person must be for the other, precisely in order that the other may address him or her as "thou."

But if the Lord is present persistently as the objects bread and wine, what is to prevent our misusing this availability? What is to prevent our seizing upon his thing-like givenness, to perform with it works of our own choosing, or even for blatantly superstitious purposes? That, again, is the Protestant question. The answer, surely, is nothing.

A person's body is that person as an object for other persons; that is, a person's body is that person's availability, indeed vulnerability, to those others whom she

---

22. E.g., the international Methodist-Catholic dialogue, *The Dublin Report* (1976), nr. 59: "Methodists could use such expressions from the Windsor Statement (i.e., the report on international Anglican-Roman Catholic dialogue) as 'mysterious and radical change . . . in the inner reality of the elements' . . . only in the sense that the bread and wine acquire an additional significance as effectual signs of the body and blood of Christ." Or there is "evangelical" Anglican response to dialogue with Roman Catholicism, as summarized by Kamath, "Convergence on the Eucharist," 84. "The Evangelicals are highly critical of this section (on real presence), because of the exclusion of receptionism. . . . Once the real presence . . . is admitted in the elements, then the related issues like the reservation and adoration would follow, which again would not be acceptable to the Evangelicals."

23. Specifically Lutheran critique of the *LC* made this point very early. So the "Stellungnahme der evangelischen Michaelsbrüderschaft zu den Arnoldshainer Thesen," *Lehrgespräch über das heilige Abendmahl*, ed. Gottfried Niemeyer (München: Chr. Kaiser, 1961), 51: "Alle Wendungen der Arnoldshainer Thesen über Christi hoheitsvolle Gegenwart bleiben im Bereich worthaft personaler Anrede, sie dringen nicht vor in den leibhaft-dinglichen Raum der Kreatur."

or he addresses. And there is never a guarantee that they will not use such availability to the person's injury. If I had no body, you could not smite me; since I do, you can. If the risen Christ has a body, and if the bread and cup are that body, then we *can* steal Jesus and try to use him as a charm; we *can* carry him about in procession, and the practices of the procession *can* very well be the practices of self-justification. It is not that such acts are impossible; it is that they are violations of the present Lord. The violators at Corinth did not by their unsisterly use of the bread make it not be the body of Christ; they made themselves guilty over against the body of Christ.

V

Therefore the legitimate Protestant concern cannot be about a too-strong identification of real presence with the elements; the legitimate Protestant concern is the practical demand noted earlier. Mutual agreement to refrain from offensive practices cannot satisfy Catholic concern, but it must satisfy Protestant concern. If it does not, that concern is shown to be unjustifiable. The legitimate Catholic question is about what can be done, as a probe of what is really there. The legitimate Protestant question is about what may be done, with what is really there. Once that is seen, closer consensus ought surely to be possible.

Why is it so enduringly not seen? I suggest that one reason Catholics are unwilling to see it, is that when they do they will have to stop deducing what liturgically is to be done with the bread and cup from metaphysically true propositions about what could be done. Thereby they will lose their sole means of justifying some very persistent, if always somewhat deprecated, Catholic practices, and will have to acknowledge that the church can adopt and even entrench itself in illegitimate practices. The temporal continuity of the church is, in part, the issue. Protestants are unwilling to see it because when it is seen, so is the Eucharist's reality as sacrifice.[24] We are at a point reached before, where the dialogues have had to discover that other, more dreaded subjects were the true assignment.

---

24. The invaluable Hans Grass has stated the connections between this chapter and the next, and Protestant alarm at the connection, with all desirable directness. Declaring his full agreement with Hugh E. W. Turner as cited above, in the name of "unseren deutschen protestantischen Haltung," he says: "Die Repräsentationslehre, nach der im Abendmahl eine Vergenwärtigung des Kreuzesopfers Christ . . . stattfindet, und zwar nicht nur im Gedächtnis der Gläubigen . . ., stellt zweifellos eine Weiterentwicklung der lutherischen Abendmahlslehre in Richtung auf die römische Lehre dar. . . . Für unser Verständnis bestehen gegen (this view) schwere Bedenken, weil man hier eben doch in die unmittelbare Nähe zu katholischen Messopfervorstellungen gelangt" (Hans Grass, "Diskussionseinleitung," *Wort und Abendmahl*, ed. R. R. Williams [Stuttgart: Evang. Missionsverlag, 1967], 20–21).

3

Eucharistic Sacrifice

I

Martin Luther's denunciations of the "abomination" of the "sacrifice of the mass" were fully equalled in vehemence by otherwise more polite Calvinists and Anglicans. Once again, therefore, we must begin with astonishment at the contemporary accord the dialogues register and promote. A commission of German Evangelical bishops recently listened to the teaching of their Catholic colleagues and said, "Over against such a statement of the relation between Christ's sacrifice on the cross and the church's eucharistic service, a statement which interprets and carries forward the doctrines of Trent, evangelical theology must say plainly: this is not the teaching which our reforming fathers condemned, or which was envisaged in the polemics of past centuries against 'the sacrifice of the mass.' "[1] The German study of the condemnations concluded without nuance. "The controversy about 'the sacrifice of the mass,' and its church-divisive character . . . have been left behind."[2]

II

The contemporary Catholic doctrine of eucharistic sacrifice that so disarmed the German Evangelical bishops, and that is the basis of concord in every major dialogue report, may for our purposes be described in three steps. The first is what Catholic theologians regularly call the "recovery" of a *sacramental* point of view, thereby, of course, acknowledging its previous temporary absence. The Catholic theologian who enabled Anglican-Roman Catholic agreement[3] in this matter can be spokesman. "One of the most precious fruits of the renovation of sacramental theology (is) affirmation of the essential participation of the eucharistic mystery in the sacramental universe, and so of the conformity of all the eucharist's aspects to the laws of that special reality."[4]

---

1. Arbeitsgruppe der deutschen Bischofskonferenz und der Kirchenleitung der Vereinigten Evangelisch-lutherischen Kirche Deutschlands, *Kirchengemeinschaft im Wort und Sakrament* (Paderborn: Bonifatius-Drückerei, 1984), 42.
2. Ökumenischer Arbeitskreis evangelischer und katholischer Theologen, *Lehrverurteilungen— kirchentrennend?* ed. Karl Lehmann & Wolfhart Pannenberg (Freiburg: Herder, 1986), 1:121.
3. Ravi S. Kamath, "Convergence on the Eucharist" (Diss. Greg., Rome, 1977), 49. The dialogue found its "solution . . . in the biblical notion of memorial, so much emphasized in contemporary eucharistic theology. It is Tillard . . . who provided the solution."
4. J. M. R. Tillard, "Catholiques romains et Anglicans: l'Eucharistie," *Nouvelle Revue Théologique* 103(1971): 607.

In this way of thinking, to be sacramental is to *be* in a particular way, to have a particular ontological mode. Thus the Eucharist *is sacramentally* whatever it is; if it is a sacrifice, it is sacramentally and not otherwise a sacrifice, and its interpretation as sacrifice must be interior to its interpretation as sacrament. The doctrine is not new, if it was long neglected.[5]

This sort of Catholicism has been able to enter a consensus, found in all the dialogues, that the sacrifice of Christ at Calvary "can be neither continued, nor repeated, nor replaced, nor complemented,"[6] since sacramental reality *never* continues or repeats or complements other-than-sacramental reality. Again to cite Tillard: by a properly sacramental understanding of the sacrifice, the misunderstanding is "dissipated . . . which sees in the Catholic position the assertion of a re-immolation of Christ. . . . We are dealing with the efficacious sacramental presence of the unique and unrepeatable sacrifice of the Cross."[7] Or, as the international Lutheran-Roman Catholic dialogue formulated, "Catholic and Lutheran Christians confess together, that in the Lord's Supper Jesus Christ 'is present as the crucified . . . , as the sacrifice which once for all was brought for the sins of the world."[8]

Note a mildly ironic twist here. As we have earlier seen, modern Protestant interpretation emphasizes the personal and dynamic character of the real presence; "body and blood" of Christ are taken to mean the person of Christ. But if the biblical texts' insistence on "body and blood" is their insistence on the sacrificial character of Christ's personal action, as the Reformation vehemently asserted, then this personal presence must be seen as the personal presence of the self-sacrificing Christ precisely in his act of sacrifice. Thus contemporary Protestant personalism produces exactly the position that contemporary Roman Catholic theology makes as the foundation of its doctrine of eucharistic sacrifice.

A move that occurs at this point in all the dialogues (and that makes the second step announced above) is a "return to . . . the notion of *memorial.*"[9] (emphasis added) In the dialogues, the Greek word so translated from the narratives of institution is often simply borrowed as *anamnesis*, or interpreted by a neologism as "re-presentation." According to the report of international Anglican-Roman Catholic dialogue, cited and affirmed also by the international Lutheran-Roman Catholic dialogue, "The notion of memorial as understood in the Passover celebration of the time of Christ—i.e., the making effective in the present of an event of the past—has opened the way to a clearer understanding of the relationship

---

5. It was Thomas Aquinas's starting point, *Summa theologiae* III,79,7. "This sacrament is not only a sacrament but also a sacrifice. For *in that* in this sacrament the passion of Christ is represented . . . it has *also* the character of sacrifice." (emphasis added)

6. Joint Lutheran-Roman Catholic Commission, *The Eucharist* (1978), 56.

7. Tillard, "l'Eucharistie," 614.

8. Joint Lutheran-Roman Catholic Commission, *The Eucharist,* 56.

9. Tillard, "l'Eucharistie," 607. Tillard has proven that it is accepted teaching of the Roman Catholic Church after Vatican II, and a legitimate interpretation of Trent, that the eucharistic sacrifice does not repeat or renew the sacrifice of Christ but perpetuates it by making anamnesis (J. M. R. Tillard, "Sacrificial Terminology and the Eucharist," *One in Christ* 28[1987]: 179–91).

between Christ's sacrifice and the Eucharist."[10] The Lutheran-Roman Catholic document then continues. "In the memorial celebration . . . more happens than that past events are brought to mind by the power of recall. . . . The decisive point is not that what is past is called to mind, but that the Lord calls his people into his presence and confronts them with his salvation. In this creative act of God, the salvation event from the past becomes the offer of salvation for the present and the promise of salvation for the future."[11]

No one has used the concept of *anamnesis*/re-presentation more bluntly to obtain consensus than the American Lutheran-Roman Catholic dialogue. "Lutherans have often understood Roman Catholics to say that the Mass adds to Calvary. . . . Catholics agree that some of the language used in the sixteenth century by Catholics could be so interpreted. Lutherans agree that it was this . . . which brought about the strenuous objections of Luther and the Lutheran Confessions. Now we can agree that this is not what Roman Catholics intend to say. . . . Catholics have used the word 're-presentation,' not in the sense of doing again, but in the sense of 'presenting again.' Lutherans can wholeheartedly agree. It was agreed that the unrepeatable sacrifice which was, now is in the Eucharist."[12] Also the German study of the anathemas has the concept at the key place. "It has proven possible jointly to state faith's conviction of the uniqueness and perfection of Jesus Christ's offering on the cross and the breadth of its *anamnesis* in the church's celebration of Eucharist."[13]

The third step is stated straightforwardly by Rome's official response to *BEM*. "When (Christ) then gives himself to the faithful as the means of sacramental communion, this is to make it possible for them to unite themselves with his self-offering to the Father."[14] It is communion with the present Jesus that is the sacramental gift of the Eucharist. But this Jesus is present specifically in the act of his self-sacrifice to the Father.

Also at this step, Tillard can provide a fuller statement of the matter. First, any teaching is rejected according to which our offering of sacrifice occurs other than sacramentally, occurs as an act allegedly separable from the act of sacramental eating and drinking. "Also the 'sacramental sacrifice' must occur as a function of (the 'sacramental signs') basic meaning, set by the biblical context. . . . But the eucharistic signs all direct us to the act of the believer who in the experience of the fraternal meal shares with his brothers the blessings of salvation." It is exactly by our participation in Christ's sacramental gift of himself as bread and cup that we are united with his sacrifice of himself—in body and blood—to his Father. Thus: "The matter of the 'sacramental sacrifice' is the same as that of the

---

10. International Anglican-Roman Catholic Dialogue, *Eucharistic Doctrine* (1971), 5; International Lutheran-Roman Catholic Dialogue, *The Eucharist* (1978), 36.

11. Ibid.

12. Kent S. Knutson, "Eucharist as Sacrifice," in *The Eucharist as Sacrifice*, vol. 3 of *Lutherans and Catholics in Dialogue*, ed. Paul Empie and T. Austin Murphy (Minneapolis: Augsburg, 1974).

13. Ökumenischer Arbeitskreis evangelischer und katholischer Theologen, *Lehrverurteilungen*, 121.

14. Secretariat for the Promotion of Christian Unity, with the Congregation for the Faith, *Response to "Baptism, Eucharist and Ministry"* (1987), III.B.2.

'sacramental eating.' . . . Offering and communion structure themselves each through the other, so that their respective finalities penetrate one another."[15] "In this perspective, the old quarrels about the propitiatory value of the mass shrink to their just proportion. If the mass has a real efficacy against sin, this derives from the fact that in it there is active the power of the unique and unrenewable propitiatory sacrifice of which we celebrate the memorial."[16]

Such new understanding of Catholic teaching has enabled wide consensus. Pioneers of the consensus were the Groupe des Dombes.

> The redemptive act of Christ on the cross . . . cannot be reiterated, but its power is eternally active in the perpetual intercession of the Son, the eternal High Priest, before the Father. . . . In giving himself in the Eucharist to the church, Christ sweeps the church along in his own movement to the Father, a movement of consecration and renunciation, of life through death. So he makes the church participate in his praise of the Father and in his power of intercession for the salvation of the world. Thereby the churchly Body of Christ the High Priest, is manifested and fulfilled as a priestly people.[17]

International Anglican-Roman Catholic dialogue formulated the consensus simply. "The eucharist is a sacrifice in the sacramental sense." This means, "In the celebration of the memorial, Christ in the Holy Spirit unites his people with himself in a sacramental way so that the Church enters into the movement of his self-offering."[18] International Lutheran-Roman Catholic dialogue proceeded more laboriously. First a general foundation was laid. "Christ instituted the eucharist, sacrament of his body and blood . . ., as the anamnesis of the whole of God's reconciling action in him. Christ himself with all that He has accomplished for us . . . is present in this anamnesis." Then the same key move is made, and in the same terminology. "The Lord present among us wants to draw us into the movement of his life."[19]

International Lutheran-Roman Catholic dialogue continues. When in the memorial celebration the past salvation-event becomes present, the celebrants are "incorporated" into Christ, and so "they are taken as his body into the reconciling sacrifice which equips them for self-giving. . . . Thus is rehearsed in the Lord's Supper what is practiced in the whole Christian life." The Eucharist is, of course, a thanksgiving, and insofar as both traditions can call it a "sacrifice of thanksgiving," "this is neither simple verbal praise of God, nor is it a supplement or a complement which people from their own power add to the offering of praise and thanksgiving which Christ has made to the Father."[20]

15. Tillard, "l'Eucharistie," 609.
16. Ibid., 614.
17. Groupe des Dombes, *L'acte sacerdotal du Christ dans l'activité sacerdotale de l'Église* (1962), 3,8.
18. International Anglican-Roman Catholic Dialogue, *Eucharistic Doctrine: Elucidations* (1979), 5.
19. International Lutheran-Roman Catholic Dialogue, *The Eucharist,* 17–18.
20. Ibid., 46–47.

III

The authors of the international Lutheran-Roman Catholic document regarded the consensus they had reached as inadequate.[21] International Anglican-Roman Catholic dialogue was more optimistic and claimed "to have attained a substantial agreement on eucharistic faith,"[22] but found their claim disputed. The Roman Congregation for the Faith responded directly to the Anglican report and therein implicitly to the Lutheran report.

> But one still asks oneself what is really meant by the words "the church enters into the movement of (Christ's) self-offering" and "the making effective in the present of an event in the past." It would have been helpful, in order to permit Catholics to see their faith fully expressed on this point, to make clear that this real presence of the sacrifice of Christ, accomplished by the . . . ministry of the priest saying "in persona Christi" the words of the Lord, includes a participation of the church, the body of Christ, in the sacrificial act of her Lord, so that she offers sacramentally in him and with him his sacrifice.[23]

Particularly with the last clauses, the congregation touched the sore point from which renewed dissensus would spring. When it is agreed that the church "participates" in Christ's sacrifice, does it follow therefrom that "the church offers" Christ's sacrifice?

Precisely insofar as one may think that this does follow, the documents are attacked from the Protestant side. Evangelical Anglicans were led to dispute even the key conceptuality, denying that "anamnesis" in the institution-texts can mean "making present," and insisting that not Christ's death but only its efficacy are present in the Supper.[24] Also of the more cautious Lutheran-Roman Catholic document, there was vigorous Lutheran critique. André Birmelé can be its spokesman. "Lutheran theology . . . cannot say with Catholic theology that the church offers the eucharistic sacrifice, that it offers Christ to God. . . . Lutheran theology . . . will not reject the offering of thanksgiving, of praise, and of the believers themselves, but it opposes every idea of a 're-presentation' in the sense of a sacrifice unbloody but propitiatory, offered by the priest and the church."[25]

Over against this situation, the group of German ecumenists who conducted the anathema study undertook a special study, "The Offering of Jesus Christ and of the Church." The relation to previous dialogue was explicit. "The useful document *Das Herrenmahl* could in this matter not yet achieve a full consensus. Additional insights now make it possible to go a step further."[26] Three such additional insights functioned in the work of this group.

---

21. Ibid., 56–60.

22. International Anglican-Roman Catholic Dialogue, *Elucidations*, 6.

23. Congregation for the Faith, "Observations on the ARCIC Final Report" B.I.1.

24. Kamath, "Convergence on the Eucharist," 51, 84.

25. André Birmelé, *Le salut en Jésus Christ dans les dialogues oecuméniques* (Paris: Cerf, 1986), 152–53. See the other Lutheran critics of the international document listed there (in the case of Albrecht Peters, to be sure, misleadingly).

26. Ökumenisches Arbeitskreis evangelischer und katholischer Theologen, "Das Opfer Jesu Christi und der Kirche: Abschliessender Bericht," *Das Opfer Jesu Christi und seine Gegenwart in der Kirche*, ed. Karl Lehmann and Edmund Schlink (Freiberg: Herder, 1983), 4.1.

First, exegesis of the ways in which acts called "sacrifices" appear in Scripture, and of the ways in which Scripture uses sacrificial terminology, yields criteria for right theological appropriation of sacrificial language. An obvious but long-unexploited point begins the analysis: in the world of religion, there is no such thing as *the* concept or practice of sacrifice. When Israel, the primal church, and the later traditions used sacrificial practices and notions, they were thus bound to no one scheme, and could and did accept, reject, and manipulate freely and eclectically. In the New Testament we find sacrificial concepts and language appropriated when they fit what Christ did and calls us to do, rejected when they do not, and if convenient transformed to *make* them fit.[27]

The general outcome of this process in the New Testament and later is that sacrifice, as Christians came to use the concept, is "the giving-over of oneself out of love. . . . Over against the usual cultic separation of priest and offering there occurs here a decisive new interpretation: Jesus Christ worked redemption, in that he poured out his own blood; he is priest and offering at once." Here occurs a "personalising of the notion of sacrifice: it is no longer a matter of giving something, but of giving oneself."[28]

Second, analysis of the history of the church's interpretation of the Eucharist as sacrifice, and of the polemics of the sixteenth-century opponents, shows both sides of those polemics hindered by a common theological disaster: the antecedent disappearance of properly sacramental ways of thinking, that is, of a conceptuality in which the identity in difference of the "sacrifice of the mass" with the one sacrifice on the cross could be grasped.[29] For both parties, *memorial* could only be understood as subjective recollection.

The reformers and counter-reformers faced late medieval practices and teachings that both parties of this study call "gross abuses"[30] resulting from "inappropriate notions of sacrifice"[31]; these practices indeed made the "sacrifice of the mass" a sacrifice other than Christ's. From the one side, the reformers were determined to prevent any suggestion that the mass repeats or supplements Christ's sacrifice; within the conceptuality available, this reformation could only be accomplished by denying altogether that the mass is a sacrifice. From the other side, the fathers of Trent, to preserve the sacrificial character of the mass, as this was after all

27. Ibid., 2.1–3.
28. Ibid., 4.2.1.
29. Ibid., 3. The Catholic members of the German bishops' Arbeitsgruppe made much the same point, *Kirchengemeinschaft im Wort und Sakrament,* 42–43. "Dass Messopfer ist also nichts zum Kreuz susätzliches . . . Vielmehr gilt 'Es ist ein und dieselbe Opfergabe . . . nur die Art der Darbringung ist verschieden.' Freilich ist nicht zu verkennen dass es das Trienter Konzil schwer tat, die unterschiedliche Art der Darbringung theologisch zu bestimmen. Es fehlte in 16 Jh. an angemessenen sakramentalen Kategorien, was in der Volksfrömmigkeit zu vergröbenden Missverständnissen und in der Theologie zum Messopfertheorien geführt hat, die von uns heute als unzureichend bezeichnet werden müssen. Heutige katholische Theologie geht von der durch die moderne Exegese neu entdeckten biblischen Idee der 'memoria' . . . aus."
30. Ökumenisches Arbeitskreis evangelischer und katholischer Theologen, "Das Opfer Jesu Christi," 1.2.
31. Ibid., 2.4.2.

taught in the entire tradition, did indeed assert, in faithfulness to Scripture and the more ancient tradition, that the sacrifice on the Cross and the sacrifice of the mass were but one, but could not conceptualize this in such fashion as to "ensure the unrepeatability of the New Testament sacrifice"; Trent, that is, could not find a theology to counter what it indeed regarded as abuses.[32]

And third, there is "above all, the 'rediscovery' of the fundamental meaning of the *communion* structure of the Eucharist, the Spirit-given fellowship of the worshipers with the risen Lord and among themselves." In this document, the notion of memorial retains a key function, but within an interpretation more generally determined by the notion of communion. And it is the latter concept that "proved the comprehensive context for fruitful new work on the classical controversies."[33]

I must barbarously and dogmatically summarize the conclusions to which use of these insights brought the study. Jesus' sacrificial act on the Cross is his giving of himself *to* the Father *for* us and inseparably his giving of himself *to* us in *obedience* to the Father. *What* he gives is therefore communion: our communion with him, and just so our communion with the Father and with one another. Just so again, the content of this encompassing communion is our sharing in Jesus' "own life and fate," which is to say, in his self-giving, his sacrifice. Precisely in that Jesus sacramentally gives himself to us in the bread and cup of the Eucharist, all these dialectics belong also to the event of the eucharistic meal, of his giving the bread and cup and our receiving them. The sacrament of his self-giving to us incorporates us as a communion, as the church, precisely into the communion of his sacrifice of himself and of us to the Father.[34]

Where these truly sacramental relations are seen, it does indeed become a question. "Are [there] not stronger convergences between the Lutheran doctrine of real presence and the Catholic doctrine of sacrifice, than were visible in the sixteenth century, in that both intend to overcome the historical distance between the sacrifice on Golgotha and the celebration of Eucharist?"[35] In my judgment, it even becomes a merely rhetorical question, insofar as "the Lutheran doctrine of real presence" and "the Catholic doctrine of sacrifice" refer to the positions espoused by the parties in contemporary dialogue. If these positions can be maintained, then the judgment of the anathema study itself is surely correct: The "controversy about 'the sacrifice of the mass' " is "left behind."

One more feature of this group's work must be noted. As the Groupe des Dombes set the doctrine of eucharistic presence in a trinitarian context, so here the doctrine of eucharistic sacrifice is set in the same context, though unfortunately not quite so persistently. The Father's role as the giver, and not merely the receiver, of the Son's sacrifice is noted, but little is made of it.[36] It is, however, fully acknowledged

32. Ibid., 3.3.1–4.3.
33. Ibid., 1.1.
34. Ibid., 4.3–4.
35. Ibid., 3.3.1.
36. Ibid., 4.2.4.

that the notion of communion, by which all the document's positions are enabled, is fundamentally a pneumatological concept. "Only with appropriate, trinitarian weighting of what is to be said about the Holy Spirit of God and Jesus, and of its concretising in what is to be said about the church, can the historical unrepeatability and the universal meaning of Jesus Christ be mediated, and only so can also the identity and difference of Jesus Christ's historical sacrifice on the cross and the Eucharist be described."[37]

Surely this trinitarian move is the right track. It is only to be regretted that the German group's exploitation of the concept of communion does not begin so decisively as did that of the Groupe des Dombes. "Gestures of Christ whom the Father sent into the world with the power of the Spirit, the sacraments introduce human creatures into the communion of Father, Son and Spirit; from there they receive their efficacy."[38]

IV

The consensus found in the dialogues is largely enabled by new Catholic theology, which both excludes previously possible, and to Protestants objectionable, Catholic understandings of eucharistic sacrifice, and should itself be affirmable by Protestants. It is noteworthy that little creative thought has been brought to the consensus from the Protestant side. And this is the more surprising since to the extent that Protestant theology affirms existing consensus on "real presence," a robust and distinctly Reformation doctrine of eucharistic sacrifice is plainly implied. I will sketch this possibility very summarily, in a succession of steps.

First, we must take seriously the fact, already decisively exploited by the German anathema study, that "sacrifice" is a very comprehensive word, both in the religious world generally and in Scripture's and the theological tradition's eclectic adaptation of sacrificial concepts and practices. What is a "sacrifice"? It would even be possible to argue for the definition: sacrifice is any action directed toward the divine. But it will be better, in order to retain "sacrifice" with a more specific meaning than "prayer," to take the word in a phenomenologically easily supported narrower sense: Sacrifice is prayer insofar as prayer is not purely linguistic, insofar as it is made also with gestures and objects.

Second, it has never been disputed between Catholics and Protestants that the Eucharist is a "sacrifice of praise and thanksgiving," that it is an overt action of prayer. Third, prayer in the understanding of Scripture is not simply our response to God's word, it is itself word of God, it is the Spirit's own response to the Father speaking in the Son. It may well be that this third point has not been to the front of Protestant consciousness, but neither has Protestantism denied it—as, indeed, it hardly could, in view of its blatantly biblical status. But finally, fourth, the whole Reformation insisted—though Calvinists and Lutherans had different reasons for the insistence—that the word of God is never purely linguistic, that it is always

---

37. Ibid., 4.4.2.
38. Groupe des Dombes, *L'Esprit Saint, l'Eglise et les Sacraments* (1979), 98.

"visible" word, embodied word. But if prayer is also word of God, then it too must come under this insight.

In what, it is then surely right to ask, is *this* word, the eucharistic prayer-sacrifice of praise, embodied? With what gestures and objects is this word of God accomplished? Even as a mere phenomenological observation, the answer is inescapable: with the loaf and cup. What are these? If they are the body and blood of Christ, is not the eucharistic "sacrifice of praise" indeed an offering of the incarnate Christ to the Father?

V

Yet the question raised by the Roman Congregation for the Faith is not simply banished by these considerations. In what sense exactly does the church "participate" "in the sacrificial act of her Lord, so that she offers sacramentally in him and with him his sacrifice"? Both sides raise the questions with equal urgency. They agree that a sacrifice is, sacramentally, offered when the Eucharist is celebrated, that Christ offers this sacrifice, and that the church participates. Does this mean that the church is a subject, an agent, of this act?

To the extent that it does seem to mean that, Protestants draw back. Typically, the Working Party of the German Catholic and Evangelical bishops states: "Controversial, or at least not clarified between us, is how the presence of Christ's self-offering is related to what the church does, and if the Eucharist can be described also as the sacrifice of the church." No doctrine could be acceptable to the Evangelical members of this dialogue, which made it appear that "no longer Christ, but the church were the subject of the sacrifice."[39] And to the extent that language about participation and the like seems designed to mollify Protestants on this point, to suggest that the church is only in some attenuated sense an acting subject of the sacrifice, Catholics draw back. Despite everything, the traditional Catholic phrase "sacrifice of the church" turns out to gather up all the divisive power of the old controversies,[40] and carry it into a new location, the understanding of the church and its agency.

Quite apparently, dissensus continues. And yet the dissensus can hardly be grasped by the formulas before us. No one has ever proposed what the Evangelical

39. Arbeitsgruppe der deutschen Bischofskonferenz und der Kirchenleitung der Vereinigten Evangelisch-lutherischen Kirche Deutschlands, *Kirchengemeinschaft im Wort und Sakrament*, 43. For gloriously blunt Protestantism on this point, we may hear the Moderamen des Reformierten Bundes, "Dialog zwischen römisch-katholischen Kirche und reformierten Kirchen," *Materialdienst* 32(1981): 33, officially responding to results of Reformed-Catholic dialogue. "Die Eucharistie wird . . . als Akt der Kirchen verstanden. . . . Die Gemeinde ist aber in diesem Geschehen ausschliesslich empfangende und nicht selbst darbringende Gemeinschaft."
40. The chairman of the Catholic side of the Arbeitskreis, now the Bishop of Mainz, Karl Lehmann, "Gegenwart des Opfers Jesu Christi im Herrenmahl," *Kerygma und Dogma* 29(1983): 146. "Die Polemik und die Ablehnung des Messopfer-Gedankens haben in dem Wort 'Opfer der Kirche' der katholischen Tradition eine exemplarische Veranschaulichung und—wie es scheint—eine plausible Bestätigung gefunden. Die Gesprächssituation ist in dieser Hinsicht auch durch die nach dem Zweiten Vatikanischen Konzil erneuerten Hochgebete der Eucharistiefeier nicht einfacher geworden. Es ist darum kein Zufall, dass die Verständigung über das mit dem Wort 'Opfer der Kirche' Gemeinte im Ökumenischen Dialog einen . . . Prüfstein darstellt."

bishops attacked, that the sacrificer is "no longer Christ." Surely the truth must be that, in the terms of an old theologoumenon, the great high-priestly intercession before the Father is that of the *totus Christus,* of Christ with and as his Body of the saints, and neither of Christ *without* his saints nor of Christ *plus* his saints. Perhaps the real difficulty is more specific.

The Roman Congregation for the Faith insisted not only on the church as the subject of eucharistic sacrifice, but on the agency of the one who acts overtly for the church at this liturgical juncture. The actuality of the sacrifice, in their formulation, is "accomplished by the . . . ministry of the *priest.*" (emphasis added) In 1967, the Groupe des Dombes found itself stopped in its progress by the inability to agree on "the role of the ministry in the communication" of Christ's mediation. The difficulty, they noted, is centered

> in the case of the eucharistic celebration. For the one party, this celebration does not suppose an other priesthood than that of the whole church. . . . For the other, it necessarily requires a specific properly priestly ministry. The difficulty of the Catholic position for Protestants (is) above all that this . . . ministry seems to obscure or repeat the mediation of Christ. . . . The difficulty of the Protestant position for Catholics (is) that the priestly power of the one Mediator does not seem, as such, to appear visibly signified for his body.[41]

The official dialogues faltered at the same point as the Groupe des Dombes, namely, not *what* is done at the Eucharist, but *who* does it. The American Lutheran-Roman Catholic dialogue, after what seemed comprehensive agreement on eucharistic sacrifice, ended with a list of unresolved questions, all of which turn out to be about the ministry.[42] The foreword to the report of the next round said that after such notable convergence on eucharistic presence and eucharistic sacrifice, it "seemed natural to take up as the next point the question of intercommunion. A weekend of conversations . . . quickly revealed that one could not even discuss the matter without considering the key question of a valid ministry in relation to the administration of the Eucharist."[43]

In a paper for the very first round of international Lutheran-Roman Catholic dialogue, Walter Kasper wrote:

> According to widespread opinion, it is a difference in understanding the churchly office which today poses the decisive difficulty for further rapprochement of the divided churches. . . . That this should be the problem, is anything but obvious. Neither the Reformers nor the Council of Trent set the question of the churchly office so decisively at the center. . . . The

41. Groupe des Dombes, *Sacerdoce et Ministère de l'Eglise* (1961). How far "the one side" can go, it is again the service of the Moderamen des Reformierten Bundes to make plain. "Auch die Behauptung . . . dass zur Spendung der Sakramente ein Spender, zu ihrer Verwaltung ein Verwalter gehöre, ist zu befragen" ("Dialog," 33).

42. "The Eucharist: A Lutheran-Roman Catholic Statement," in *Eucharist as Sacrifice,* conclusion.

43. "Foreword," *Eucharist and Ministry,* vol. 4 of *Lutherans and Catholics in Dialogue,* ed. Paul Empie and T. Austin Murphy (Minneapolis: Augsburg, 1974).

displacement of the problematic is all the more surprising, in that it is now generally supposed that the doctrine of justification . . . no longer represents a church-divisive difference. Should that not have consequences also for a common understanding of office?[44]

Should it not indeed?

44. Walter Kasper, "Zur Frage der Anerkennung der Ämter in den lutherischen Kirchen," Evangelium-Welt-Kirche, ed. Harding Meyer (Frankfurt: Otto Lembeck, 1975), 401.

Part 2

CONVERGENCES ABOUT THE CHURCH

4

The Churchly Office

I

Early in the American Roman Catholic-Reformed dialogue an essayist burst out, "And always the real stumbling block turns out to be the problem of ministry and order."[1] André Birmelé's historical account of Lutheran-Roman Catholic dialogue notes, first, that its whole course has led toward ecclesiology, and, second, that this statement of the case is too general. "Within ecclesiology there is a further cristallization-point to which all dialogue between the two Christian families leads: the question of ordained ministry."[2] In the Roman Congregation for the Faith's observations about the report of international Anglican-Roman Catholic dialogue, most of the negative comments are objections to the report on ministry and ordination.[3]

Nevertheless, the starting point of our discussion must be that an established dialogical-ecumenical doctrine of ordained, "special," or "hierarchical" ministry does exist, however incomplete or overdone various churches may judge it. The chief document to date of multilateral dialogue, *Baptism, Eucharist and Ministry* (*BEM*), lays it out quite fully and with useful restraint. I will make that document the framework of this chapter.[4] I will present the doctrine of *BEM* as a series of consenses, not always in the order of the document.

II

The context of ordained ministry is straightforwardly identified as the ministry of the whole people of the church, in its sending to the world.[5] It is "in order to fulfill" this mission, that the church needs ordained officers.[6] Thus ordained ministry can have "no existence apart from the community. Ordained ministers

1. Daniel J. O'Hanlon, "A New Approach to the Validity of Church Orders," American Reformed-Roman Catholic Dialogue, *Reconsiderations* (New York: World Horizons, 1967).

2. André Birmelé, *Le salut en Jésus Christ dans les dialogues oecuméniques* (Paris: Corf, 1986), 130.

3. Congregation for the Faith, "Observations on the ARCIC Final Report," *Origins* 11(1982): B.II-III.

4. Birmelé, *Le salut*, 461: "The third part of the Lima-document . . . recapitulates the convergences which appear in the bilateral dialogues."

5. Faith and Order Paper, *Baptism, Eucharist and Ministry* (Geneva: World Council of Churches, 1982), 1, 5.

6. Ibid., 9.

can fulfill their calling only in and for the community."[7] This unequivocal affirmation of the "priesthood of all believers" is universal in the dialogues. International Anglican-Roman Catholic dialogue is especially straightforward. "The goal of the ordained ministry is to serve this priesthood of all the faithful."[8]

If Roman Catholic theology ever talked of the ordained clergy as if they could be the church by themselves, or as if the laity's ministry were derived from or subordinate to theirs, Roman Catholic representatives in the dialogues do so no longer. The international Lutheran-Roman Catholic dialogue, with direct reference to the teaching of Vatican II, could say, "The doctrine of the common priesthood of all the baptized and of the serving character of the ministries in the church . . . represents in our day a joint starting point . . . in (the) attempt to clarify as yet open problems regarding the understanding of the ordained ministry."[9] Moreover, there is an official Roman Catholic response to *BEM*, and the latter's affirmations on this matter are not among the many to which this response takes exception. So far as consensus-propositions can reach, the Reformation's concern at this point is fully satisfied.

Within the priesthood of believers, *BEM* discerns a plurality of ministries construed by the Pauline doctrine of charisms, of plural, differing, and mutually reinforcing permissions and empowerments of the Spirit.[10] This procedure, too, is general in the dialogues[11]; it represents one of the places where biblical study has indeed provided categories in which frozen positions could be transcended. The official Roman Catholic response gives explicit approval.[12]

Within this context, *BEM* then stipulates the referrent of the term *ordained ministry*. Ordained ministers are "persons who have received a charism," later to be specified, "and whom the church appoints for service by ordination through the invocation of the Spirit and the laying on of hands."[13] Ordained ministry, according to this consensus, is constituted in a specific charism and is given by a specific rite, that which we find in the Pastoral Epistles of the New Testament and which historically has been called ordination. We should note both the decisive coordinate mention of charism and rite and the careful abstention from any precise stipulation of their relation. In the remainder of the document, this description of ordained ministry is amplified in various contexts, and the same restraint is mostly maintained.

III

The document is in fact entertaining, and being cautious about, an understanding of ordination as *sacramental*. The rite of ordination is regularly called a "sign"; that is, ordination is located in the class within which Western theology has

7. Ibid., 12.
8. International Anglican-Roman Catholic Dialogue, *Ministry and Ordination* (1973), 7.
9. International Lutheran-Roman Catholic Dialogue, *The Ministry in the Church* (1981), 15.
10. Faith and Order Paper, *Baptism, Eucharist and Ministry*, 3, 5.
11. E.g., International Lutheran-Roman Catholic Dialogue, *The Ministry in the Church*, 20.
12. Secretariat for the Promotion of Christian Unity, with the Congregation for the Faith, *Response to "Baptism, Eucharist and Ministry," in Churches Respond to BEM*, ed. Max Thurian (Geneva: World Council of Churches, 1988), 4:28.
13. *Baptism, Eucharist and Ministry*, "Ministry," 7.

traditionally located sacraments as a subclass. "The laying on of hands is the sign of the gift of the Spirit."[14] "Ordination is . . . at one and the same time invocation of the Holy Spirit (*epiklesis*); sacramental sign; acknowledgment of gifts and commitment."[15] Moreover, ordination is regularly described materially as that *sort* of sign which, within the larger class, has been called sacrament: the sort that conveys what it signifies. At ordination, the church prays for the gift of those relations to and in the Spirit that are constitutive of ordained ministry. The total rite is

> a sign of the granting of this prayer by the Lord who gives the gift of the ordained ministry. Although the outcome of the Church's epiclesis depends on the freedom of God, the Church ordains in confidence that God, being faithful to his promise in Christ, enters sacramentally into contingent, historical forms of human relationship and uses them for his purpose. Ordination is a sign performed in faith that the spiritual relationship signified is present in, with and through the words spoken, the gestures made and the forms employed.[16]

Just so, it is—against the actual practice of several signatory groups—explicitly stated, "In recognition of the God-given charism of ministry, ordination . . . is never repeated."[17]

Nevertheless, the document throughout tends to evade an outright statement of the relation between rite and gift. It does not explicitly choose between a doctrine that the rite *grants* the relevant charism or charisms, and one that the rite is "an *acknowledgment* by the Church of the gifts of the Spirit in the one ordained."[18] (emphasis added) So also it is never said straightaway that "ordination is a sacrament." Here *BEM* reaches a limit of multilateral consensus, a hesitation apparently caused by fears and concerns at cross-purposes.

However cautious *BEM* is in its use of labels, it nevertheless develops a fairly complete doctrine of ordination as sacrament, including a doctrine of the "matter" of this "sacramental sign," of the *res* that the *signum* communicates. "The laying on of hands is the sign of the gift of the Spirit, rendering visible the fact that the ministry was instituted in the revelation accomplished in Christ."[19] It is a sign "that the new minister be given the power of the Holy Spirit in the new relation which is established between this minister and the local Christian community and, by intention, the church universal."[20] Thus the matter of this sacrament, the reality

14. Ibid., 39.
15. Ibid., 41.
16. Ibid., 43.
17. Ibid., 48.
18. Ibid., 44. The issue is stated clearly by the response of the Seventh-day Adventists, "General Observations," which objects to a "pervading theology of sacrament. . . . 'Ministry,' to be sure never states simply that ordination . . . is a sacrament. . . . There is need, however, to pay close attention to . . . use of sacramental terms like 'sign' . . . ,'signify' . . . , 'represent' . . . , 'express' . . . , 'point to'. . . . Sacramental churches could understand these terms as efficacious signs . . . , whereas churches born of the Reformation would understand simply 'signs.' "
19. Ibid., 39.
20. Ibid., 42.

communicated by it as sign, is on the one hand a relation to Christ and on the other hand a relation to the community. It is apparent how formal this doctrine is; also, this is a classic characteristic of doctrines about a sacrament. What the doctrine practically means depends on what these relations in fact are, and that will indeed be stipulated.

The advanced dialogues universally, but cautiously, understand the rite of ordination as sacramental. I may instance the Groupe des Dombes. "The ministry of the word and sacraments is not reducible to ecclesial . . . organization; it is a gift of the Spirit and is signified and realized by a sacramental act of ordination. The ministry of the communication of the Spirit is itself received from the Spirit through the church."[21] Even international Reformed-Roman Catholic conversation reported: "The liturgical validation at the time of the act of ordination includes the invocation of the Holy Spirit . . . with the laying on of hands. . . . The laying on of hands is an *efficacious sign* which initiates and confirms the believer in the ministry conferred."[22] (emphasis added) For an additional and, in this context, weighty instance, the ecumenical Working Party of German Catholic and Evangelical church governments could agree that ordination grants "a charism of the Holy Spirit" that is "authorization and blessing" for the specific ministry, and that this charism puts the "person" of the one ordained wholly in the "service of his office" for the whole of life. Even the Catholic doctrine of an "indelible character" granted by ordination is found unproblematic.[23]

The Roman Catholic response to *BEM* identifies the question of "sacramental ordination" as a point at which the document is "unsatisfactory." Nevertheless, in its actual comments to the specific texts, it affirms the stated consensus. The response notes with satisfaction that the text clearly "points in the direction of a sacramental understanding" of ordination. Indeed, the response can even say that "the essentials of a sacramental understanding can be recognized in the broad treatment . . . in this text." Where these essentials are present, the Catholic response does not seem to think it necessary that the very phrase "a sacrament" be used. Catholics indeed "would like it to be stated clearly that ordination is not only a sign, but an effective sign."[24] Even this admonition is, however, remarkable for its restraint.

In the chief bilateral dialogues there is much less guarded agreement that the sign of ordination is "effective," namely, that ordination is sacramental. Perhaps we should cite one more consensus-statement on the matter, the international Lutheran-Roman Catholic dialogue. "Through the laying on of hands and through prayer . . . the gift of the Holy Spirit is offered *and conveyed* for the exercise of ministry."[25] (emphasis added)

21. Groupe des Dombes, *L'Esprit Saint, l'Eglise et les Sacrements* (1979), 79.
22. International Reformed-Roman Catholic Dialogue, *The Presence of Christ in Church and World* (1977), 98.
23. Arbeitsgruppe der deutschen Bischofskonferenz und der Kirchenleitung der Vereinigten Evangelisch-lutherischen Kirche Deutschlands, *Kirchengemeinschaft im Wort und Sakrament* (Paderborn: Bonifatius-Drückerei, 1984), 63–64, 70–72.
24. Secretariat for the Promotion of Christian Unity, *Response*, 34.
25. International Lutheran-Roman Catholic Dialogue, *The Ministry in the Church*, 32.

IV

The content of the ordination-charism is double, as *BEM* evokes it. First, within the total community of the church, ordained ministry represents something to that community: that Christ and the church, while one, are also two, and that in that difference the church is radically dependent on Christ. The ordained are "publically and continually responsible for pointing to (the church's) fundamental dependence on Jesus Christ."[26] They "are representatives of Jesus Christ to the community" who are to "proclaim his message of reconciliation" and "call the community to submit to the authority of Jesus Christ."[27] Precisely that someone must be set apart in the community, to speak *for* Christ *to* the community, represents to the community that it is not its own founder or authority, that it is not itself its Christ.

Merely this consensus has gone far to bridge the Catholic-Protestant division on ordination. For within Roman Catholicism responsible theologians hold that "the theologically decisive criterion for right understanding of the ecclesial office . . . is whether one understands the office both as an entity within the community of the faithful and as one that also stands over against the congregation and presents a sign of the uncontrollable prevenience of salvation."[28]

Second, the ordained are there to "provide . . . within a multiplicity of gifts, a focus of unity."[29] Their office is essentially and not merely incidentally *pastoral*. "Under Jesus Christ the chief shepherd" they "assemble and guide the dispersed people of God."[30] In recently fashionable terminology, ordained ministry is to provide a focus of and is to work to preserve both the church's synchronic and diachronic unity.

These same two motifs dominate wider consensus in the dialogues. The Groupe des Dombes has again been paradigmatic, both in stipulating the two charisms and in displaying their unity. "Whatever may be the diversity . . . of charisms and functions in a Christian community, the property of the pastoral ministry is to assure and signify the dependence of the church over against Christ, who is the source of its mission and the basis of its unity. Member of the Christian community, the minister is also over against it a 'messenger' whom it receives from Christ. His functions mark, within the church's life, the priority of the divine initiative and authority, the continuity of the mission in the world, the bond of communion established by the Spirit between the many communities in the unity of the church."[31]

---

26. *Baptism, Eucharist and Ministry*, "Ministry," 8, 11.
27. Ibid., 11.
28. Walter Kasper, "Zur Frage der Anerkennung der Ämter in den lutherischen Kirchen," *Evangelium—Welt—Kirche*, ed. Harding Meyer (Frankfurt: Otto Lembeck, 1975), 108 9.
29. *Baptism, Eucharist and Ministry*, "Ministry," 8.
30. Ibid., 11.
31. Groupe des Dombes, *Pour une réconciliation des ministères* (1972), 20–21. See also, e.g., *Ministère de communion dans l'Eglise universelle* (1985), 6: "Dés sa naissance, l'Eglise a vu se développer, sous l'impulsion de l'Espirt, des ministères et des charismes destinés à assurer sa continuité et son extension dans le monde. En étudiant l'histoire de cette Eglise, marquée par le péché des hommes mais gardée par la fidélité de Dieu, nous sommes invités à discerner et à reconnaître ce qui vient de l'Esprit Saint."

V

The referrent of "ordained ministry" and something of the content of "ordained" thus established, *BEM* proceeds to a major dogmatic consensus. "In order to fulfill its mission, the Church needs persons who are publicly and continually responsible for pointing to its fundamental dependence on Jesus Christ, and thereby provide, within a multiplicity of gifts, a focus of its unity. The ministry of such persons, who since very early times have been ordained, is *constitutive* for the life and witness of the Church."[32] (emphasis added) It is the words *needs* and *constitutive* that carry the dogmatic weight, a weight Protestantism has not always been willing to allow.[33]

The cautious construction of the second sentence just cited reckons with the known history, and dispenses with some Catholic ideology. The ministry of persons with the *responsibility* and *position* described in the first sentence is constitutive of the church, for it cannot be affirmed with certainty that from the very beginning persons were given this ministry by any rite plausibly to be called ordination. The question is finessed as to whether this ministerial function, once vested in an ordained ministry, must always be thus located, though the tenor of *BEM* certainly suggests that it must be.

In the chief bilateral dialogues, where more sectarian Protestantism need not be so fully reckoned with, less qualified consensus about the church-constitutive character of specifically ordained ministry is usual, even as the historical variability of its forms is also invariably acknowledged. So we find in the international Lutheran-Roman Catholic dialogue: "Thus while the existence of a special ministry is abidingly constitutive for the church, its concrete form must always remain open to new actualizations."[34]

In this same text of *BEM* a connection appears to which the text does not call explicit attention but which is nonetheless decisive for it, and for the ecumenical situation. The link is between the assertion of ordination's *constitutive* character and the assertion of its *continuity* through the history of the church. The connection between ministerial succession and ministerial necessity is ubiquitous in theological tradition and in the dialogues. In fact, it determines the very structure of *BEM,* which immediately follows the paragraph just cited with three paragraphs developing a doctrine of ministerial succession.

Before reporting that doctrine, I should note two points. In the tradition, the dialogues, and *BEM* a further twist postpones full discussion of ministerial succession: Catholic conviction that succession of certain ministers directly responsible for succession itself, namely, bishops, is essential. Also, the further nexus between the sacramentality of ordination and the succession of ordinations is ecumenically decisive.

32. *Baptism, Eucharist and Ministry*, "Ministry," 8.

33. E.g., the response of the Evangelical Church of Lutheran Confession in Brazil, "Concerning the Contents of the Text," 3.1. "There are . . . some statements difficult to accept, such as . . . that the ordained ministry is 'constitutive for the life and witness of the church.' "

34. International Lutheran-Roman Catholic Dialogue, *The Ministry in the Church*, 18.

How essential is succession through time to the integrity of the ministry? What would it mean to agree that such succession must be established sacramentally? Joseph Cardinal Ratzinger, in a much-noted statement, laid it down. "For the catholic church of East and West the conviction is fundamental, that the church does not, like worldly institutions . . . , hand on in its own right that authority which is decisive for it as the church, that it can do this only in a spiritual, i.e., sacramental way. The grant of priestly office occurs through . . . the sign of the laying on of hands, taken over from the New Testament, with prayer for the Holy Spirit. In this form of office-granting, the church expresses faith that it is a creature of the Holy Spirit, that forever continues to live by his gifts."[35]

I may begin the approach to these questions by noting and repairing a strange near-omission in *BEM*. The bilateral dialogues have achieved a differentiated doctrine of apostolicity that our document has only marginally incorporated and that surely would have made its teaching easier to accept. International Lutheran-Roman Catholic dialogue has stated this wider doctrine with especial straightforwardness. Noting that "apostolic succession" usually refers to episcopal-ministerial succession, the report continues, "But apostolic succession is also often understood to refer in the substantive sense to the apostolicity of the church in faith." Then a consensus is formulated that must have great consequence for all ecumenical discussion of the church. "The starting point must be the apostolicity of the church in the substantial sense. The basic intention of the doctrine of apostolic succession is to indicate that, throughout all historical changes in its proclamation and structures, the church is at all times referred back to its apostolic origin."[36]

Knowledge of the history of ordered ministry in the church has undermined earlier ideology about succession on both sides. It is a great virtue of *BEM*, and itself a considerable ecumenical fact, that it explicitly and, for the most part, adequately reckons with the known history. This turns out to affirm the central Catholic position but with firm Protestant restraints. "The basic reality of an ordained ministry was present from the beginning . . . the actual forms of ordination and of the ordained ministry, however, have evolved in complex historical developments."[37] Exactly similar historical sketches are a regular feature of bilateral dialogues.

According to *BEM*, the beginning of "differentiated roles in the community" was the apostolate.[38] It is acknowledged that the apostolate was itself unrepeatable; here a concern of Reformation understanding is adopted.[39] But in that "as Christ

35. Joseph Cardinal Ratzinger, "Fragen zur Sukzession," *KNA—Kritischer Ökumenischer Informationsdienst* 28/29:5.

36. International Lutheran-Roman Catholic Dialogue, *The Ministry in the Church*, 59–60. The Groupe des Dombes is, as so often, exemplary: "The fulness of (apostolic) succession involves continuity of transmission of the ministerial mandate, fidelity to the apostolic witness and conformity of life to the gospel. . . . All these aspects are inseparable from one another" (*La succession apostolique* [1968], 28).

37. *Baptism, Eucharist and Ministry*, "Ministry," commentary (11).

38. Ibid., 9.

39. Ibid., 10.

chose and sent the apostles, Christ continues through the Holy Spirit to choose and call persons into the ordained ministry,"[40] the apostolate "prefigures" and founds the ordained ministries.[41]

Stronger versions of this consensus appear in the bilateral dialogues. One might expect such positions in Anglican-Roman Catholic dialogue,[42] but also international Lutheran-Roman Catholic dialogue agreed: "In addition to their unique function in founding the church, the apostles also had a responsibility for building up and leading the first communities, a ministry that later had to be continued. The New Testament shows how there emerged from among the ministries a special ministry which was understood as standing in the succession of the apostles. . . . One can, therefore, say that according to the New Testament the 'special ministry' established by Jesus Christ through the calling and sending of the apostles" was and is essential in the church.[43]

We may surely take the teaching of Vatican II, and its exposition by the prefect of the Congregation for the Faith, as authentic expositions of contemporary Roman Catholic understanding of ministerial succession. The foundational passage of *Lumen gentium* reads: "That divine mission, which was committed by Christ to the apostles, is destined to last until the end of the world . . . since the gospel, which they were charged to hand on, is, for the church, the principle of all its life for all time. For that very reason the apostles were careful to appoint successors in this hierarchically constituted society."[44] Here, Cardinal Ratzinger points out, the successive concepts are mission, gospel, tradition, and the life of the church. "The starting point is the sending of the apostles, but this sending is itself the handing on, the tradition, of the gospel. Apostolate and handing on the gospel are two sides, the personal and the material, of the same thing."[45]

Ratzinger begins with a position that is also decisively established in the dialogues. "Apostolic succession is not a purely formal authority, but participation in the mission for the gospel." And then he concludes directly to the Catholic position. "*Therefore* the concepts for succession and for tradition blended in the

---

40. Ibid., 11.
41. Ibid., 10.
42. International Anglican-Roman Catholic Dialogue, *Ministry and Ordination* (1973), 1–8.
43. International Lutheran-Roman Catholic Dialogue, *The Ministry in the Church*, 17. The point was argued with special stringency by the Arbeitsgruppe der deutschen Bischofskonferenz und der Kirchenleitung der Vereinigten Evangelisch-lutherischen Kirche Deutschlands, *Kirchengemeinschaft im Wort und Sakrament*, 60. "Wie die Kirche ihren Ursprung und Grund im Ganzen des Christusgeschehens hat, so ist auch das kirchliche Amt mit dem Heilswerk Christi mitgesetz und gestiftet. . . . Als Weiterführung der apostolischen Sendung geht es der Kirche insofern vorauf, als Kirche immer neu aus der Verkündigung und der Spendung der Sakramente wächst; andererseits hat es seinen Ort in der Kirche. Das Verhältnis eines Amtsträgers zu seiner Gemeinde spiegelt nicht nur das paulinische Gegenüber des Apostels zu den von ihm gegründeten Ortskirchen wider, sondern auch die Vielzahl von Charismen unter den Getauften."
44. *Lumen gentium*, III, 20.
45. Joseph Cardinal Ratzinger, *Theologische Prinzipienlehre* (München: Erich Wewel, 1982), 255–56.

ancient church; therefore Vatican II rightly binds them firmly together. The *successio*-structure is an expression of the catholic church's binding to tradition and idea of tradition."[46] (emphasis added)

It is hard to see that the Catholic position, so described, demands anything not generally agreed in the dialogues. If indeed ordination is, as the dialogues generally agreed, sacramental (or something so very like being sacramental as to be indistinguishable therefrom by the naked eye), the following should also be agreed: "The sacrament of ordination is thus an expression of and simultaneously a warrant for communal standing in the tradition."[47] But we will see that it is not so simple.

VI

Let us recall a vital but mostly implicit point in *BEM:* The dialogical process was led into the doctrine of ministry by precisely the extent of consensus in the doctrine of the Eucharist. It is the question of presidency at the Eucharist around which also circle *BEM*'s discussions of the ministry's representation of Christ to the community and of the pastoral ministry of unity.

These connections surface in *BEM* under the rubric of ordained ministry's "responsibility." "The chief responsibility of the ordained ministry is to assemble and build up the body of Christ by proclaiming and teaching the Word of God, by celebrating the sacraments, and by guiding the life of the community."[48] The main clause of this definition substantively repeats what is said about the content of the ministry's charism; the operative statements are the prepositional phrases that follow. Three responsibilities are listed. The first two reiterate the teaching of the Augsburg Confession, and of all the Reformation and Protestant theology that has followed it, in defining the ministry by "Word and Sacrament"; the third is an operative version of the definition of the ministerial charism as *pastoral.*

BEM then continues: "It is especially in the eucharistic celebration that the ordained ministry is the visible focus of the . . . communion between Christ and the members of his body. . . . If the ordained ministry is to provide a focus for the unity . . . of the Church, it is appropriate that an ordained minister should be given this task."[49]

With both of these propositions *BEM* evokes positions widespread in the dialogues and elsewhere more systematically developed. Thus, whereas *BEM* merely adds "ministry of Word and Sacrament" and "pastoral ministry" together, for the Groupe des Dombes the "pastoral ministry" "*includes* that of the Word and the Sacraments"[50] (emphasis added), therewith attempting an actual synthesis of Catholic and Protestant concerns.

The Reformation's definition of ordained ministry as "ministry of Word and Sacrament," while in itself surely true, and acceptable to Catholics, has often

46. Ibid., 256–57.
47. Ibid.
48. *Baptism, Eucharist and Ministry*, "Ministry," 13.
49. Ibid., 14 and commentary to 14.
50. Groupe des Dombes, *L'autorité pastoral dans l'Eglise* (1959), 17.

seemed either to be inadequate to distinguish the ministry of the ordained from
that of all believers, or—by an ironic reversal—to give ordained ministry a monopoly of the means of grace. It has thus tempted Protestantism to understand the
distinction between ordained and unordained ministry in a "functional" way, or
even to think of ordained ministry as "delegated" or otherwise derived from the
priesthood of believers.

When the notion of *pastor* is made encompassing, these temptations disappear.
The Groupe des Dombes shows the extent of consensus that then becomes possible.
"The pastoral ministry . . . draws its authority from the fact that it is, in the
church, a service of Christ in the power of the Spirit. It follows 1) that the authority
of the ministry belongs to the being of the church, 2) that it is entirely directed
to the growth of the body of Christ . . . , and 3) that, without being delegated
by the community, it is dedicated to the community's edification in love and
unity."[51]

Nor is this solution limited to this institutionally less committed dialogue. The
1984 report of the Working Party of the German Catholic and Lutheran authorities
has exactly the same synthesis. "The pastoral office, the service of the unity of
the church, is carried out through proclamation of the gospel and administration
of the sacraments."[52] The group argued further. "This office roots in the assignment
to the shepherds of the congregations to preserve and hand on the legacy of the
apostles . . . , since this was then threatened by . . . false teaching. And since
also the unity . . . of the congregations was thereby threatened, this function
becomes simultaneously a "pastoral" function. Especially the Pastoral Letters see
the task of the office in this way. Thus the churchly office is not founded in the
social needs of the congregations, but . . . in the apostolic sending."[53]

Catholic and Protestant concerns are synthesized from the other direction with
this emphasis on the pastoral role of ordained ministry. Ecumenists have long
agreed that in practice an ordained minister should always preside at Eucharist[54];
they have not agreed why this is so. An older Catholic theology that founded the
ordained minister's presidency in his "priestly" character was and is unacceptable
to Protestants—though both parties have usually been sufficiently vague about
what "priestly" means—while the Protestants themselves often had no justification
at all for their normative practice.

---

51. Ibid. Even delegation-theories, while dead in the dialogues and in responsible theology, are alive
in the churches. So the response to *Baptism, Eucharist and Ministry* of the United Church of Canada,
"Conclusion," C: "The ordained person . . . is not the 'visible focus' of the sacrament. She or he acts
as the representative of the community. She or he is designated by the community, for the sake of order,
to preside."

52. Arbeitsgruppe der deutschen Bischofskonferenz und der Kirchenleitung der Vereinigten evangelisch-lutherischen Kirche Deutschlands, *Kirchengemeinschaft im Wort und Sakrament*, 84.

53. Ibid., 63–64.

54. Though even this can be denied, and by putatively "mainline" groups. So the response to
Baptism, Eucharist and Ministry from the United Church of Canada, 2.(a): "The United Church of
Canada, in recent years, has tended to see ordination as the normative but not unique way in which
individuals are authorized . . . to preside at the sacraments. . . . When, for example, a lay person is
presiding officer of a church court, it is often the case that the presiding officer will officiate at the
court's eucharistic celebrations."

In the dialogical consensus, the necessary presidency of an ordained minister at Eucharist is not founded in the minister's priestly character (even though Catholics continue to assert the existence of such a character and even though it may now be granted also by many Protestants) but in the ordained minister's pastoral role as guardian and symbol of the church's oneness, namely, of that very communion established and displayed in the Eucharist. As the international Anglican-Roman Catholic report put it, "Hence it is right that he who has oversight in the Church and is the focus of its unity should preside at the celebration of the eucharist."[55]

The controversy occasioned by the 1979 report of an unofficial dialogue group, the joint *Oberseminar* of Munich's ecumenical institutes, put this explanation of ordained presidency decisively on the ecumenical table. The group, to general offense, proposed that nothing stood in the way of prompt mutual recognition of Roman Catholic and Evangelical ministries. A key proposition of its stated consensus read: "Catholic and Lutheran Christians agree that the celebration of the Eucharist is to be led by an ordained holder of the ecclesial office. It belongs to this office to represent the total church over against the individual congregation, and the individual congregation within the total church. Celebration of the Supper, by Catholic and Lutheran conviction, always represents the celebration of the church as a whole. . . . Therefore the . . . ordained holder of the ecclesial office leads the Supper. Therein he acts, as Catholic and Evangelical theology can formulate together, in the place of Christ. . . . Presidency in the celebration of the Supper is thus not delegated by the celebrating congregation." That this conception is not only fruitful but still problematic became apparent in the reaction from all sides.[56] Here is an opening into chapter 5.

VII

I have already trespassed thoroughly on this chapter's final rubric: the *authority* of ordained ministry. *BEM* begins with a firm and very catholic affirmation. "The authority of the ordained minister is rooted in Jesus Christ, who has received it from the Father . . . and who confers it by the Holy Spirit through the act of ordination." Then a Protestant worry receives its due. "Since ordination is essentially a setting apart with prayer for the gift of the Holy Spirit, the authority of the ordained ministry is not to be understood as a possession of the ordained person but as a gift for the edification of the body in and for which the minister has been ordained."[57]

Finally, let us examine a key point from the more general dialogical consensus, which might easily be taken for mere platitude. "Ordained ministers . . . are bound to the faithful in interdependence and reciprocity."[58] The last phrase directly

---

55. International Anglican-Roman Catholic Dialogue, *Ministry and Ordination,* 12.

56. For the text and comment, see Karlhein Schul, ed., *Amt in Widerstreit* (Berlin: Morus Verlag, 1983). A particularly important comment, on the side of the institutes, was by Karl Rahner, "Vom Sein und Auftrag des kirchlichen Amtes," *Amt in Widersheit.*

57. *Baptism, Eucharist and Ministry,* "Ministry," 15.

58. Ibid., 16.

paraphrases the Groupe des Dombes on "the reciprocal dependence of the community and the ordained ministers."[59] But the consensus achieved in the Groupe des Dombes uses this (in itself, obvious or even banal) point far more explicitly and profoundly, to overcome the ancient and tiresome Protestant-Catholic question whether it is "the community as a whole which is responsible" for "teaching" and "delegates qualified people" or whether "there is a distinctive responsibility of the pastoral ministry" not derived from the community.[60] For the Groupe des Dombes, it is through this reciprocity that "the church receives the acts of Christ . . . and that she expresses her recognition of her Lord."[61] In consequence, "Ordained ministers act . . . inseparably as ministers of Christ and of the church,"[62] and therefore have "the authority which corresponds to their pastoral responsibility, to set forth through the faith of the church the sign of Christ's act."[63]

We may summarize the dialogical results on this point as follows. Ordained ministers are authorized by Christ to maintain his authority in the church. The gospel is not the "Christian tradition" but the message about Christ; the sacraments are not our ritual expression but his gifts. In that the ordained are at once servants of Christ and servants of the congregation, it is their pastoral role to make these ownerships plain; even, if need be, to defend the authenticity of the gospel and its sacraments against wishes or fears of the congregation.

This doctrine of ministerial authority, together with the dialogues' double specification of the ministry's charism, effectively attribute to the ordained what traditional language calls *magisterium*, the authority to say what is right teaching of the gospel and what is not. Once it is agreed that pastors must have the authority needed to carry out their role, then the Catholic argument becomes undeniable. "The pastors who are responsible for the well-being of the community have a special responsibility regarding its common confession of faith. When conflicts arise as to the terms of its creed . . . those with pastoral responsibility must have the authority to judge which of the conflicting opinions is in accord with the faith of the church."[64] The argument could be attacked only by supposing that "common confession" is not a necessary part of the flock's unity; groups who could faithfully take this position are outside the dialogues.

Yet dissensus in fact reappears so soon as the word *teaching* falls. Thus Reformed-Roman Catholic dialogue said, "So far as instruction is concerned, for the Reformed it is the community as a whole which is responsible and which delegates qualified people; whereas for the Catholics there is a distinctive responsibility of the pastoral ministry."[65] Such recalcitrance over against the plain

59. Groupe des Dombes, *L'Esprit Saint, l'Eglise et les Sacrements* (1979), 106: "la dépendance réciproque de la communauté et des ministres ordonnés."
60. International Reformed-Roman Catholic Dialogue, *Christ in Church and World*, 107.
61. Groupe des Dombes, *L'Esprit Saint*, 106.
62. Ibid., 107.
63. Ibid., 108.
64. Francis A. Sullivan, *Magisterium: Teaching Authority in the Catholic Church* (Mahwah, N.J.: Paulist Press, 1983), 30.
65. International Reformed-Roman Catholic Dialogue, *Christ in Church and World*, 37. That the opposition as stated is ludicrously false history in what it says of the Reformed communities is itself extremely interesting.

import of established agreement is undoubtedly connected with the circumstance that for Catholicism the *magisterium* is specifically tied to one form of ordained ministry, the episcopacy—and within the episcopacy to the papacy. We have come again to a point where new problems arise.

VIII

The consensus just laid out is extensive, and it would seem that Catholic and Protestant concerns are equally and remarkably satisfied. Yet in fact this consensus has not proven acceptable on either side. Moreover, both sides attack the same point.

In the Catholic response, we read that "a crux in the endeavours towards Christian unity" consists in the "issue of sacramental ordination related to (the) issue of the historic episcopal succession." "Ordination is a sacrament. The competent minister of this sacrament is a bishop who stands in the authentic apostolic succession."[66] But Protestant responses make most objection[67] to the cautious approaches that *BEM* takes toward relating episcopal ministry and sacramental ordination. Some Protestant responses even wonder why ordination, which is "only" after all a sign, should be so insisted upon.[68] We may instance the response of the North Elbian German Evangelical Church. "By ordination we understand an act of calling, sending, authorizing and blessing. . . . The biblical gesture of the imposition of hands and the . . . unrepeatability of ordination are signs of this. But we do not regard ordination as a sacrament . . . nor its lifelong validity as irrevocable." The key proposition of *BEM*—that "ordination is a sign performed in faith that the spiritual relation signified is present in, with and through the words spoken, the gestures made and the forms employed"—the North Elbian Lutherans "have hesitations about accepting at all."[69]

This pattern of remaining difficulty is reflected in an otherwise puzzling structure of *BEM*. Following the fundamental sections from which most of the preceding was drawn, a section on "The Forms of Ordained Ministry" discusses episcopal ministry. This discussion then necessitates a whole renewed consideration of "Succession in the Apostolic Tradition," which turns out to contain *BEM*'s main discussion of ordination's sacramental character.

We have come to another one of the points where dissensus rises from the matter at hand and resettles; though this time the leap is, as it were, centripetal rather than centrifugal. At the end of achieved consensus, it seemingly turns out not to

---

66. Secretariat for the Promotion of Christian Unity, with the Congregation for the Faith, *Response,* 35.

67. E.g., a mainline body in a third-world location, response to *Baptism, Eucharist and Ministry* by the Evangelical Church of Lutheran Confession in Brazil, "Concerning the Contents of the Text," 3.1: "Concentration on the ministry of the bishop . . . and the great weight attached to the formal apostolic succession can undermine the primacy of the Christological dimension."

68. E.g., at some random, the generally very careful and open response of the Presbyterian Church of Wales; Secretariat for The Promotion of Christian Unity, with the Congregation for the Faith, *Response,* 2:164–76.

69. Ibid., 1:50–51.

be the doctrine of ordained ministry that is the problem, or even the sacramental character of ordination. The problem now seems to be a specific form of ordained ministry, its succession, its position as the ministry of sacramental ordination, and its specific role in the teaching authority of the ministry.[70]

These matters require a chapter of their own. For all but the last point just listed, *BEM* can again provide the framework.

5

Episcopacy

I

The question Must we have bishops, in the historically dominant sense of the designation? seems initially straightforward. That is, is the existence within the ordained ministry of bishops *and* presbyters—with the bishops standing in their own sacramentally qualified and significant succession, and exercising functions of episcope specific to them—essential to the integrity of the ordained ministry? The question is often described as a question about the threefold ministry of bishops, presbyters, and deacons, but since all Christian bodies are in the modern situation confused about deacons, only the matter of bishops is divisive.

Most of Protestantism has thought that bishops in this sense are *not* essential, and even that Catholic insistence that they are is itself church-divisive. Much of Protestantism continues to reject dialogue results to the contrary. So the response of the Church of Norway to *Baptism, Eucharist and Ministry (BEM)*: "Such distinctions within the framework of the one ministry . . . rest, in our view, primarily on the basis of practical-theological considerations. . . . It is not intrinsic to the nature of the church that the ministry be divided into . . . categories of bishop, presbyter and deacon."[1]

The matter has weight. The dialogues agree that the ordained ministry is constitutive of the church. What then if episcopal ordering is in turn constitutive of the ministry? A semiofficial commentary assigned by the then Roman Secretariat for the Promotion of Christian Unity approved the results on ministry from international Lutheran-Roman Catholic dialogue except for one chief point. The author could see no way around the invalidity of orders conferred otherwise than by bishops in sacramental succession.[2]

II

BEM begins with and bases itself upon an agreed report of history. Equally contrary to much episcopalian or congregational ideology, "The New Testament does not

---

1. Response to *Baptism, Eucharist and Ministry* of the Church of Norway, 3.5. Or we may read the response of a quite different church, The Methodist Church in the United Kingdom, 4.3.4: "(T)he ends imperfectly realised through the historic episcopate have been and are realised equally well by other structures, with the result that we see the historic episcopate as one possible form of church order, with considerations that commend it . . . but neither normative nor clearly superior to any other."

2. P. Lecuyer, " 'Le ministère dans l'église' selon la rapport Catholique-Luthérrien," *Documentation Catholique* 79(1982): 932–36.

describe a single pattern of ministry which might serve as a blueprint or continuing
norm for all future ministry in the church. In the New Testament there appears
rather a variety of forms which existed at different places and times." Only as
time went on were "certain elements from this early variety . . . further developed
and . . . settled into a more universal pattern of ministry. . . . During the second
and third centuries, a threefold pattern of bishop, presbyter and deacon became
established." Both the contingency of this development and its establishment
"throughout the church" are acknowledged.[3]

But this pattern of ministry was not yet the episcopal pattern that is in ecumenical
dispute, for these second- and early third-century bishops were pastors of eucharistic communities that in current terminology would be called local congregations. This role, however, provided the basis for the future development that
occurred, since therein each bishop provided "a focus of unity" for his congregation
and for the unity of his congregation with others.[4]

Thus the report continues. "Soon . . . the functions were modified. Bishops
began increasingly to exercise episkope over several local communities at the
same time," to provide precisely a "focus" for the more comprehensive churchly
unity that their function in fact posited, for "unity in life and witness within areas
comprising several eucharistic communities." *BEM* provides neither a historical
explanation of this development nor a full rationale for its appropriateness; for
dogmatic purposes the former may not be needed, but the absence of the latter is
a weakness.[5]

The bishops' new role of *episkope* over a larger than congregational flock was
not itself a new phenomenon in the church; "in the first generation" it had been
an essential role of the *apostles*. Moreover, this apostolic role had in the meantime
continuously been filled, in that such persons as "Timothy and Titus are recorded
to have fulfilled a function of *episkope*" in wider areas.[6]

The episcopal office that thus developed, given its existence, is then normatively
describable. Bishops are to "preach the Word, preside at the sacraments, and
administer discipline in such a way as to be representative pastoral ministers of
oversight, continuity and unity in the church."[7]

So far, one may think, so good. To agree that the church has mostly been
governed by bishops of the "historic" sort, to agree on the history of this form
of governance, and to agree that if there are such bishops, they should have the
role just described, should not be hard, but it probably carries us very little toward
meaningful consensus. For two hard questions remain.

3. *Baptism, Eucharist and Ministry*, "Ministry," 19. The frequency with which official churchly
responses blandly ignore that the document itself insists on this point is amazing. Thus, e.g., the
American Lutheran Church somehow thought it useful to argue, "Observations on Ministry," 5: "Lutherans have traditionally regarded matters of polity and structure as adiaphora, as . . . not foundational
or prescribed. . . . The New Testament itself discloses wide varieties of polity or structure."
4. *Baptism, Eucharist and Ministry*, "Ministry," 20.
5. Ibid., 21.
6. Ibid.
7. Ibid., 29.

III

The first such question is, Given that the church came to be episcopally governed, must it always be so governed? As André Birmelé put it, "Are the visible, juridical and institutional forms handed on in the actuality of episcopal ministry constitutive of the church under the same rubric as are the word and the sacraments?"[8]

At this point we need a terminological—and somewhat more than terminological—excursus. In the old polemical language the present question would have been, Is the episcopacy *iure divino,* "by divine law," or merely *iure humano,* "by human law"? Over the centuries, this terminology has occasioned a great deal of discussion at cross-purposes as well as of genuine contradiction, and has the capacity to do both still. Moreover, modern scholarly developments have compelled a shift in the scope of the terminology; this produces new possibilities both of confusion and consensus.

In the conflicts of the Reformation, assertion that something in the church existed *iure divino* meant both that it was necessary to the church and that it was part of the church as instituted at some one time for all. Moreover, the second requirement was taken to be decisive for the first,[9] so that necessity for the life of the church and emergence by historical development within the church's once-instituted life were taken to be inconsistent. Thus Roman Catholics insisted that episcopal order was at least *in nuce* present in the church from its founding by Christ, and the continental reformers insisted that it was only a later development.

Modern historical knowledge makes it impossible to assert dominical institution of the episcopacy. This at first would seem to favor the Protestant side of the old controversy. But the same knowledge makes it equally impossible to assert dominical institution of much else that both sides nevertheless insist is *iure divino.* Even the two dominical sacraments as we know them—for all parties the very paradigm of what is *iure divino,* as may be seen in the citation from Birmelé—emerged in a history much of which follows any plausible founding of the church. If Baptism and the Supper as we know them are *iure divino,* then something can emerge in the already founded church's historical development and yet be mandated by the church's divine foundation.[10] Recognizing the facts at this point works out differently for the two sides.

---

8. André Birmelé, *Le salut en Jésus Christ dans les dialogues oecuméniques* (Paris: Cerf, 1986), 194.

9. For the discussion that has been decisive in ecumenical conversation, see George Lindbeck, "Papacy and the Ius Divinum: A Lutheran View," in vol. 3 of *Lutherans and Catholics in Dialogue,* ed. Paul C. Empie and T. Austin Murphy (Minneapolis: Augsburg, 1974), 193–202. There is some authoritative recognition that the old conceptuality will not hold. The "Cartigny-Bericht I" of the Lutheran World Federation, *Lutherische Rundschau* 21:222, argues: "Das Evangelium kann nur in lebendiger Beziehung mit den jeweils gegebenen gesellschaftlichen Wirklichkeiten Kriterium für die kirchliche Ordnung sein. . . . Auf Grund dieser Einsichten müssen die Begriffe *ius divinum* und *ius humanum* neu durchgedacht werden. . . . Was *ius divinum* und *ius humanum* ist, lässt sich auch niemals adequat unterscheiden. Wir besitzen das *ius divinum* nur in jeweils geschichtlichen Vermittlungsformen."

10. George Lindbeck, "Doctrinal Standards, Theological Theories and Practical Aspects of the Ministry in the Lutheran Churches," in *Evangelium—Welt—Kirche,* ed. Harding Meyer (Frankfurt: Otto Lembeck, 1975), 280–81.

Protestants lose the means by which they have often justified departing from the ancient order. George Lindbeck, who has perhaps been more decisively involved at this point than any other Protestant ecumenist, has delivered what is surely the just verdict. In attempting to distinguish the strictly congregational pastorate from "other ministerial offices, we can no longer make use of the sixteenth century form of the disjunction between the first as *de iure divino* and the others as *de iure humano*."[11] Roman Catholics may now indeed ask of Reformation churches whether ecclesial institutions of later development may not nevertheless be *iure divino* by analogy to "a contemporary theological concept of dominical institution of the sacraments."[12]

Birmelé doubtless did not intend it so, but his question opens to an affirmative answer, or even solicits it. Also by Protestant lights, we must now consider it plausible that some handed-on "visible, juridical and institutional forms" are constitutive of the church under precisely the "same rubric as are the word and the sacraments," in the only way in which that "rubric" can now be meaningful.

Catholics lose a sure means of identifying what is in fact *iure divino*. Since not everything that has emerged in the history of the church can be *iure divino*, how do we know that, to our matter, episcopacy is? Nor will it do to say those historic emergents are *iure divino* that the church's teaching organs certify as such, since these very organs with their authority to make such certifications are the chief historical developments in question.

The classic distinction of *iure divino* from *iure humano* having thus been undone, the possibility is at least posed of finding a better concept of divine ordination, indeed, of seeking one that meets the concerns and embarrassments of both Catholic and Protestant. Lindbeck has proposed the first two steps of such a definition. All must surely agree that "historically relative and conditioned" emergents may nonetheless be called *iure divino* at least in the sense that they are "functionally urgent, i.e., contingently but really necessary 'for the sake of the gospel.' "[13] But neither side, he supposes, will be satisfied with this as a full definition of *iure divino*. In Lindbeck's observation, both sides show they want "irreversibility" added to the definition. To assert that an institution that has emerged historically in the life of the church is *iure divino* is to say that the development by which it emerged may not be undone. Then, he fears, having agreed on the new concept, Catholics and Protestants will simply disagree on what or if any developments in the life of the once founded church can, in fact, be irreversible.[14]

It is indeed likely that consensus can be, or already has been, achieved on such a revised concept of divine ordination. Thus the Roman Congregation for the Faith, responding to the report of international Anglican-Roman Catholic dialogue

---

11. Ibid.
12. Joseph W. Baker, "The Petrine Office: Some Ecumenical Projections," *Papal Primacy and the Universal Church*, vol. 5 of *Lutherans and Catholics in Dialogue*, ed. Paul C. Empie and T. Austin Murphy (Minneapolis: Augsburg, 1974), 215.
13. Lindbeck, "Papacy and the Ius Divinum," 202.
14. Ibid., 203.

on papal primacy, wrote that "the power of jurisdiction over all local churches
. . . belongs inalienably (which is what *iure divino' means*) to this office."[15]
(emphasis added) The disagreement Lindbeck predicted also occurs, as the discussion of *BEM* shows on every hand.

The one point to be added is that this disagreement results from the loss of an
old *criterion* and from crossing "fears and concerns" about a new one. What must
a temporal emergent be like, in the life of the church, to be, though contingent
beforehand, thereafter irreversible? In other words, how does something occur in
time so as to be transcendent to time's following possibilities? Exactly at this
point, the discussion of episcopacy's *"ius"*—as that of other institutions—opens
to the depth at which my study finally aims.

IV

We return to *BEM*, which presents three steps of consensus about episcopacy.
First, it is agreed that "a ministry of episcope" is indeed a constitutive element
in the church, in that such a ministry is "necessary" among the "diversity of gifts
or ministries" through which the Spirit constitutes the church.[16] This is a wide-
reaching agreement; yet we should note its abstraction. It is not the historically
realized episcopate, but rather "a" ministry defined by the *function* episcope,
which is said to be constitutive. Thus the most that can be said normatively is
that "every church needs this ministry of unity *in some form* . . . to be the church
of God."[17] (emphasis added).

This form of agreement in the dialogues is old. The American Lutheran-Episcopal dialogue already agreed in 1971 that "apostolicity" is essential to the church
and that "apostolicity is manifested in various ways in all areas of the church's
life, and is guarded especially by common confession and through that *function*
of the church designated as *episcope.*" (emphasis added) This agreement became
the basis on which one of the few actual, if qualified, restorations of fellowship
achieved by the dialogues came to pass, since it could thereupon be agreed that
the sixteenth-century decisions of both communions were, under their very different
circumstances, appropriate to preserve the church's temporal and geographic unity
in the gospel—the continental decision to reorder the ministry and the English
decision not to.[18] Perhaps more surprisingly, international Anglican-Roman Catholic dialogue could also agree. "It is enough for our purposes that, from the beginning
of the Christian Church, there existed *episcope* in the community, however its
various responsibilities were distributed."[19]

Second, *BEM* affirms that the settling of the church into a "more universal
pattern of ministry," the threefold ministry, occurred as "the Holy Spirit continued

---

15. Congregation for the Faith, "Observations on the ARCIC Final Report," B.III,2, *Origins*
11(1982): 752–56.

16. *Baptism, Eucharist and Ministry*, "Ministry," 23.

17. This exact same pattern appears throughout the dialogues, e.g., in International Reformed-Roman
Catholic Dialogue, *Towards a Common Understanding of the Church* (1990), 142.

18. American Lutheran-Episcopal Dialogue, *A Progress Report,* ed. Peter Day and Paul Opsahl
(FM Maxi Books, 1972), 20–21.

19. International Anglican-Roman Catholic Dialogue, *Elucidations* (1979), 4.

to lead the church."[20] It is a bit hard to know exactly what this says, and that may be intended; but read without undue suspicion, the passage would seem to say that the Spirit led the church to adopt episcopal order instead of some other.

These two teachings taken together—that the church must have a ministry of *episcope* and that the particular historically developed form of such ministry called episcopacy occurred under the guidance of the Spirit—yield a third step: a stated presumption for historically episcopal ordering. This appears as a cautiously stated recommendation. Churches presently without the threefold ministry "will need to ask themselves whether the threefold pattern as developed does not have a powerful claim to be accepted by them."[21]

As was to be expected, bilateral dialogues have achieved less guarded and more argued versions of this consensus. As doubtless was again to be expected, the international Anglican-Roman Catholic report is especially useful. "The Holy Spirit . . . gives to some individuals and communities special gifts . . . which entitle them to speak and be heeded. . . . Among these gifts . . . is the *episcope* of the ordained ministry. . . . (The ordained) exercise their authority in fulfilling ministerial functions related to 'the apostles' teaching and fellowship, to the breaking of bread and the prayers. . . . This pastoral authority belongs primarily to the bishop, who is responsible for preserving and promoting the integrity of the *koinonia*."[22]

Then follows a rationale, only implicit in *BEM*, for the existence of a ministry of episcope covering more than the local eucharistic assembly. "The *koinonia* is realized not only in the local Christian communities, but also in the communion of these communities with one another. The unity of local communities under one bishop constitutes what is commonly meant in our two communions by a 'local church.' " Moreover, "each bishop" must cultivate "the universal communion" of such local churches among themselves; his ministry "expresses" this unity.[23] At whatever level there is communion, there must be pastors, shepherds of the unity; as the communion must transcend the immediate eucharistic fellowship, so there must be pastors of this larger flock.[24]

This rationale depends on a specific ecclesiological concept: the church is understood *essentially* as *koinonia*, so that the local congregation's own integrity must be invested in its communion with other congregations. What has been called the communion-ecclesiology is widespread both in the dialogues and in current scholarly ecclesiology; we will return to it repeatedly.

The responses to *BEM* by nonepiscopal or almost episcopal churches do not reveal any great self-interrogation on the lines suggested. The test will, of course, be the response to actual proposals for restoration of fellowship by extension of historic episcopate to nonepiscopal ministries. Just such a proposal is now before

20. *Baptism, Eucharist and Ministry*, "Ministry," 19.
21. Ibid., 25.
22. International Anglican-Roman Catholic Dialogue, *Authority in the Church* (1976), 5.
23. Ibid., 8.
24. Ibid., 9.

two major communions, in the *Niagara Report* (1987) of the international Anglican-Lutheran dialogue and in the *Concordat of Agreement* (1991), which the American Lutheran-Episcopal dialogue has devised to implement the *Niagara Report* on its territory.

To the Evangelical Lutheran Church in America and to the Episcopal Church the concordat proposes the following for adoption: "Each church hereby promises to invite and include on an invariable basis at least three bishops of the other church, as well as three of its own, to participate in the laying-on-of-hands at the ordination of its own bishops."[25] To the Episcopal Church the concordat proposes this for adoption: "The Episcopal Church hereby recognizes now the full authenticity of the ordained ministries presently existing with the Evangelical Lutheran Church in America." It is further proposed that the Episcopal Church enact a temporary suspension, in this case only, of the canons that provide that no one can exercise presbyteral ministry in the Episcopal Church unless ordained by bishops in the succession.[26]

It is hard to know which fellowship is given the harder potion to swallow. Insofar as Lutheran bodies have come to think of themselves as Protestant churches, they will doubtless balk at any suggestion that they do not have something ecclesial but should. But the ecumenically decisive question is nevertheless that posed to the episcopal churches: whether they can indeed recognize "the full authenticity" of existing ministries not yet episcopally ordered. For to the extent that churches without episcopacy are compelled to disavow the authenticity of their previous ministry in order to reenter fellowship with episcopal churches, such fellowship will be very long in coming.

V

In my judgment, the problematic of the previous section, taken for itself, is resolvable. Let me propose a resolution.

The dialogues generally agree that the existence of the ordained ministry, as this emerges in the Pastoral Epistles, is constitutive of the church and is an irreversible development. Ordained ministry is *iure divino* by any standard according to which anything could now have that status. The Reformation has always contended that this divinely ordained office is fundamentally *one* office, a *pastoral* office of word and sacrament.[27] Whether this was also the teaching of Roman

---

25. American Lutheran-Episcopal Dialogue, *Concordat of Agreement between the Episcopal Church and the Evangelical Lutheran Church in America* (1991), 2.

26. Ibid., 4, 5.

27. E.g., Arbeitsgruppe der deutschen Bischofskonferenz und der Kirchenleitung der Vereinigten Evangelisch-lutherischen Kirche Deutschlands, *Kirchengemeinschaft im Wort und Sakrament* (Paderborn: Bonifatius-Druckerei, 1984), 75. A statement of the Lutheran participants: "Die evangelisch-lutherische Kirche spricht nur von *einer* Ordination zum kirchlichen Amt . . . die ubertragung von kirchenleitenden, in diesem Sinne also episkopalen Amtern gilt als Installation, auch dort, wo ihnen allein die Ordination ubertragen ist und sie faktisch als Konsekration vollzogen wird. . . . Dieser Unterschied, der zweifellos dogmatisches Gewicht hat, muss auf dem Hintergrund der Entwicklung im 16. Jahrhundert gesehen werden. Auch die Wittenberger Reformation suchte das geistliche Amt im Rückgriff auf die altkirchlich Ordnung neu zu verstehen, indem sie das Amt der Leitung in der Stadtkirche als Bischofsamt deutete und den Gottesdienst der Ordination in weitem Unfang als Wieder-aufnahme der altkirchlichen Bischofsweihe strukturierte."

Catholicism may have been unclear until Vatican II, but now it is clear. Also, according to Roman Catholicism, there is, in the singular, "the divinely instituted ecclesiastical ministry" that is "exercised in different orders by those who from ancient times have been called bishops, priests and deacons." In the present teaching of Roman Catholicism, some such differentiation of the one office as the historical distinction of bishop from presbyter is essential, but not, apparently, necessarily always under the titles of "bishops, priests and deacons."[28]

Lumen gentium teaches that the bishop is "invested with the fullness of the sacrament of Orders,"[29] so that presbyters "depend on the bishops in the exercise of their own proper power."[30] This teaching, which once would have been a decisive offense to the Reformation, becomes in its new theological context an ecumenical opening. It now says that the one ecclesial office has its full and foundational expression in the office of *pastor*, of care for diachronic and synchronic unity in the local flock and between local flocks.[31] That the pastor in his flock is the paradigmatic instance of ordained ministry has always been the vehement insistence of the Reformation, against what it until now took to be Roman Catholic teaching.

The next step is to note that in the New Testament the nature of the church realizes itself at three levels. *Ekklesia* in the New Testament (notably in the Pauline canon—so decisive for the Western church generally and for the Reformation in particular) indifferently denotes a local fellowship, or many such fellowships as a class, or all such fellowships as one great fellowship.[32] Consensus at this point is therefore wide and old in the dialogues. We may cite international Lutheran-Roman Catholic dialogue. "The one church of Jesus Christ assumes concrete form

---

28. *Lumen gentium*, 28. To the passage see, e.g., Hans Jorissen, "Inwieweit sind die Dialoge und ihre Ergebnisse verbindlich für die Kirche?" *Les dialogues oecuméniques hier et aujourd'hui*, ed. Centre Orthodoxe du Patriarchat Oecuménique (Chambésy: Centre Orthodox, 1985), 278f: "Bei der Aussage 'presbyterale Ordination/Sukzession' sollte man sich bewusst halten, dass die Unterscheidung zwischen 'bishöflicher' und 'presbyteraler' . . . Ordination/Sukzession auf dem Hintrgrund der historischen Aufgliederung des kirchlichen Amtes zu verstehen ist, dass sie aber nicht notwendig einen dogmatischen Unterschied zum Ausdruck bringt. Diese Auffasung . . . lässt sich . . . von den Aussagen des Zweiten Vatikanum her legitimieren. In der Kirchenkonstitution (LG 28) spricht das Konzil von dem auf göttlicher Stiftung beruhenden kirchlichen Dienstamt . . . das 'in vershiedenen Ordnungen ausgeübt wird von jenen, die schon von altersher . . . Bischöfe, Presbyter, Diakone heissen'. Offensichtlich geht das Konzil von der Einheit des kirchlichen Amtes aus. Von diesem einen Amt wird die göttliche Stiftung ausgesagt. Nun lehrt das Konzil zwar, dass der Bischof die 'Fülle des Weihesakramentes' . . . (LG 26), des ordinierten Amtes also, besitze, es betont ferner die Unterordnung der Presbyter unter den Bischof in Ausübung ihrer Vollmachten (LG 28), es will aber dadurch, und zwar nach Ausweis der Konzilsverhandlungen mit voller Absicht keine Aussage über . . . einen sakramentalen Unterschied zwischen Episkopat und Presbyterat machen."

29. *Lumen gentium*, 26.

30. Ibid., 28.

31. To this, one must observe the invariable language of *Lumen gentium* through the relevant sections. See also the entirety of *Christus dominus*, otherwise significantly titled "Decree on the Pastoral Office of Bishops in the Church." What is possible on the basis of contemporary Catholic teaching appears, as usual, early and decisively in the work of the Groupe des Dombes, *Le ministère épiscopal* (1976), 102: "Cette revalorisation du ministère de l'épiscopé, qui inclut la personalisation, devrait conduire les Eglises de la Réforme à retrouver le sens et la nature spécifique d'un ministère d'unité essentiellement destiné à promouvoir la réconciliation, entretenir la communion et orienter la mission globale de l'Eglise."

32. E.g., I Corinthians 1:1; 7:17; 12:28.

in local churches which participate in the diversity of historical, cultural and racial situations in which the people live to whom the gospel is proclaimed in word and sacrament. The church is therefore a communion (*communio*) subsisting in a network of local churches."[33]

Again the ecumenical communion-ecclesiology emerges. Consensus in this motif is truly widespread, opening also into dialogue between East and West. Its foundation, moreover, is everywhere *trinitarian*, opening into the proposals I will make to this book's final problem. I cite here only the so-called *Munich Report* of international Orthodox-Roman Catholic dialogue. "Because the one and only God is the communion of three Persons, the one and unique church is a communion of many communities and the local church a communion of persons."[34] Cardinal Willebrands has seen here a key for dialogue and eventual restored fellowship both with the East *and* within the West. "The church . . . finds its origin, its model and its goal in the mystery of the Trinity. From this insight of faith, the secret of 'One in Many' can be opened in its deep context of being and life, both for the relation of local churches among themselves and for their relation to the universal church."[35]

But note that while it belongs essentially to the church, as the New Testament describes it, to exist congregationally, regionally (locally), and universally, it cannot be *iure divino* to which of the first two levels the chief pastoral order of ministry. (That is, the episcopal order) cannot be coordinated *iure divino*.[36] For this order was born and formed at what at least then became the parochial level, yet later, without any suggestion that the earlier pattern had been wrong, was transferred to a more regional level. Alternatively stated, while it may be *iure divino* that the chief pastor, the bishop, shepherds the local church, it cannot be *iure divino* whether it is the parochial or more regional manifestation that functions as the local church, since both have done so within the period of history during which the general legitimacy of development is undisputed.

At the time of the Reformation, most continental reformers transferred the chief pastoral office from the dioceses as these were then defined, to town parishes and

---

33. International Lutheran-Roman Catholic Dialogue, *Facing Unity*, 5.
34. International Roman Catholic-Orthodox Dialogue, *Le mystère de l'église et de l'eucharistie à la lumière du mystère de la Sainte Trinité* (1982), III.2.
35. Jan Cardinal Willebrands, "Die Bedeutung der Verhandlungen der römisch-katholischen Kirche mit den orthodoxen Kirchen und der Anglikanischen Gemeinschaft für die Lehre von der sakramentalen Struktur der Kirche," *Die Sakramentalität der Kirche in der ökumenischen Disskussion*, ed. Johann-Adam-Möller Institut (Paderborn: Bonifatius-Druckerei, 1983), 17.
36. Arbeitsgruppe der deutschen Bischofskonferenz und der Kirchenleitung der Vereinigten Evangelisch-lutherischen Kirche Deutschlands, *Kirchengemeinschaft in Wort und Sakrament*, 76–77: "Dazu lässt sich wohl sagen, dass im Rückblick auf das N. T. and die frühe Kirche es nicht ausschlaggebend sein kann, ob das Bischofsamt auf der lokalen oder auf der regionalen Ebene angesiedelt ist. Der Bischof ist ursrprünglich der Leiter einer Ortsgemeinde. Deshalb sollte es auch heute keine ins Grundsätzliche reichende Differenz sein, dass der Vollauftrage des kirchlichen Amtes in der Römische-katholischen Kirche wie in der Orthodoxie im jetzt regionalen Bischofsamt am klarsten heraustritt, in der lutherischen Kirchen im lokalen Pfarramt, das im theologishcne Verständnis wesentliche Elemente des altkirchlichen Bischofsamtes aufgenommen hat."

central congregations of cities, while maintaining functional and cultic continuity. Only so, as they diagnosed the situation, could they salvage the integrity of the church at their place and time. This was done, clearly, *iure humano,* thereby in effect partly restoring the most ancient form of the episcopacy. If the foregoing argument has any force, nothing that Catholic teaching now certifies as *iure divino* can have been violated by this action taken for itself.

But what was done *iure humano* can be undone by the same right, and without compromise of principle. Moreover, excellent *iure humano* reasons exist for saying that normally it will be better to correlate the paradigmatic and constitutive pastoral office to the diocesan rather than the parochial level—not least among them the demands of ecumenical reconciliation.

The church has always manifested the three levels that appear in the New Testament. But the church has also regularly been disturbed by ideological and practical struggle among the three for sovereignty, for recognition as that assembly of believers in which the others paradigmatically find themselves. At which level should we locate those shepherds who are, in the terms of Vatican II, "invested with the fullness" of the one ministerial order?

Nor is this struggle adventitious to the nature of the church, for it results from the pull between two equally vital characters of churchly *koinonia:* its eucharistic location and its promised catholicity. The church is itself in celebration of the Eucharist; must not that level of community that can regularly gather be "the" church? The church is catholic, it is in its fulfillment but one great assembly; must not the one universal church therefore be "the" church?

It seems an obvious solution. Surely the most appropriate level of assembly to be invested with paradigmatic and communally constitutive status will be that which can, however imperfectly, manifest both of these poles. The one catholic church will gather for service only on and after the last day; the parochial congregation that regularly gathers does not by itself manifest that there is one catholic church. But the regional church, if of proper size for its pastor to practice a pastoral role, is sometimes an actual eucharistic assembly, and yet is in itself a widening communion of plural continuing eucharistic fellowships.

Let us move to the final difficulty in this matter. Even the question of how we may know that the episcopacy belongs to those historical emergents that may not be reversed is, in the context now established, soluble. Indeed, the solution is already present in the literature. The dialogues establish that the pastoral office (now agreed to be paradigmatically realized in the bishop's role) exercises magisterium, to speak authoritatively to what is and what is not the truth of the gospel. But that is to say, "When we are talking about the universal reception of bishops as authoritative teachers whose decisions on matters of faith were recognized as binding on the faithful, we are talking about the reception by the Church of a norm of its faith." A church "that is indefectible in its faith" cannot "have been mistaken when it determined what was going to be the norm of its faith."[37]

---

37. Francis A. Sullivan, *Magisterium: Teaching Authority in the Catholic Church* (Mahwah, N.J.: Paulist Press, 1983), 30–31.

This last argument is surely valid. A simpler form cuts even more decisively through Protestant hesitations. George Lindbeck has stated it with lapidary precision. "It is to (the) episcopally unified church . . . that all the major Christian traditions owe their creeds, their liturgies, and above all their scriptural canon. If these latter are unexpungable, why not also the episcopate?"[38] The famous threesome of canon, creed, and episcopate emerged simultaneously, in joint response to a single crisis in the life of the church, and were in their origin mutually interdependent aspects of one historical structure. If any one of the three is to be regarded as the result of a reversible development, so must the other two.

The notion of the church's indefectibility has just appeared. Even the bugaboo of infallibility is just around the corner. Again, questions at the heart of this study beckon. For now, however, it will suffice to note that also Protestantism has, in obedience to Christ's promise, believed that the gates of hell will not prevail against the church, that the church cannot fall definitively from faith. Moreover, precisely Protestantism, which insists on proclamation of the gospel as the center of the church's life, must identify false teaching as that above all to which the church can never fall definitively.

Those proposals do not make the existence and authority of the episcopal office itself a matter of merely human right. What *is* of human right is whether this office is exercised at the more parochial or regional level. All must admit that this is the case, since within the history of the undivided church this office was moved from one level to the other. In contrast, once it is clear that the episcopal office is not another office than the ordained ministry but its paradigmatic and fully realized order, and that it has this status because it is the paradigmatically pastoral order of the office, the divine right of the episcopate cannot be challenged by any principle of the Reformation.

VI

The second of the hard questions is, Even if the episcopal ordering of the ministry is, in the way just specified, essential to the ministry, does that order essentially involve continuous ritual and intentional succession in office? Is apostolic succession, in the sense of location in the ancient train of episcopal consecrations, essential to the irreversibly mandated episcopal order?[39]

This question reaches even more deeply into the matters with which this book must finally labor than does the issue of irreversibility. While convincing solutions may be offered within the present terms of discussion, it is almost inconceivable that many will within the present terms of discussion be convinced. We need new terms of discourse.

38. George Lindbeck, "The Church," *Keeping the Faith: Essays to Mark the Centenary of Lux Mundi,* ed. Goeffrey Wainwright (Philadelphia: Fortress, 1988), 199.

39. Arbeitsgruppe der deutschen Bischofskonferenz und der Kirchenleitung der Vereinigten Evangelisch-lutherischen Kirche Deutschlands, *Kirchengemeinschaft im Wort und Sakrament,* 77: "Das eigentliche dogmatische Problemm (kommt) erst bei der Ordinationsvollmacht des Bischofs in den Blick im Zummenhang des katholischen Verständnisses von 'apostolischer Sukzession.' "

There is multilateral consensus to a certain point. *BEM* begins with somewhat slighted recognition of an imperative Reformation concern. "The primary manifestation of apostolic succession is to be found in the apostolic tradition of the Church as a whole."[40] Or as the Groupe des Dombes stated it earlier, apostolic succession "must be taken in the context of the total continuity of the church, as she is founded by the apostles . . . , and in virtue of the Lord's promise . . . and the Spirit's assistance, carries through history . . . the responsibility for proclamation of the gospel."[41]

Then the multilateral consensus continues. "Within the Church the ordained ministry has a particular task of preserving and actualizing the apostolic faith. The orderly transmission of the ordained ministry is therefore a powerful expression of the continuity of the Church throughout history."[42] Once episcopacy was there, "the succession of bishops became one of the ways . . . in which the apostolic tradition of the Church was expressed." Later, the document speaks of episcopal succession as "serving, symbolizing and guarding" the church's apostolic tradition.[43] Later again, the one is a "sign, though not a guarantee" of the other.[44] As with ordination itself, *BEM* thinks that episcopal succession has sacramental character—however episcope itself is realized—but is loathe to assert it.

Episcopal succession *expresses* churchly continuity; it is its *sign* and *symbol*. The question is, Is this sign, while of course no guarantee, an *effective* sign? If it is, it has that quality that the general Western tradition has labeled sacramental.

There is a clearly developed contemporary Catholic position that begins by tracing the multilateral consensus; I will here draw it from the ecumenical writings of Walter Kasper and Joseph Cardinal Ratzinger. Its starting point is in my judgment fully agreeable to the Reformation. "The church as a whole is apostolic, insofar as it stands in succession of the apostolic faith. Succession in office must be understood within this *successio fidei* of the total church; it is a weighty sign of this succession, but is not itself the matter of the sign. It is in this sense that apostolic succession was understood in the ancient church and in this sense it is now again increasingly understood in Catholic theology."[45]

---

40. *Baptism, Eucharist and Ministry*, "Ministry," 35.

41. Groupe des Dombes, *La succession apostolique* (1968), 1: "Cette succession doit être comprise dans le context de la permanence de l'Église tout entière." *International Lutheran-Roman Catholic Dialogue, The Ministry in the Church* (1981), 59–60, defined a "substantive sense" of apostolic succession as "the apostolicity of the church in faith" and formally agreed that "the starting point must be the apostolicity of the church in the substantive sense." Walter Kasper, "Zur Frage der Anerkennung der Ämter in den lutherischen Kirchen," *Evangelium—Welt—Kirche*, ed. Harding Meyer (Frankfurt: Otto Lembeck, 1975), 405–6, states the position of much contemporary Roman Catholic theology. "Die gesamte Kirche ist apostolische, insofern sie in der Sukzession des apostolischen Glaubens steht. Die Sukzession der Amtsnachfolge muss innerhalb dieser *successio fidei* der Gesamtkirche verstanden werden; sie ist dafür ein wichtiges Zeichen, aber sie ist nicht die Sache selbst, um die es geht. In diesem Sinn wurde die apostolischen Sukzession in der Alten Kirche verstanden, und in diesem Sinn wird sie heute in zunehmenden Mass in der katholischen Theologie wieder verstanden."

42. *Baptism, Eucharist and Ministry*, "Ministry," 35.

43. Ibid., 36.

44. Ibid., 38.

45. Walter Kasper, "Zur Frage der Anerkennung," 405–6.

But then the Catholic argument moves to the exact point at which *BEM* hesitates: taking episcopal *collegiality* as constitutive for episcopal ministry. The *diachronic* aspect of collegiality is understanding that every bishop occupies a previously occupied see and is consecrated by those who are already bishops. If a bishop as chief pastor holds the magisterium, if he "is a man who can explicate the voice of the universal church in matters of doctrine,"[46] then just as the bishops' contemporaneous unity will effect the church's sychronic unity in the gospel, so their unity through time will effect the church's gospel-unity through time. Consecration of bishops by those who are bishops "is at once the expression and the warrant of joint perseverance in the tradition from the beginning."[47] "Apostolic succession is thus no merely formal authority, but participation in the continuing mission of the gospel. In the ancient church, the concepts of succession and of tradition therefore overlap. "The successio-structure" is but the person-aspect of the "catholic church's general binding by tradition and of its idea of tradition."[48]

Roman Catholicism's official response to *BEM* closely followed this theology and in its terms defined Catholicism's ecumenically minimum position. In the existing multilateral consensus, according to this response, "Episcopacy is rightly described as 'a focus of unity.' " The consensus fails by slighting the "essential *collegial* aspect of episcopacy" (emphasis added), without which the many bishops would not in fact be a focus of unity between their local churches.[49] When we see the essential collegiality of episcopal ministry, then we can also see how the bishop's "ministry is a sacramental sign of integration and a focus of communion," across both space and—to our concern—time. The succession of ordinations is the temporal form of episcopal collegiality. Thus the bishop's ministry, precisely by virtue of the bishops' succession one upon another, "embodies and actualizes" not only "communion lived in each generation," but "catholicity in time."[50]

Some bilateral dialogues have come very close to these propositions. The Groupe des Dombes states: "In the present and for the future (the bishops' ministries) assure the continuity of the church's path. . . . In light of this understanding of episcopal ministry . . . we are able to affirm that the succession of the apostolic ministry realizes itself principally through the episcopal succession."[51] Yet to the key question, the response of, say, the Church of Norway is as clear as that of

46. Joseph Cardinal Ratzinger, *Église, oecuménisme et politique,* trans. P. Jordan, P.-E. Gudenus, and B. Müller (Paris: Fayard, 1987), 103, in comment on international Anglican-Roman Catholic dialogue.
47. Joseph Cardinal Ratzinger, "Die Kernfrage im katholisch-reformatorischen Disput: uberlieferung and Successio apostolica," *Theologische Prinzipienlehre* (München: Erich Wewel, 1982), 256.
48. Ibid., 257.
49. *Churches Respond to BEM,* ed. Max Thurian (Geneva: World Council of Churches, 1988), 6:31.
50. Ibid., 33.
51. Groupe des Dombes, *Le ministère épiscopal,* 93. International Anglican-Roman Catholic concord is perhaps less surprising, *Ministry and Ordination* (1973), 16. "Moreover, because (the bishops who ordain a new bishop) are representatives of their churches in fidelity to the teaching and mission of the apostles and are members of the episcopal college, their participation . . . ensures the historical continuity of this church with the apostolic church. . . . The communion of the churches in mission, faith, and holiness, through time and space, is thus symbolized and maintained in the bishop."

Rome and precisely contrary. "The matter of a personal succession of the so-called 'historical episcopacy' can never be anything more than a sign of doctrinal continuity."[52]

There is, of course, something logically strange in positions like that of the Church of Norway. If they accept that the ministry itself is constitutive of the church,[53] then within the context of contemporary Roman Catholic understanding of the episcopal office, as the paradigmatic and foundational exercise of the *one pastoral* ministry, Catholic assertion that succession in this office is an effective sign of "catholicity in time" in fact contains nothing to which they can reasonably object. But something about this precise matter cripples the persuasive force of mere logic.

The Lutheran members of the German bishops' ecumenical group have perhaps stated the maximum consensus currently possible between Roman Catholicism and any Protestant group outside the Anglican communion. It is agreed

> that there are successions of office and of ordination, and that the unity of the church through history can be understood as a weave of tradition and reception in a succession of teaching. The firm order—which could be broken only in extreme situations of necessity—that ordinations are performed by those already ordained . . . creates in fact also in evangelical-Lutheran churches a succession-chain among the latter. Again, it seems only a small step to bring into connection the rule . . . , also firmly established in church law, that ordination belongs to the ministry of occupants . . . of episcopal offices, in order to come very close indeed to the practice which underlies the doctrine of 'apostolic succession.' And the impression of convergence is strengthened, in that we today agree that the continuity of a chain of consecrations does not guarantee community with the apostles, but does indeed testify to it and *effectively signify* it.[54] (emphasis added)

It is hard to see what these erudite Lutherans can possibly mean when they affirm that episcopal succession "effectively signifies" the church's apostolicity yet seem to think they are holding something back from consensus by denying that it "guarantees" it. For of course even Baptism and the Eucharist do not "guarantee" salvation or brotherly love. Yet something has moved the Lutherans to make the distinction. Then the statement concludes with a reservation that reflects back on what otherwise seemed agreed. "But does such a succession of ordination belong to the necessary marks of the church? Would not that bind the validity of churchly office inappropriately to an inner-worldly criterion?"[55]

Joseph Cardinal Ratzinger has seen the precise issue. "One could formulate the real question" that stands between the Reformation and Catholicism: "Can the authenticity of the Word and the authenticity of the church come forward

---

52. *Churches Respond to BEM*, 2:12.

53. Lutherans, like the Norwegians, in any case, are in no position to hang back. It has been Lutheran teaching for centuries that God uses "the ecclesial office" to *create* the church, that the ministry is the church's *"causa efficiens instrumentalis"*; e.g., Johann Gerhard, *Loci theologici* XXII, v, 37, 40.

54. Arbeitsgruppe der deutschen Bischofskonferenz und der Kirchenleitung der Vereinigten Evangelisch-lutherischen Kirche Deutschlands, *Kirchengemeinschaft im Wort und Sakrament*, 303.

55. Ibid.

where there is a break with the concrete continuity of the church, as it is episcopally governed?"[56] Does the concrete historical continuity of the church belong to the church's character *as* church?

56. Joseph Cardinal Ratzinger, "Fragen zur Sukzession," *KNA—Kritischer Oekumenischer Informationsdienst*, 28/29:6. The German Arbeitsgruppe, Kirchengemeinschaft "Beide Kirchen stimmen darin überein . . . dass für die Wortverkündigung and für die Sakramentenverwaltung das Amt gestiftet ist und Ämter in der Kirchen notwendig sind. . . . Kontrovers ist zwischen uns aber, ob und inwiefern zu diesem Amt . . . eine bestimmte geschichtliche Gestalt gehört, um gültiges Zeichen der Einheit sein zu können."

⑥

Roman Primacy

I

Supposing that bishops in their collegiality and succession are essential to the church, must one of their number be first among them and must this one possess a universal ministry, with its appropriate charism? If this is needful, does the universal bishop need to be precisely the bishop of Rome? Must there be "the papacy"?

With two—to be sure, major—exceptions, the dialogues have proceeded on the usually tacit supposition that the question of Roman primacy should be saved for last. The postponement is understandable. For centuries, if Protestants could find no other way to justify their separation from the main body of Western Christianity, they have simply refused, in the name of Christian freedom, to be subject to the Pope. The form in which the first Vatican Council dogmatized papal supremacy was guided in part by determination to define the office that this refusal would reliably continue. The dialogues have perceptibly feared that here was the stone that could not be budged by dialogue, and have delayed attacking it in hope that it would somehow roll over of its own.

Yet plainly, unless there is a catastrophe of the world in which the church now exists such that all predictions must be abandoned, no reunion of the church can take place unless one unifying factor is the primacy of the bishop of Rome. This fact may indeed pose the singular obstacle that only a new extraordinary act of God's mercy can solve. Notoriously, at the very beginning of modern Roman Catholic ecumenism, Paul VI said, "We are aware, that the pope is undoubtedly the greatest obstacle in the path of the Ecumene."[1]

Yet, somewhat paradoxically, the papacy poses few actually new theological problems for dialogue. For the traditional questions about primacy, universal ordinary and immediate jurisdiction and infallibility are but specifications of questions already posed by the ecclesial office generally and the episcopacy more particularly, or at least so the problematic presents itself now, after Vatican II.[2] Insofar as the definitions of the first Vatican Council were thereafter most often interpreted by the "ultramontane" theology of genuine papal imperialists, Roman Catholic theology understood bishops on a presumed model of the Pope. But

---

1. Paul VI, to the Secretariat for Christian Unity, *Acta apostolicae sedis* 59(1967): 498.
2. Once again, our guide can be J. M. R. Tillard, in this matter with his *The Bishop of Rome*, trans. John de Satgé (Wilmington: Michael Glazier, 1983).

Vatican II made it necessary to understand "the pope's function by looking at the bishops and not the other way around."[3]

II

Two dialogues have tackled the matter: the international Anglican-Roman Catholic dialogue and the American Lutheran-Roman Catholic dialogue. I will consider each separately, the Anglican dialogue first.

The consensus this dialogue reported is surely all that is possible within present parameters of discussion—or perhaps rather more than all. The question is located under the rubric of "authority in the church."[4] Churchly authority is interpreted generally by an understanding of the church as *koinonia*, "which consciously seeks to submit to Jesus Christ"[5] and therefore involves relations of authority and obedience, and by a doctrine of "gifts of the Spirit for the edification of the church." Among these latter is "the *episcope* of the ordained ministry." This ministry must have the sorts of authority necessary for the exercise of its charisms.[6]

At this point a step-by-step argument begins. The warrant at each step of the argument is the character of the church as *koinonia:* at each successive level the mutual unity of the church requires a specific episcope.

Step one: The pastoral authority of the ordained ministry "belongs primarily to the bishop," the pastor of the "local" church,[7] in that he "is responsible for preserving and promoting the integrity of (its) *koinonia*."[8] Step two: Churchly "*koinonia* is realized not only in the local Christian communities, but also in the communion of these communities with one another."[9] Accordingly, it occurred "early in the history of the church" that "a function of oversight of the other bishops of their regions was assigned to bishops of prominent sees." This oversight is to serve the constitutive *koinonia* of the church, in that it serves unity among the "local" churches.[10] Step three: "Within the context" of this development of a system of metropolitan and patriarchal sees, "the see of Rome . . . eventually became the principal center in matters concerning the church universal." In "analogy with the position of Peter among the apostles," the particular oversight of the bishop of Rome is to promote universal fellowship, "to guard and promote the faithfulness of all the churches to Christ and one another."[11]

Finally, in response to questions and objections, it is made explicit that the "*episcope* of a universal primate" is consensually affirmed to be "the will of God," and that this affirmation is a "doctrinal" and not merely a "historical"

---

3. Ibid., 37.
4. Anglican-Roman Catholic Conversations, *Authority in the Church* (1976).
5 Ibid., 4.
6. Ibid., 5.
7. That is, of whatever smaller than "metropolitan" eucharistic community is in a historical period the basic pastoral unit.
8. Ibid.
9. Ibid., 8.
10. Ibid., 10.
11. Ibid., 12.

statement.[12] The argument is intended to establish that the church by its divinely willed nature "needs . . . a universal primate as servant and focus of visible unity in truth and love."[13]

So far—and it is, of course, very far—so consensually. But here Anglican fears emerge. These fears turn out to be precisely those that Protestant groups display about the episcopacy more generally.

Thus we have seen wide consensus that a ministry of episcope belongs essentially to the church. Protestants typically, however, doubt that the historically developed form of this ministry, the diocesan episcopate in sacramental succession, is similarly essential. Ecumenists agree that episcope is *iure divino*, but do not so readily agree that the actual episcopal system is. Entirely analogously, Anglicans in the dialogue agree that a universal episcope is essential, and that such an *episcope* obviously cannot be exercised by competing ministers; but that it must be precisely the bishop of Rome who holds the position is stated with great circumspection: "The only see which makes any claim to universal primacy and which has exercised and still exercises such *episcope* is the see of Rome, the city where Peter and Paul died. It seems *appropriate* that in any future union a universal primacy such as has been described should be held by that see."[14] (emphasis added)

Therewith, of course, the dialogue embroils itself in the ambiguities of the possible divine right of historical emergents. If indeed the papacy is the final stone of ecumenical stumbling, it is because the appearance of a papacy with universal jurisdiction is the most practically obtrusive case of an indisputably later historical development for which irreversibility is claimed. The Anglicans could agree that "the primacy of the bishop of Rome can be affirmed as part of God's design for the universal *koinonia*,"[15] that it exists by divine providence. Then the commission suggested, "It is reasonable to ask whether a gap really exists between the assertion of a primacy by divine right (*iure divino*) and the acknowledgement of its emergence by divine providence (*divina providentia*)."[16]

Within the argument of the report, this hopeful—and, I think, ultimately true—approximation of divine right and divine providence depends on a particular interpretation of the two Vatican councils. Vatican I laid it down that the papacy exists by "divine right";[17] the Anglicans make it plain that they cannot accept the definition if it must mean "that as long as a church is not in communion with the bishop of Rome, it is regarded by the Roman Catholic Church as less fully a church."[18] But as the dialogue interprets Vatican II, the teaching of *this* council "allows it to be said that a church out of communion with the Roman see may lack nothing from the viewpoint of the Roman Catholic Church except that it does

---

12. Anglican-Roman Catholic Conversations, *Elucidations* (1981), 8.
13. Anglican-Roman Catholic Conversations, *Authority in the Church II* (1981), 33.
14. Anglican-Roman Catholic Conversations, *Elucidations*, 8.
15. Anglican-Roman Catholic Conversations, *Authority in the Church II*, 15.
16. Ibid., 13.
17. Indeed, according to *Pastor aeternus*, c. ii, "*Si quis ergo dixerit, non esse . . . iure divino, ut beatus Petrus in primatu super universam ecclesiam habeat perpetuos successores . . . , anathema sit.*"
18. Anglican-Roman Catholic Conversations, *Authority in the Church I*, 24.

not belong to the visible manifestation of full Christian communion which is maintained in the Roman Catholic Church."[19]

But just this argument, which makes consensus possible for Anglicans, and evidently for Catholics on the dialogue commission, has proven unacceptable to Roman Catholic authority. The Roman Congregation for the Faith, in its evaluation of the dialogue's report, explicitly rejected the key interpretation of Vatican II, and said that according "to Catholic tradition, visible unity is not something extrinsic added to the particular churches, which already would possess . . . in themselves the full essence of the church; this unity pertains to the intimate structure of faith,"[20] so that a local church lacking something that is acknowledged to be the appropriate sign of universal communion must merely for that reason be indeed regarded as "less fully a church."[21]

Ensuing on the Roman See's claim to primacy is its claim of jurisdiction. Vatican I laid it down that the pope possesses an authority throughout the universal church that is "properly episcopal," "ordinary," and "immediate."[22] That is to say, the bishop of Rome is a functioning bishop for all local churches, his episcopal authority in them is not derived from that of the local bishops but is inherent in his own office, and he need not work through the mediation of the local bishops. This claim is understandably said to be "a source of anxiety to Anglicans,"[23] whose self-understanding and ecclesial justification have historically been constituted by a decidedly decentralized understanding of episcopal governance.

The dialogue again finds comfort in an interpretation of the two Vatican councils, according to which the authority of the pope is not intended to override "the authority of the bishops in their own dioceses" and does not "imply submission to an authority which would stifle the distinctive features of the local churches."[24] Primacy and "conciliarity"[25] must be understood and practiced as "complementary

---

19. Anglican-Roman Catholic Conversations, *Authority in the Church II*, 12.

20. Congregation for the Faith, "Observations on the ARCIC Final Report," II,2. Moreover, Joseph Cardinal Ratzinger has made this point his own. "The report of ARCIC must be contradicted, when it says that Vatican II allows it to be taught that, from the point of view of Rome, a particular church without communion with Rome lacks nothing to be the church but adhesion to the visible manifestation of Christian community. . . . For there is indeed a pre-eminence of the universal church over the particular church." "Problèmes et espoirs du dialogue Anglicans-Catholiques," *Église, oecuménisme et politique*, trans. P. Jordan, P.-E. Gudenus, and B. Müller (Paris: Fayard, 1987), 103–4.

21. Let me for the sake of my conscience say here that the congregation is clearly, of course, correct in principle. Since unity is a creedal predicate of the church, for any "local" church to be out of fellowship with any body that it acknowledges as church is for its own churchly reality to be called into question; that is the very dynamic of the ecumenical movement. Rome seems unable to admit that it has the same problem, having once at all acknowledged the churchly character of other communions.

22. *Pastor aeternus*, c. iii. To the historical interpretation of this language, see Gustave Thils, *Primauté et infaillibilité du pontife romain à Vatican I* (Leuven: Peeters, 1989), 61–106.

23. Anglican-Roman Catholic Conversations, *Authority of the Church I*, 24. It frightened a large number of the Catholic bishops at the council in exactly the same way; Thils, *Primauté et infaillibilité*, 61–91.

24. Ibid., 12.

25. Ibid., 19–20.

elements of *episcope*," and errors not repeated whereby "it has often happened that one has been emphasized at the expense of the other."[26]

In struggling with this question, the dialogue made a decisive contribution by developing an explicit doctrine of the authority "attributed to . . . those exercising *episcope* at different levels." This authority is in each case "determined by the specific functions which (a bishop) is required to discharge in relation to his fellow bishops."[27] "Each bishop is entrusted with the pastoral authority needed for the exercise of his (sort of) *episcope*."[28] Thus, although the scope of a *universal* jurisdiction "cannot be precisely defined canonically, there are moral limits to its exercise: they derive from the nature of the Church and of the universal primate's pastoral office," the latter of which is "the task of safeguarding the . . . unity of the universal Church."[29]

However, this valuable doctrine by itself is probably not sufficient for generally viable consensus. "Jurisdiction" is a legal concept, and must necessarily carry some legal meaning. A person's jurisdiction is his or her legitimate ability to state what is the law, within a territory or sphere of competence. A legal competence that cannot be legally (in churchly language, canonically) defined is defined as totalitarian.

A universal jurisdiction of any bishop is, moreover, a notion anciently ominous to most of the church. So in Orthodox-Anglican dialogue, on behalf of the Orthodox: "The Ecumenical Councils ascribe a position of special seniority . . . not only to the See of Rome but also to that of Constantinople; and this fact needs to be taken into account in any Christian reunion. The Ecumenical Patriarch does not, however, claim universal jurisdiction over the other Churches, such as is ascribed to the Pope . . . and Orthodox see any such claim as contrary to the meaning of seniority."[30] In *this* dialogical context, it could be said straightforwardly also for the other partner. "The Anglican Communion has developed on the Orthodox rather than the Roman Catholic pattern."[31]

"Anglicans," they say in the dialogue with Roman Catholicism, "are entitled to assurance that acknowledgement of the universal primacy of the bishop of Rome

26. Ibid., 22.
27. Anglican/Roman Catholic Conversations, *Authority of the Church II*, 16.
28. Ibid., 17.
29. Ibid., 19.
30. "The Mystery of the Church," *Anglican-Orthodox Dialogue*, ed. Kallistos Ware and Charles Davey (London: SPCK, 1977), 27. For a pure statement of the Orthodox understanding, unperturbed by the exigencies of dialogue with Rome. "Les éveques sont, de droit divin égaux entre eux. . . . Cependant, bien que du point du vue de l'autorité épiscopale les évéques soinent égaux . . . , la vie du l'Église, déjà dés les trois premiers siècles, amena à une différentiation entre l'honneur dû aux différents sièges. Les éveques de certaines Églises locales qui, pour différentes raisons, avaient acquis une autorité plus grande, jouissaient du'un honneur particulier et exerçaient un rule plus important dans les affaires ecclésiales. . . . C'est d'un tel primat d'honneur que jouissait tout particulièrement l'éveque de Rome. . . . C'est pour cette raison que, selon l'enseignement des Églises orthodoxe et vieille-catholique, quelcuus des décisions postérieures qui conférèrent à l'éveque de Rome un pouvoir absolue . . . et qui le considèrent infaillable . . . n'est acceptable" (Orthodox-Old Catholic Conversations, "Chambesy Document," *Episkepsis* 14[1983] 11).
31. Ibid., 29.

would not involve the . . . imposition of . . . alien traditions."[32] It is hard to see what such an assuring limitation of papal jurisdiction could consist in, if it cannot be canonical. Communions other than the Anglican will not be as hopeful. Thus the Church of Norway, in official response to international Lutheran-Roman Catholic dialogue, rejected even that dialogue's far less compromising proposals for gradual integration and joint nomination of the episcopacy, "if it is not intended that bishops who come from a Lutheran ecclesial connection, together with their churches, will be freed from the jurisdiction of the pope. Subjection to the papal office in its present form does not come into question."[33]

Finally there is the matter of infallibility. Notoriously, Vatican I decreed it to be divinely revealed truth. "When the Roman pontiff . . . in the exercise of his office as shepherd and teacher of all Christians . . . defines a doctrine concerning faith or morals to be held by the whole church, he possesses . . . that infallibility which the divine Redeemer willed his church to enjoy. . . . Therefore, such definitions of the Roman pontiff are of themselves, and not by consent of the church, irreformable."[34] Against this may again be set the consensual opinion of the rest, and majority, of the church. So international Anglican-Orthodox dialogue reads: "Both Anglican and Orthodox agree that infallibility is not the property of any particular institution or person in the Church, but that the promises of Christ are made to the whole church."[35] The decisive question, of course, is whether these two propositions are irretrievably contrary.

The Anglican-Roman Catholic commission did labor mightily. They agreed that the church is, to use current terminology, *indefectible,* that her magisterium "will . . . not fail to reach its goal,"[36] and that the church will be preserved "from fundamental error."[37] They agreed that this "requires that at certain moments the Church can in a matter of essential doctrine make a decisive judgment which becomes part of its permanent witness."[38] They agreed that "universal councils" and "a universal primate" are "instruments" of this indefectibility, so that through these "agencies the Church can make a decisive judgment in matters of faith, and so exclude error."[39] They even agreed that "it is not through reception by the people of God that a definition first acquires authority,"[40] thus satisfying the Vatican decree's "not by consent of the church." Finally, they agreed that it "inheres" in the office of a universal primate that in order to carry out this ministry "he should

32. Ibid., 22.

33. General Synod of the Church of Norway, "Facing Unity"—Response of the Church of Norway, "Unity in the Ecclesial Office?"

34. *Pastor aeternus,* c. iv. The hardest part is, of course, "*Romani pontificis definitiones ex sese, non autem ex consensu ecclesiae irreformabiles esse.*" To this definition see now Thils, *Primauté et infaillibilité,* 117–255.

35. Anglican-Orthodox Conversations, *Moscow Statement* (1976), 17.

36. Anglican-Roman Catholic Conversations, *Authority of the Church II,* 23.

37. Ibid., 28.

38. Ibid., 24.

39. Ibid., 26.

40. Ibid., 25.

have . . . the appropriate gifts of the Spirit."[41] Infallibility, should there be such a thing, would be classified under this rubric.

Protestant concerns are reckoned within other agreements; these circle around the question of the "consent of the church." The dialogue agreed that "neither general councils nor universal primates are invariably preserved from error even in official declarations,"[42] so that a criterion is needed to know when in fact "the Church's authoritative decision . . . has been truly preserved from error." They agreed that this criterion is finally the "assent of the faithful," even though this assent "does not give a magisterial decision its authority."[43]

Yet by all this, the dialogue thought, the question is not yet exhausted, "whether there is a special ministerial gift of discerning the truth . . . bestowed at crucial times on one person to enable him to speak authoritatively . . . to preserve the people of God in the truth."[44] Roman Catholics posit "the guaranteed possession of (a) gift of divine assistance in judgment necessarily attached to the office of the bishop of Rome by virtue of which his formal decisions can be known to be wholly assured before their reception by the faithful. . . . Anglicans do not."[45]

III

The American Lutheran-Roman Catholic dialogue very early produced a consensus document on primacy.[46] Perhaps it came *too* early in this dialogue, which went directly from ministry in general to papal ministry, leaping over the question of episcopacy. Since the papal office is self-defined as episcopal, and since understanding its jurisdiction and teaching authority as other than merely totalitarian depends on taking this self-definition very seriously, this leap must surely skew the dialogue's results.[47] The question about infallibility was left for later.

The American dialogue, as so many, had agreed that the ecclesial office is there to serve the unity of the church.[48] One arrives at the question of the papacy when one then asks about "the role of particular persons, offices or officeholders in exercising responsibility for the unity of the *universal* church." (emphasis added) The dialogue agreed that in the New Testament, just such a role is in various ways attributed to Peter, and that the church in its subsequent history was therefore right in making him "the image of a pastor caring for the universal church." The dialogue thus found it "appropriate to speak of a 'Petrine function,' " meaning a ministry that "serves to promote or preserve the oneness of the (universal) church by symbolizing unity, and by facilitating communication, mutual assistance or correction, and collaboration in the church's mission."[49] Such a role has been

41. Ibid., 33.
42. Ibid., 27.
43. Ibid., 25.
44. Ibid., 23.
45. Ibid., 31.
46. *Papal Primacy and the Universal Church*, vol. 5 of *Lutherans and Catholics in Dialogue*, ed. Paul C. Empie and T. Austin Murphy (Minneapolis: Augsburg, 1974).
47. In an ironically "ultramontane" fashion!
48. Ibid., 1–3.
49. Ibid., 4.

variously filled in the church's history, but "the single most notable representative of this Ministry toward the church universal . . . has been the bishop of Rome." Nor, the Lutherans could say, need they protest this.[50]

Nevertheless, the actual claims made for the Roman primacy remain problematic. Does the New Testament show that "Jesus conferred on Peter a unique role of leadership in the whole church *for all times* and in this sense provided for succession in the Petrine function"?[51] (emphasis added) Closely linked to this exegetical question is the "theological issue" of whether Roman primacy is of divine or human right.[52] Finally, the characterizations of the primacy as "supreme," "full," "ordinary," and "immediate" have all been "vehemently" contested.[53]

The American dialogue attempts to deal with all these questions by one key notion, that of a historical "trajectory." The Petrine projectory is said to start with "a prominence" of Peter in the New Testament that "modern scholarship" can trace "back to Peter's relationship to Jesus in his public ministry and as the risen Lord." The equation governing[54] the trajectory—if I may put it so—is then set by "the thrust of the images associated with Peter in the later New Testament books." When "a 'trajectory' of these images is traced . . . one can see the possibility of an orientation in (the) direction" of the later papacy, "when shaped by favoring factors in the subsequent church."[55] The trajectory thus biblically defined is then traced through the main stages in the known history by which the modern papacy emerged.[56]

The virtue of describing the situation in this way is that it is possible both to affirm a trajectory in itself, and even to affirm it as divinely ordained, and nevertheless to reject much of what has come to pass along it.[57] In the present case, moreover, both parties can then join in tracing the trajectory into a future in which "papal primacy, renewed in the light of the gospel, need not be a barrier to reconciliation."[58] Lutherans can "recognize the need for a Ministry serving the unity of the church universal" and "acknowledge that . . . the church should use the signs of unity it has received, for new ones cannot be invented at will."[59] And the lines of renewal necessary to that outcome can be recognized by Catholics in the way Vatican II bends the trajectory:[60] in particular, the principles of "legitimate diversity" in the life of the church, of "collegiality" in the exercise of churchly authority, and of "subsidiarity" in the church's governance will be vital.[61]

50. Ibid., 5.
51. Ibid., 6.
52. Ibid., 7.
53. Ibid., 8.
54. The dialogue does not, to be sure, use this terminology. But it is plainly the sort of thing they must have in mind, if they have anything very clearly in mind at this point.
55. Ibid., 13.
56. Ibid., 14–20.
57. Ibid., 20–21. The dialogue itself never quite said this as clearly as required for its own point.
58. Ibid., 32.
59. Ibid., 28.
60. Ibid., 20.
61. Ibid., 22–25.

Insofar as this dialogue came to actual outcomes, these differ very little materially from those of the Anglican dialogue, but are rather less developed. Interestingly, the dialogue uses the notion of a historical trajectory. To be sure, as the dialogue itself uses the notion, its ontic status is unclarified, and it seems a slippery notion indeed. As the dialogue itself uses the notion, it states the problem more than suggests a solution.

But a clarification seems possible that could make the notion a powerful ecumenical tool. For what has a trajectory is often that which has been *aimed* at something. The notion of trajectory could serve to set the question of historical identity and continuity within an *eschatological* context. To see what is true about— to continue with our immediate matter—the place of Peter in the history of the church, and about the institutions that have historically derived their self-understanding from the church's memory of Peter, surely we might well ask what God wills to *come* of this history, when it devolves into the kingdom. Here, too, the dialogue results open into the final problematic of my study.

IV

This chapter will also carry the discussion somewhat further than the dialogues have been able to carry it. Three questions continue to occasion dissensus. Why should there be a Roman primacy at all? What "assurance" could there be that Protestant, or Orthodox, acceptance of Roman primacy would not mean submission to an autocracy that the modern papacy has too often practiced? If there is to be a Roman primacy, how can its infallibility and immediacy be understood or justified?

The first two questions, it seems to me, will be resolved simultaneously or not at all. The ecumenically viable reasons why there should be a Roman primacy themselves provide standards of its exercise.

In the centuries of the undivided church, the local Roman *church*, not the papal office, was accorded special authority by the other local churches; the bishop of the Roman church enjoyed primacy among the bishops *as* the pastor of Rome, the minister to unity in and for the church of that particular place.[62] In yet another of J. M. R. Tillard's precisely Catholic and therefore clarifying formulations, "The office of the bishop of Rome . . . is derived from the mission of his local church within the communion of churches."[63] Nor should acceptance of this ancient position by modern Catholicism be impossible, since it has been emphasized in statements of recent popes.[64]

The fact and character of a special mission of the Roman local church derived, in patristic teaching and canonical law, from the Spirit-led historical course of the apostolic mission. Rome was the church glorified by the teaching and martyrdom of the two apostles between whom the New Testament, in the Acts of the Apostles,

---

62. The evidence for this and the subsequent paragraph has been gathered many times, now conveniently by Tillard, *The Bishop of Rome*, 67–119.
63. Ibid., 90.
64. E.g., Paul VI, "Petrum et Paulum," in *Documentation Catholique* 64(1967): 88.

divided the story of the Spirit's mission to the ecumene. In the understanding of
the fathers, the founding history of each local church is a particular creative act
of the Spirit that lives on in a special character of that church. The life of each
local church is a *memorial*, a sacramental presence, of its particular emergence
within the gospel's mission. The existence and life of the church at *Rome* is thus
a memorial "of the great and glorious confession of Peter and Paul." The congregation in which Peter and Paul finally united their witness, and which maintains
the memorials of their martyrdoms for that witness, was for the ancient church
just so a Spirit-chosen "touchstone and . . . point of reference for the apostolic
faith."[65] The Roman bishopric is the office by which this authority can be present
among the other churches.

Plainly, if this patristic understanding is true, there is reason *iure divino* why
Protestants, and Orthodox, should join with Roman Catholicism in reestablishing
ecumenical fellowship around Roman primacy. If renewed fellowship were established on *this* basis, the specific charisms and historically derived characters
and concerns of other local churches would be equally established. The freedom
of other churches from "imposition of . . . alien traditions" would be seen as
founded by the same act that founded primacy. Even canonical channeling of papal
authority would be not only possible but already given in the ancient canons that
foundationally assert Roman primacy itself.

The question, to be sure, is whether the ancient church's doctrine of Roman
primacy *is* true. That is, does the continuing history of a local church make a
sacramental memorial of the Spirit's unique apostolic mission to that place? We
have again arrived at the area of reflection to which this whole study tends.

As to the nest of questions posed by the doctrines of Vatican I, beneath them
all, it seems to me, is but *one* question, to be answered yes or no by the dialoguing
parties. Is the one catholic church itself, in the language of the Augsburg Confession, an "assembly"? Is the one church itself a congregation that one might
expect like any congregation to have its pastor and other ministers to carry on an
activity of teaching, and to do so in obedience to the magisterium of its pastor?

To this question the Catholic party simply says yes. The one church is a single
communal entity in a reasonably straightforward sense, recognizable in much the
same way as is a parochial congregation. Thus it needs a pastor, and this pastor
will, like all pastors, hold a teaching office and a jurisdiction.[66]

To the same question, Protestantism has mostly, if often convolutedly and
implicitly, said no. The one church is thought to subsist on a different ontological
plane than do parochial congregations, synods, presbyteries, or even denominations

65. Ibid., 86. It should be noted that this theological evaluation of Rome does not depend on whether
or not both Peter and Paul were, in historical fact, martyred there, but only on the equally historical
fact that the ancient church believed they had been; and that the tradition of their martyrdom at Rome
is at least as reliable as most other testimony unanimously accepted by history.

66. Notably, Martin Luther appears on this side of the question! *"Ecclesia est numerus seu collectio
baptizatorum et credentium sub uno pastore, sive sit unius civitatis sive totius provintiae, sive totius
orbis"* (WA 30/II, 421,19).

and territorial churches. Thus the one church can be one without needing a pastor specific to it, or a teaching office specific to this pastor, or a specific jurisdiction. How would one decide between these answers? Perhaps by beginning with the reason why the Protestant answer is initially compelling. The particular "assembly of all believers" that is the one catholic church cannot actually assemble—not, at least, until the eschaton. The one catholic church can now exist only insofar as actual gatherings of Christians, parochial congregations, dioceses, or synods anticipate the last great assembly and *so* each instantiate the one catholic church.

But just here is the reason that also the Catholic answer is compelling. *Anticipation* is in the biblical view of reality the causal relation that most decisively establishes reality. If the one catholic church now exists as anticipation within history of the last day's assembly, then the one catholic church is now the solidest of realities.

Must not then the one catholic church's anticipation of the final assembly be *itself* somehow historically actual? And what could that historical actuality be, if not provision of those things by which the presence of any congregation is historically recognizable? Must there not therefore be a pastor of the one church? That is, must not the great pastor who will shepherd the last assembly, so long as he is not yet returned, have exactly a historical "vicar"? Must not this vicar undertake historically actual identifications of the one "eternal gospel" the final pastor will then speak? In other words, must he not undertake doctrinal definitions that are indeed "irreversible"?

The decisive question is, we see on yet one last occasion, about time. Just how realized is the eschaton, in the church between the times? Is the one catholic church, the assembly that will gather but once at the end, now anything other than the plural local and parochial churches that will then come together?

If the question just posed could be given a clear answer, the specific questions about jurisdiction and magisterium would already be answered. Since the papacy is a Catholic concern, I will take as my hypothesis a Catholic answer to the prior question and try to show how on that basis the more particular questions could be dealt with.

Insofar as the pope is to exercise a jurisdiction, he is called to do what all bishops are to do—and indeed what all who govern the church in fact do, whether Catholic or Protestant. Churchly law is not in the first instance a mere necessity of order; it is a necessity of the gospel. If God gives the church consent in the teaching of the gospel and offices to serve such *koinonia*, then God institutes obedience to mutual consent and its offices. Thus it lies in the very concept of the ecclesial office that it have jurisdiction, that is, the authority that invokes communal obedience. So far, there can surely be no legitimate occasion of dissent between Catholics and others. The question is not whether persons in the church are to exercise "juris-diction," but what is the true character of the law, the *ius*, that they state.

The character of churchly law depends entirely on the way in which the church and its offices are themselves understood and practiced. If the church is understood fundamentally as *communion*, then its laws must be understood as emerging through the life of the communion itself, from the mutuality of its charisms and offices. Like the common law of England, the *koinonia*'s law is imposed by no single power but has many lawgivers, whose legitimacy resides in their collegiality, across both locality and time. This indeed is the empirical character of canon law, whatever contrary theories may from time to time have been enunciated. The legitimate demand of the Reformation cannot be that there be no such law, but only that existent church law, wherever found, be subject to critique and reform.

Within an understanding of the church as communion, it should be possible to agree: It is *iure divino* that there *be* law in the church, that there be canons. Surely, for example, the church's ancient decision that infants can be baptized—a legal ruling if ever there was one—is (if correct) *not* separable from God's mandate of this sacrament itself, is (if correct) a law of the gospel.

It should also be possible to agree: It is *iure divino* that only such laws should have force in the church as are appropriate to the church's essential charisms and offices. Finally, it should be possible to agree: The actual canons that at any time exist in the church are binding in their various degrees and ways so long as they are in force, *iure divino*, but are subject to reform by the purposes for which God intends them.

It follows also that the reality of churchly law is subsidiary to the reality of churchly office. And here we must remember the consensus of all dialogues, that the ecclesial office is defined as *pastoral*. Critique of any ministerial office's practice of jurisdiction has therefore a clear criterion and just so becomes possible. Is the office understood or practiced as endowed with a less than pastoral authority, perhaps with merely administrative authority? Violation of this norm can occur either in the clericalist way to which Catholicism may have been especially tempted or by those uncritical approximations to secular models that have been the bane of Protestant churchly governance. Ecumenical agreement on this issue should also be possible.

As for the immediacy and ordinariness of papal jurisdiction, if indeed the one church is in any sort an actual congregation, the perceived problems disappear. If the pope is the *pastor* of the one universal congregation, then *of course* his authority, whatever that may materially turn out to cover, is immediate and ordinary. For he is then not pastor only of the pastors of the local assemblies but of the people.

Even the question of papal infallibility would not be so insoluble if there can be a universal pastor because there is a universal congregation. It surely cannot be a matter of churchly dissensus, that the church is—in the currently used language—"indefectible." The church lives by Christ's promise that the gates of hell will not prevail against her, that she cannot fall decisively from her mission. Her mission—exactly according to Reformation principle—is to speak the gospel; it is, therefore, precisely doctrinal error into which by Reformation principle the church cannot fall decisively.

To a pastoral office belongs the magisterium, the task of authoritative teaching of the gospel. On our present hypothesis, the congregation whose unity the pope is to shepherd is the one church; and the unity of the one church transcends not only geography but time. If now there is a pastor whose congregation is the one church, the temporal unity that pastor has to shepherd comprehends the whole of the church's time, from its foundation through the last assembly. That is, this pastor's teaching must anticipate the outcome of all the church's teaching, must anticipate the so to speak "final enunciation of the gospel." What would one call the charism of such teaching if not "infallibility"?

Infallibility does not, of course, guarantee every utterance for which a pope may claim it, nor of every council claiming to be ecumenical. It cannot even be guaranteed that a heretical pope cannot appear, so that his teaching as a whole must be subject to severe *post facto* critique.[67] Nor are either of these propositions ecumenically controversial. The consequence of such considerations is that the operational content of a possible dissensus over infallibility is located in the nest of questions about reception.

"Actually, there are two different questions . . . : 1) what conditions are objectively required for an infallible conciliar or papal definition? and 2) how can we know in any particular case, that all of these conditions have been fulfilled?"[68] It would seem that the fact that a pope has *claimed* to be speaking "ex cathedra" cannot *merely* by itself prove that the "objective conditions" for the utterance to have such authority have been fulfilled,[69] since precisely a heretical pope might be expected to make such claims rather lavishly. As to what would constitute evidence that some objective condition was lacking, Vatican II seems to have settled this matter by teaching that "the assent of the church . . . can never fail to be given to those definitions on account of the activity of the . . . Holy Spirit, by which the whole flock of Christ is preserved in the unity of faith."[70] According to this teaching, the failure of reception must show that a council or pope had not in fact spoken "with that infallibility which the Divine Redeemer willed his church to enjoy."

At this point an outsider may inquire what, operationally, can be left of the teaching that the pope can make decisions that "are of themselves, and not by consent of the church, irreformable." Joseph Cardinal Ratzinger, precisely to the ecumenical point, has exegeted Vatican II on the matter.

> The first Vatican Council said that the Pope could make definitive decisions not only on the basis of the church's agreement, but also by himself, *ex sese*. . . . Although at the first Vatican Council there were many efforts to interpret this blunt and easily misunderstood formula so as better to bring out its real content, this could then not be done. . . . Now, it seems to me, what then remained a mere wish is undertaken. It is no longer simply said that the

---

67. The possibility of a heretical pope cannot be disputed by Roman Catholicism for the excellent reason that on Catholicism's own account there has already been one: Honorius I, condemned as a "monothelite" by an acknowledged ecumenical council and Pope Leo II.

68. Francis A. Sullivan, *Magisterium: Teaching Authority in the Catholic Church* (Mahwah, N.J.: Paulist Press, 1983), 99.

69. Among others, ibid., 108.

70. *Lumen gentium*, 25: *"Istis autem definitionibus assensus ecclesiae numquam deesse potest. . . ."* See Sullivan, *Magisterium*, 109.

teaching office can decide by itself—*ex sese*. Much more correctly, it is now said that the work of the teaching office always takes place on the background of the faith and prayer of the whole church, and nevertheless cannot be restricted to the expression of an already established common opinion but, bound to 'the written and traditional word of God,' must under certain circumstances take the initiative: it must be able to declare this Word, which may demand the consent of all, over against the confusion of a church without consensus.[71]

Now, *if* there is a universal pastor, must it not be this pastor's office to do exactly that? What else is a parish pastor called to do in his or her congregation?

V

Yet all these solutions depend upon an affirmative answer to the question Is the one universal church somehow a congregation? Is that answer indeed correct? It depends on just how, within the temporal history of the church, the outcome of that history is present.

71. Joseph Cardinal Ratzinger, "Ökumene in der Sackgasse? Anmerkungen zur Erklärung 'Mysterium Ecclesiae'," *Theologische Prinzipienlehre* (München: Erich Wewel, 1982), 247.

7

The Church's Mediation

I

There is at present something close to consensus about the location of a Catholic-Protestant *Grunddifferenz*. It is thought to lie between opposed understandings of the church's role in the life of faith. Multilateral international study concluded, "Today we see the real difference that led to division more in the conception of the church" than in any of the standard items of controversy "viewed in themselves."[1] I may let a Protestant who became notorious for ecumenical nay-saying at this very point assert the alleged clash at its bluntest. "Justification on the one hand, and the church on the other, each in its way claims the whole. . . . For the Reformation . . . the question can only be: Which shall rule (faith)? The church or justification?"[2] *Why* exactly the church and the doctrine of justification should thus be rivals is often more assumed than stated by those who see them so[3]; it is one task of this chapter to dig out some of the assumptions.

In this special aspect of the doctrine of the church we must seek a Protestant-Catholic "basic difference" may well seem confirmed by the fate of the dialogues that have worked their way to it. Thus the international Reformed-Roman Catholic report on ecclesiology is a simple failure: a laborious recital of pieties, good intentions for future dialogue, and vaguely discerned remaining difficulties.[4] The international Lutheran-Roman Catholic dialogue is currently embroiled in the same

1. So the World Council of Churches, *Confessing One Faith*, conclusion, 3.
2. Gustave Maron, *Kirche und Rechtfertigung* (Göttingen: 1969), 251.
3. Perhaps the best statement of what may be the matter comes from the very beginning of the dialogues; George Lindbeck, "Doctrinal Standards, Theological Theories and Practical Aspects of the Ministry in the Lutheran Churches," *Evangelium—Welt—Kirche*, ed. Harding Meyer (Frankfurt: Otto Lembeck, 1975), 238. "It seems that there is still one insurmountable barrier. Is it not true that Roman Catholics are irrevocably committed to the view that the legitimacy of the office ultimately guarantees the authenticity of the Word, while the sons of the Reformation are equally committed to the converse, that the authenticity of the Word is the only guarantee for the legitimacy of the office? Catholics, it would seem, must deny that the ministry of the church can become so unfaithful that it is obligatory (or at least legitimate) on occasion to establish discontinuous ministerial orders, as was done in the sixteenth century; and this, according to the sons of the Reformation, shows that Catholics make the ministry into something other than sheer service of the Word and instead regard it as a privilege, as possessing power over the Word."
4. International Reformed-Roman Catholic Dialogue, *Towards a Common Understanding of the Church* (1990).

topic. It appears[5] that decidedly more will have been achieved in this dialogue; nevertheless, the price in labor and lost hopes has been high. While the dialogues indeed strike tender nerves in this area, we will not at the end find in this area anything deserving to be called a basic difference.

I said in the introduction that the process by which divisive impetus moves from locus to locus circles back to the beginning; here occurs the circling. J. M. R. Tillard, who has pointed out many ecumenical issues for us, gave the alarm. "It seems to me . . . that the question of justification again tenders itself, but this time in a new form. It is no longer a matter of *sola fide* . . . but rather of the role of the church in the act of justification. . . . Is the church external to justification?"[6] It is easy to share the alarm of Catholic ecumenist Otto Herman Pesch. "Has ecumenical-theological work on the theme (of justification) with which . . . the conversation seemed to enter its most hopeful phase, in the meantime become a . . . Sisyphean labor?"[7]

II

As the Protestant-French Roman Catholic dialogue provided a paradigm of the notion of basic difference, so its identification of a candidate can be the pattern of this chapter. The dialogue's report identifies the mediation or instrumentality of the church as the sensitive concept. Then it formulates, using a Catholic terminology. "The difference between us is . . . not over the fact of the church's instrumentality in the transmission of salvation, but over *the nature of that instrumentality: is the church sanctified in such a way as itself to become the subject of sanctifying acts?*"[8] According to the report of this dialogue, Catholics believe it is and Protestants do not. Protestants can countenance no "idea of 'cooperation' by the church in the mystery of salvation" since this would "blunt salvation by grace alone. . . . The church is . . . always the object of grace, never its subject."[9]

Bernard Sesboüé, leader of the Catholic team, laid down the Catholic affirmation in an analysis published by the dialogue. "The church, the first fruit of saving grace, becomes through that foundation the minister of Christ's mediation."[10] To

---

5. To the personal observation of the author; so much can surely be said without violating confidentiality.

6. J. M. R. Tillard, "Vers une nouvelle problématique de la 'justification'?" *Irenikon* 55(1982): 1856–57. See also André Birmelé, *Le salut en Jésus Christ dans les dialogues oecuméniques* (Paris: Cerf, 1986), 309.

7. Otto Herman Pesch, "Rechtfertigung und Kirche," *Ökumenische Rundschau* 37(1988): 22–23.

8. Comité mixte catholique-protestant en France, *Consensus oecuménique et différence fondamentale: Réflexions et propositions* (1986), no. 11. "l'Église est-elle sanctifiée de manière à devenir elle-même sujet sanctifiant?"

9. Ibid., no 5. "L'Église est . . . toujours objet de la grâce, jamais son sujet." Just how bizarrely sensitive Protestants can be on the subject of churchly "mediation" can be seen in responses to *Baptism, Eucharist and Ministry;* e.g., that of the American Lutheran Church, *Churches Respond to BEM*, ed. Max Thurian (Geneva: World Council of Churches, 1986), 2:83. "We find problematic, however, the assertions . . . that . . . the presence of ordained ministers 'reminds the community of the divine initiative . . . and of the dependence of the Church on Jesus Christ,' and that 'in them the church sees an example of holiness and loving concern.' . . . This raises the issue of mediatorship."

10. "Nos différences ecclésiales: leur enjeu dans la recherche de l'unité" (1986), "Analyse catholique," by Bernard Sesboüé, published in *Consensus oecuménique et différence fondamentale* (Paris: le Centurion, 1987), 59.

this ministry, "Christ has entrusted his gifts," so that it is "an active ministry, that is, a ministry that is not a sheer announcing or attesting . . . but that involves the doing of concrete saving acts."[11] To state gruffly what is at issue, we may again summon Tillard's deliberately provocative formulation. Agreed that the individual's justification comes from outside, without his or her own merit, does this very justification come *from* "God by himself or from God and the church?"[12]

Undoubtedly the French team here represents authentic and unnegotiable Catholic conviction. Vatican II taught that the church "by receiving the word of God in faith becomes herself a mother. By preaching and baptism she brings forth sons . . . to a new and immortal life." And Catholicism is willing to make emphasis on this churchly agency an ecumenical sticking point: even the international Anglican-Roman Catholic dialogue, not notably given to the Reformation's more Protestant ecclesiologies, drew high-level Roman critique. "Are not such expressions as . . . 'the Church will be used by God' to realise God's plan . . . too imprecise? Could not one find another expression, to avoid any . . . accusation of passivity" on the part of the church?[13]

André Birmelé explicated the Protestant objection to such teaching. "That God needs his church to speak the word and administer the sacraments, that the church is God's instrument, is affirmed . . . by both traditions."[14] But the church cannot be understood to "perform acts of which it as a subject is the agent and which sanctify its members in respect of their salvation."[15] The problem of human "cooperation" in salvation, seemingly resolved to Protestant satisfaction when "the question is about the cooperation of the *individual* in his salvation," becomes virulent when the question is about "the active cooperation of the *church* in the salvation of its members."[16] (emphasis added) This question, because it is corollary to the doctrine of justification, "touches the fundamental identity of the churches born of the Reformation."[17] International Reformed-Roman Catholic dialogue can

---

11. Ibid., 56.
12. J. M. R. Tillard, "Vers une nouvelle problématique de la 'Justification'?" *Irenikon* 55(1982): 187. Or we may hear Erwin Iserloh, "Luther und die Reformation in katholischer Sicht," *Luther et la réforme Allemande dans une perspective oecuménique* (Chambésy: Centre Orthodoxe, 1983), 380. "Diese Frage des Synergismus . . . ist bis heute nicht erledigt. Es wird uns nicht beantwortet, wieso die Aussage Luthers, der Glaube sei 'werk Gottes, in uns ohne uns' . . . den Menschen nicht zu einem Klotz macht. . . . Es geht auch hier nicht um das Heil in Jesus Christus selbst, sondern um seine *Vermittlung* und *damit* um die Kirche." (emphasis added)
13. Donato Valentini, "Contribution pour le lecteur du rapport de la Commission Internationale Anglicane-Catholique Romaine 'Le salut et l'église,' " *Service d'Information* 63(1987): 53.
14. André Birmelé, *Le salut*, 250.
15. Ibid., 153. Also careful Roman Catholic analysts of the Reformation regularly make the same diagnosis, e.g., Hans Jorissen, "Ökumenische Erschliessung Martin Luthers," *Martin Luther im Spiegel heutiger Wissenschaft*, ed. Knut Schäferdiek (Bonn: Bouvier), 217: "Warum es Luther . . . geht, ist der Ausschluss jeder menschlichen, kirchlichen Subjekhaftigkeit im Heilsgeschehen. Die Kirche ist (Heils-)Subjekt."
16. Ibid., 291.
17. "Nos différences ecclésiales: leur enjeu dans la recherche de l'unité" (1986), "Analyse protestante," by André Birmelé, published in *Consensus oecuménique et différence fondamentale* (Paris: le Centurion, 1987), 40.

speak for the whole course of dialogue. "The Reformed commonly allege that Catholics appropriate to the Church the role proper to Christ," and "Roman Catholics . . . commonly accuse the Reformed of holding the Church apart from the work of salvation. . . . Both these views are caricatures, but they can help to focus attention on genuine underlying differences of perspective."[18]

Indeed, some Protestant ecumenists have responded strictly antithetically to Catholic affirmation of the church as the "mother" who bears believers as her children, making use and rejection of this language something close to a Catholic-Reformation *Grunddifferenz*. Thus in an influential article, Eberhard Jüngel said that the whole question about the acceptability to Reformation Christianity of contemporary Catholic ecclesiology must be decided in the negative because of these formulations.[19]

Jüngel claimed Martin Luther's authority for this judgment, even though Luther himself freely used the phrase "mother church." I will take time to note the Luther text Jüngel cites, and his reading of it, since what I must regard as Jüngel's misreading nicely reveals the problematic of this whole discussion. The cited Luther passage begins with a definition of the church's motherhood, in classically "Lutheran" terms. "Thus she bears heirs without cease . . . when she exercises the ministry of the word." Then Luther continues. "So we are all mutually fathers and sons, for we are all born from all. I, born of others by the gospel, in turn bear others, who again bear others; and thus this bearing (*generatio*) will continue to the end of the world."[20]

Jüngel interprets. "Thus Mother Church does not *stand over against* the individual believers. Mother Church—that simply *is* the Christians in the mutuality which God's Word creates."[21] Reading only the first sentence of the second Luther citation, we might suppose that Luther indeed says what Jüngel tells us he says. But reading on, we discover that what Luther in fact asserts is *not* a synchronically mutual begetting among existing believers but the dependence of each and all believers from a diachronic *generatio* that temporally transcends them all. One must, I think, even note the change from Luther's masculine-gender language about believers in the plural to his use of the feminine *generatio* to match his use of "she" for the church. In our Luther passage, the *tradition* of the gospel generates us; and it is this tradition that is identified with the church as "mother church."[22]

18. International Reformed-Roman Catholic Dialogue, *A Common Understanding*, 112.

19. Eberhard Jüngel, "Die Kirche als Sakrament?" *Zeitschrift für Theologie und Kirche* 80(1983): 450–56.

20. Cited by Jüngel from WA, 40/I, 664. "Generat autem ipsa liberos sine intermissione usque ad finem mundi, dum exercet ministerium verbi." "Sic omnes invicem sumus patres et filii, generamur enim alii ex aliis. Ego ex aliis per Evangelium genitus iam alios gigno, quit deinceps alios gignent, Et sic ista generatio durabit usque ad finem mundi."

21. Jüngel, "Die Kirche als Sakrament?" 452. Jüngel's assertion is widely shared; see André Birmelé, "La peccabilité de l'église comme enjeu oecuménique," *Revue d'Histoire et de Philosophie Religieuses* 67(1987): 409. "Ce sont les chrétiens eux-mêmes qui sont la mère Église."

22. Indeed, the Luther passage taken whole assumes precisely that "Gegenüber" of church and believers that Jüngel denies. Luther consistently and insistently speaks of the church in the singular, with feminine gender for all pronouns, and of believers in the plural, with invariably masculine gender.

But now we surely have before us something very like the Catholic position, or at the very least like an Orthodox position with which contemporary Catholicism should be able to identify.[23] The dialectic that emerges here again raises the issue to which our study repeatedly opens. How exactly are the short lives of believers "born" within the long life of the church?

In general, despite the apparent bluntness of the oppositions between saying the church is a subject of grace and saying she is not, between saying that the church's mediation is active and saying it is not, between saying the church is our mother with respect to salvation and saying she is not, the opposition so simply formulated proves slippery. What exactly could it mean to mediate something merely passively, where the mediating entity is not impersonal? Surely when the church preaches and baptizes, these are events that the church *does*? Events of which she is therefore precisely an agent, in any plausible sense of "agent"? Are then the saving events some *other* events than these? Yet if the church is a distinguishable agent of salvation, she must be liable to choose where God has not chosen and attach conditions he has not. Is there really anyone who wishes to assert this? That is, to assert either that the church can legitimately modify God's intention or that the church is not reliable? It is a favorite Protestant formulation of the matter at issue in the dialogues. "Every act of the church must be transparent for the prior action of God."[24] Doubtless, but what exactly can transparent *mean* in this context?

III

The elusiveness of the superficially simple Catholic-Protestant dissensus over churchly mediation has regularly turned discussion to the search for more operational versions of the issue; and this chapter must shortly make the same turn. But first let me propose a possible clarification of the general problem and then, indeed, a solution that probably can carry consensus only a little way.

Catholic-Protestant conflict about the church's mediation has a center, from which we were initially pointed to the generalized problem and to which it may here be clarifying to recur. Can we say that the church at the Eucharist offers Christ? Clearly the congregations with their ministers are agents at Eucharist. Is the presentation of Christ's salvific self-giving to the Father encompassed in this agency? Perhaps the most urgent request in the Roman Catholic Church's response to *Baptism, Eucharist and Ministry* was for more straightforward statement "that there is an offering of the one acceptable sacrifice made by the church in union with Christ," that "through the eucharist we are enabled to associate ourselves with the passover of Christ to his Father."[25]

Tillard has provided a concise and nuanced statement of typical contemporary Catholic teaching, which it will be useful to cite with some fullness.

<hr />

23. See pp. 135–137.
24. André Birmelé, "La peccabilité de l'église," 407.
25. *Churches Respond to BEM*, 6:20–21.

The church's consent to the event of salvation, its entry into the Servant's movement, who gives it the grace of being carried along in his self-giving to the Father and thus associates it with his mission—these things are not empty steps without consequence. The participation of the church in the work of salvation is implied in them . . . even as one must always insist that this happens only in Christ and represents a fruit of the Spirit. At the Memorial, this mysterious participation surpasses that of ordinary prayer or daily witness.[26]

Yet doubtless the most comprehensive and accurate statement of Catholic conviction is also the simplest. "That the Eucharist is an offering to the Father which is presented by *the whole Christ* (*totus Christus*), by the Head and the members."[27]

Even after the clarifications and new positions described in the chapter on eucharistic sacrifice, Lutheran or Anglican sorts of Protestantism regularly say they are unable to agree with this. The German Lutheran churches responded to the report of international Lutheran-Roman Catholic dialogue. "There remains a substantial difference between the evangelical understanding . . . that the church subjects itself to Jesus Christ's atoning intervention before God . . . and the Catholic proposition . . . which understands the church as an active subject in bringing Christ's offering. That the congregation offers Christ, is now as before an unacceptable statement for Lutheran theology."[28]

Yet perhaps just the circumstance that the conflict's existential heart is a *liturgical* act, that it is located in *assembly*, may provide guidance. Perhaps the issue may be grasped in terms of the *meeting* of Christ and believers and of believers among themselves.[29] That the risen Christ and the church are at least insofar two that they can confront one another, that they can be face-to-face, is surely agreeable to both parties, so they appear at the Eucharist. In that meeting between Christ and the church, Christ is salvifically active and the church receptive; so much may surely also be agreed. I suggest that the real question may then be formulated so: Does this meeting between Christ and the church *itself* occur inside or ouside the church? Does it not occur *within* that eucharistic assembly which is itself the creature of such meetings and itself the reality of the church?[30]

Plainly, also in the eucharistic assembly the church and its Lord stand over against each other; otherwise the church would have no Lord. Protestantism has insisted on this point. But this meeting itself takes place within and so depends upon the assembly that, precisely according to Reformation conviction, is the reality of the church. Within the event of that assembly the meeting is in phenomenological fact mediated by the meeting between different role-bearers in the

---

26. J. M. R. Tillard, "Catholiques romains et Anglicans: l'Eucharistie," *Nouvelle Revue Théologique* 103(1971): 618.

27. *Churches Respond to BEM*, 6:20.

28. " 'Das Herrenmahl:' Lutherische Stellungnahme zu dem römisch-katholischen/evangelisch-Lutherischen Studiendokument," *Materialdienst* 33(1982): 116.

29. In his article "La peccabilité de l'église," 399–419, André Birmelé in fact works with the same language. Indeed, one can move either way: from the question of the church's confrontation with Christ to that of the church's sinfulness, or vice versa.

30. Jüngel, "Die Kirche als Sakrament?" 452.

church-community. If the reality of the church displays this dialectic, must it not be so that a meeting also occurs between Christ through the church on the one side and the aggregate of individual believers on the other? Catholicism has insisted on this point.

Surely the insistences of both sides are biblically right. To see how they can be, it may be helpful to introduce a classic distinction of social theory,[31] since the problem is now posed as a problem about the public structure of a collective. As a mere association of individuals—a group gathered by the common characteristics or activities of certain individuals, in this case that they are believers—the church stands over against Christ exactly as does each of those believers. But as a community in the strong sense, as a reality distinguishable from the collective of its parts, in which each member finds his or her own reality only from and with the others, the church is the reality of Christ over against each and all of its individual members. Something like the latter, after all, must be meant when the New Testament calls this community the "body" of the risen Christ, for in biblical usage a person's body is simply that person as present and available to other persons.[32] Finally, let me propose that, in these terms, it is the great mystery of the church that alone among created communities she is perfectly and inseparably at once association and community.

IV

We must now examine several attempts to formulate more operationally the apparent Catholic-Protestant dissensus about the church's mediatorial role. Of these, the most straightforward and perhaps most profound has been proposed by Cardinal Ratzinger, in a much-noted interview and in a response to comment occasioned by that interview. The "basic decision" that founds Protestantism is "the individualizing of the act of faith," so that "faith in its own nature is no longer, as it is for the Catholic, an act of believing with the whole church. . . . For the Catholic, the church is itself comprised in the deep source of the act of faith: it is only in that I believe with the church that I share in that certitude in which I may rest my life."[33] "Christian faith is always a knowing-together-with" Christ. Therefore, since the church is Christ's body, "Faith . . . is essentially faith-together-with the church." Indeed, this togetherness with the church constitutes a "new and wider self" of the believer; and it is this self that is the subject of faith, "the self of the *anima ecclesiastica*, that is, the self of that person through whom the whole community of the church expresses itself."[34]

31. It is Max Weber's famous distinction of "Gesellschaft" and "Gemeinschaft" that I will exploit.

32. See below, pp. 125-128.

33. Joseph Cardinal Ratzinger, "Luther und die Einheit der Christen," *Communio* 12(1983): 575–76. Cardinal Ratzinger attributed this founding "decision" to Luther himself, undoubtedly a scholarly error.

34. The citation is from Cardinal Ratzinger's response to the debate provoked by the *Communio* interview; Joseph Cardinal Ratzinger, *Église, oecuménisme et politique*, trans. P. Jordan, P.-E. Gudenus, and B. Müller (Paris: Fayard, 1987), 173. We may note how Catholic polemics can at this point turn Reformation arguments back on Protestantism; Erwin Iserloh, "Luther und die Reformation in katholischer Sicht," *Luther et la réforme Allemande*, 379.

The question is: Granted that there would be no gospel to believe, did not the church preach and administer sacraments; granted even that faith in the gospel would be impossible except in the community of the church, can the church be unthematic for faith once present? Are faith in Christ and identification with the church-community distinguishable spiritual acts? Or is the Christ who is both the ground and object of faith the *totus Christus*, the embodied person whose body is the church?

That many Protestants think as the cardinal supposes they do appears precisely in their ecumenical policy. The Augsburg Confession says that "for the true unity of the church it is enough to agree in the preaching of the gospel and the ministering of its sacraments,"[35] and intends this proposition as a corollary of the doctrine of justification. According to this rule, the mere ecumenical negotiation of what is not part of the *gospel,* if church unity is made to depend on its success, already violates the doctrine of justification. So far the argument must be correct, if the Reformation was correct. The problem appears when some Protestants hold that negotiation about the *church* falls under this interdict; that is, when they suppose, deliberately or subliminally, that the existence, apostolicity and catholicity of the church are not contents of the gospel. The problem appears again, from a slightly different angle, as Protestants sometimes set their ecumenical attitudes by the rule that while the unity of the church is indeed desirable, fidelity to the gospel must be the first concern; a Catholic response would be that the *koinonia* penultimately experienced as the church is the very blessing promised by the gospel, so that fidelity to the gospel and unwillingness to accept the disunity of the church must be the very same thing.

André Birmelé states the position from the Protestant viewpoint. Catholics indeed agree with Protestants "on the necessity of accord in the preaching of the gospel and the celebration of the sacraments" for the unity of the church, "but they *also* think a common understanding of the church is necessary" (emphasis added); thereby, according to Birmelé, they have irreconcilably different criteria of churchly unity than Protestants have.[36] The problematic is in the "also": is indeed "a common understanding of the church" an *addition* to "accord in the preaching of the gospel"? A presumed affirmative answer to the latter question determines the ecumenical posture of entire Protestant denominations.

If the basic decision is formulated as the cardinal formulates it, then in my judgment the Catholic side has the straightforward right of it. The further question, however, must be about the way in which the church, a community that temporally transcends the birth and death of each of its members, determines the selfhood of any one of them. Again, it is *time* that opens as the horizon of our inquiry.

V

The French dialogue's own operational formulation of the basic difference works with a central ecclesiological formulation of Vatican II, that the church is "sacrament—as it were" (*uti sacramentum*), in that it is a "sign and instrument" of

---

35. Augsburg Confession, art. VII.
36. Birmelé, "Nos Différences . . . ," 34.

"communion with God and unity among humans."[37] The French Catholic commission affirms this teaching, of course. In their presentation, the church is like a sacrament in that its ministration "serves the mediatorship of Christ, whom it makes efficaciously present." It is only *like* a sacrament in that the church is not, like water or bread and wine, considered as such, an impersonal entity personalized only as embodiment of the risen Christ, but "a spouse who obeys her husband," so that her instrumentality for Christ is that of one "free subject" for another.[38]

According to the Protestant team, "Also the churches issuing from the Reformation . . . conceive the church as a sign and instrument of God and his reign." But they cannot "conceive the church as sacrament."[39] Unlike "the sacraments, baptism and the Holy Supper, the church can never in any way become a source or author of human salvation. . . . Any understanding of the church as a prolongation of Christ, any notion of a ministerial mediation from which the presence of Christ would depend" is an "attack on the sole sovereignty of God."[40]

Many expected that the teaching of Vatican II about the church as sacrament would present not a new ecumenical difficulty but a new ecumenical opportunity; it was anyway so intended by the council.[41] The intent and widespread actual effect on subsequent *Catholic* theology was to provide a "model for the church's self-understanding" that could "express the unity of the historical and the spiritual, of the visible and the invisible, of the temporal and the eschatological," that could overcome Western Christianity's perennial oscillation between misunderstanding the church "as an historically empirical association" and misunderstanding her as a sheerly "invisible community."[42]

But the extent to which the ecumenical promise of the *uti sacramentum* is fulfilled has been limited. This is perhaps in part explained by failure among Protestant theologians to distinguish the very simple teaching that was promulgated by the council and that Catholics have advocated in ecumenical discussion, from the developed ecclesiological theories of pre–Vatican II theologians who promoted the terminology in Catholic parlance, and whose positions are sometimes indeed unacceptable by the Reformation.[43]

---

37. *Lumen gentium*, I, 1.
38. Comité mixte catholique-protestant en France, *Consensus oecuménique et différence fondamentale*, 12.
39. It may be worth wondering parenthetically what the difference is supposed to be between "sign and instrument" and "sacrament."
40. Ibid., no. 13.
41. Also Birmelé, "Nos Différences . . ." 225, acknowledges that Vatican II's use of *uti sacramentum* was its way to avoid the previous dialectics of Roman Catholic doctrine, to "permet un réel rapprochement avec les Églises nées de la Réforme." But then he recurs to his great question. "Le question fondamentale qui demeure est celle de la définition précise de l'Église comme sacrement du salut. De quelle manière l'Église est-elle signe et instrument du salut? Quelle est la nature de l'instrumentalité de l'Église pour le salut des hommes?"
42. Jan L. Witte, "These über die Kirche in Zusammenhang mit dem Interkommunionsproblem," *Evangelium—Welt—Kirche*, ed. Harding Meyer (Frankfurt: Otto Lembeck, 1975), 443.
43. It is important, e.g., to grasp that neither *Lumen gentium* nor subsequent Catholic ecumenical use of the concept takes the church as "a sacrament," and nor then as "the one sacrament" or the "basic sacrament" in the way that Martin Luther, in *De captivitate Babylonica ecclesiae*, WA 6:501, called *Christ* the one great sacrament. See Birmelé, *Le salut*, 211ff.

It may also be explained in part by Protestant misidentification of where the difficulty really lies. The French dialogue's statement of the Protestant position is typical. It identifies the application of the concept of sacrament as itself the offense to Protestant concern. But if one looks at the same dialogue's statement of the Catholic position it is plain that what *ought* to worry those concerned about making the church an independent subject of salvation is precisely Catholic *restriction* of the concept's applicability. It is as the Catholic statement introduces into the same discourse the image of the church as Christ's bride, who is one free subject over against Christ as another, that Protestant concern might appropriately appear. Indeed, it would seem that Protestant critics of the *uti sacramentum* are very close to having it exactly backward. As a Protestant ecumenist has noted, Catholics who promoted this conceptuality did so thinking that it must "ward off precisely that inappropriate understanding of the church which critics of the concept see implied in it: a simple identification of the church with Jesus Christ."[44]

Vatican II's own use of *uti sacramentum* locates the language in two contexts. The context of the first occurrence is the church's mission; it is the *world* to which God speaks by erecting the church as a sign and so, insofar as this sign is an effective sign, it is the world that is effected. Surely Protestantism should have seen its own concerns fulfilled here. As the Lutheran ecumenist just quoted has written, "the basic intention of all ecumenical discussion of the church and its unity" is to understand these as having "their sense and goal beyond themselves," as pointing "beyond themselves to the world into which the church is sent as an instrument of salvation." Just this—surely Protestant!—orientation "tends toward this new conceptuality" of sacrament.[45]

A second occurrence in *Lumen gentium* has a biblical and christological context. "Sacrament" functions within the New Testament's fundamental specification of the church as the *body* of the risen Christ.[46] Here again should have been a perhaps even greater ecumenical opportunity.

The New Testament's proposition that the church is the body of Christ claims ontological seriousness.[47] If we obey that claim, then the relation between the risen Christ and the church must be understood as the relation between his selfhood

---

44. Günther Gassman, "Kirche als Sakrament 193. The kind of theology that Roman Catholics attach to *uti sacramentum* can be exemplified by this from Jan L. Witte. "Die pilgernde Kirche (hat) wesentlichen geshichtlichen Charakter. . . . Die eine Kirche Christi ist das ewige Heil im Gemeinschaft, wenn auch in zeitlicher, unvollkommener Gestalt: deshalb gehört es zu ihrem Wesen, Sakrament des Heiles zu sein. In dieser irdischen Gestalt ist aber die Sündhaftigkeit ihrer Glieder ihr ebenso wesenseigen wie die Heiligkeit ihrer Glieder. Deshalt ist diese Gemeinschaft . . . Zeichen des Widerspruchs: sie kann nur geglaubt werden. . . . Wir meinenh . . . dass die Einsicht in den eschatologischen—and damit auch in den sakramentalen und geshichtlichen Charakter der einen Kirche Christi—gerade entscheident ist für die Frage, ob das mystische Leib Chrsti exklusiv identisch ist mit der römische-katholischen Kirche" "Thiesen . . . ," 441–42.

45. Günther Gassmann, "Kirche als Sakrament," 172. This article provides an excellent summary of the history of ecumenical reception of *uti sacramentum*.

46. *Lumen gentium*, VII, 48: "Christ . . . set up his Body which is the Church as the universal sacrament of salvation."

47. To this and the immediately following, see the further developments at pp. 125-128.

and his body, as the self-body relation is generally construed in the language of the New Testament. In such understanding lies the possibility of an ecclesiology that at once emerges from the deepest spirit of Catholicism and answers fully to Reformation critique—what might be called an *ascetic* understanding of Christ and the church. The risen Christ, like all living human persons, *is* his body; and yet, like all living human persons, he must direct and discipline his body. But his body is the church.

A certain amount of actual dialogue consensus has accepted *Lumen gentium*'s "new conceptuality." Perhaps most notable is the statement of the American Lutheran-Roman Catholic dialogue, which speaks consensually of "the one body of Christ, whose mission is to be an anticipatory and efficacious sign of the final unification of all things."[48] What seems, however, to be at present the general limits of this acceptance appears neatly in the report of international Reformed-Roman Catholic conversation. Under the heading "The Church as the *Effective* Sign of Christ's Presence in the World," the actual consensus-proposition reads instead, "the Church is a *persuasive* sign."[49] (emphasis added) Always there are such simple rejections of the *uti sacramentum* as that of a notable Reformation scholar. "For us the church is decidedly not a mysterious reality, given antecedently to the person. For us, the church occurs in joint listening to God's Word."[50]

It will be useful to pause with the very "Lutheran" second sentence of this statement. In the same article earlier cited, Eberhard Jüngel has developed the proposition with greater nuance; and again in such fashion as clearly to reveal its problematic. The idea that the church is *uti sacramentum*, in that its actions are God's actions, is not, according to Jüngel, to be rejected out of hand.[51] The Reformation must affirm a certain "identity between divine and human action," for "the preacher must . . . say, '*Haec dixit Dominus.*' "[52] Yet the church's action must also be shaped so that "God himself . . . is experienced as the proper agent."[53] Therefore, we must formulate a rule for both understanding and practice: The church is "by its *ratio essendi . . . listening* church and *only* as *listening* also *speaking* church."[54]

But thereupon the alleged dissensus once again becomes dialectical. For to *what* does the church "listen"? Not, according to Reformation Christianity, to an inner voice or a voice from heaven or to the Scripture merely as text. But to what then?

48. *Papal Primacy and the Universal Church*, vol. V of *Lutherans and Catholics in Dialogue* ed. Paul C. Empie and T. Austin Murphy (Minneapolis: Augsburg, 1974), 10.

49. *The Presence of Christ in Church and World* (1977), no. 60. We may note also the international Reformed-Roman Catholic dialogue, 113, which after a straight report of Catholic teaching, can say no more than that perhaps it and "the" Reformation doctrine might "become the poles of a creative tension between our churches."

50. Kurt Aland, *Evangelium und Kirche*, ed. Kirchliches Aussenamt der Evangelischen Kirche im Deutschland (Frankfurt: Otto Lembeck, 1983), 82.

51. Jüngel, "Die Kirche als Sakrament," 442.

52. Ibid., 448.

53. Ibid., 447.

54. Ibid., 449.

Surely, the church at any time can hear the gospel only by listening to its own past speaking of the gospel.[55] When Jüngel says, "In the form of the listening church . . . *representatio Christi* occurs,"[56] what content can this have—if it is to have *any*—but that the communally actual occurrence of *tradition* is "representation of Christ"? Is not that the Catholic position or very like it? For the rest, we are yet again with *time* and the nature of its continuities and discontinuities, as the horizon of ecumenical confusions.

At this point, it may be useful to note explicitly how tight the connections indeed are between consensus or dissensus in a "sacramental-ontological doctrine of the church"[57] and consensus or dissensus in earlier topics. Sesboüé has made the connection between the sacramentality of the church and ministerial succession. "One may thus say that the church is a sacrament of its founding event, that is, an efficacious . . . sign of god's gift. . . . *Therefore* apostolic succession is essential to the church, for this is the sign of the church's connection with this founding event."[58] (emphasis added) A Lutheran ecumenical skeptic, after correctly describing the new Catholic doctrine of eucharistic sacrifice and consensus enabled by it, and (perhaps not so precisely) contemporary Catholic ecclesiology, lays it down. "It is a question, whether the Reformation controversy over the mass as sacrifice is really laid to rest. . . . The possibility of overcoming the until now sharp oppositions depend on how far . . . we can accept the ecclesiology just sketched. . . . Anyone who can acknowledge this sacramental-ontological doctrine of the church as legitimate . . . can have no further ground to contradict the doctrine of the mass as sacrifice, as this doctrine is here presented."[59]

VI

Convinced that the French dialogue has correctly pointed to the *Grunddifferenz*, but uneasy with the formulations it uses to do the pointing, André Birmelé,[60] with others,[61] has found sharper statement by referring to yet another slogan, Luther's description of the church as "a great sinner."[62]

---

55. A leading Catholic participant in American Reformed-Roman Catholic dialogue defined tradition, according to Catholic understanding, as "the reflection of the church on the gospel and the proclamation of the gospel by the church." "One may think of tradition as the response of the Church to the living voice of the gospel which resounds in her, as her awareness of herself" (John L. McKenzie, "Scripture and Tradition: A Roman Catholic View," *Reconsiderations* [New York: World Horizons, 1967], 23).
56. Ibid., 449.
57. Albert Mauder, "Zur Bedeutung des gemeinsamen lutherisch-katholischen Documentes 'Das Herrenmahl' für den christlichen Gottesdienst," *Materialdienst* (1979): 114.
58. Sesboüé, "Analyse catholique," 54.
59. Mauder, "Zur Bedenung . . ."
60. Birmelé, "La peccabilité de l'église," 399–409.
61. E.g. and again most sharply, Jüngel, "Die Kirche als Sakrament," 453–57. For a diagnostic summary of the discussion, see Harding Meyer, "Sündige Kirche?" *Ökumenische Rundschau* 38(1989): 397–410. Perhaps the international Reformed-Roman Catholic dialogue's statement, 122, that "we differ in our understanding of the nature of sin in the church" should be noted here; the dialogue itself was unable to clarify the difference.
62. Martin Luther, WA 34/I, 276: "*non est tam magna peccatrix ut Christiana ecclesia.*"

Catholic theology is perfectly able to speak of the church as "sinful," insofar as it is a group whose members sin. Thus Vatican II taught that the church, "during its pilgrimage on earth," is "still in its members liable to sin,"[63] that "clasping sinners in her bosom," she is "at once holy and always in need of purification."[64] But it is precisely the insistence on such qualification as "in its members," in which some Protestants find "a different ecclesiological vision."[65] "It is the church in the fulness of her mystery, in her holiness and in her character as the bride of Christ, which Luther calls the '*ecclesia peccatrix*.' "[66]

But this move surely creates more muddle rather than less. Is it possible to speak of the church in this context *otherwise* than "in its members"? If the Protestants here in question hold that it is not, as it sometimes seems they do,[67] then there is no difference between their position and that of Catholicism. Then between calling the church "sinful," which, to repeat, Catholicism is willing and eager to do, and "a sinner," there is no distinction. It would appear, however, that the objection to Catholic teaching consists in supposing that calling the church "*a* sinner" goes beyond saying that the church is a sinful *group*,[68] that a singular subject is posited here, whose liability to sin is the matter in dispute.

But who can this subject be? A *group* is made a community and so indeed is personalized only by and in some antecedent person.[69] In the case of the group that is the church, that person must be Christ or the Spirit—we need not at the moment decide which. Thus the person of the church who over against God is available to be or not to be "a sinner" can only be Christ or the Spirit over against the Father. Surely no one wishes to identify either as the singular "great sinner" of Luther's slogan. Perhaps one might call the *totus Christus* "a sinner" in the sense of Luther's own doctrine of atonement, in which Christ indeed is the singular great sinner, but such a move would lead in the Catholic direction, since in Luther's theology Christ's status as the great sinner is soteriological.

Hidden behind this entire discourse is Luther's formula for the individual believer, *simul iustus et peccator*, in an analogical application to the church as

---

63. *Unitatis redintegratio*, 3.
64. *Lumen gentium*, 8. For example of how Catholic theology moves at this point, Witte, "Thesen . . . , 441: "Wir sind der . . . uberzeugung, dass die Kirche der Ort ist, in dem Gottes rettendes Heilsangebot den Menschen begegnet, meinen aber dass die bejahende Antwort der glaubenden Gemeinschaft mit zum Wesen der Kirche gehört. Dies bedeutet, dass die pilgernde Kirche wesentlichen geschichtlichen Charakter hat. Die eine Kirche Christi ist das ewige Heil im Gemeinschaft, wenn auch in zeitlicher, unvollkommener Gestalt; deshalb gehört es zu ihrem Wesen, Sakrament des Heiles zu sein. In dieser irdischen Gestalt ist aber die Sündhaftigkeit ihrer Glieder ihr ebenso wesenseigen wie die Heiligkeit ihrer Glieder. Deshalb ist diese Gemeinschaft . . . Zeichen des Widerspruchs: Sie kann nur geglaubt werden."
65. Birmelé, "La peccabilité de l'église," 411.
66. Ibid., 410.
67. Ibid. "L'Église est pécheresse car elle est une communauté de croyants qui ne sont pas impeccables."
68. Ibid. "L'Église demande pour elle-même, et non seulement pour certains de ses membres, le pardon des pèchés."
69. Here, not entirely by the way, may be the legitimate form of the doctrine, so much insisted on by Orthodoxy, of the *monarchia* of the Father over against the Son and the Spirit.

community. That the church like the believer is *iustus* only by faith is now ecumenically uncontroversial. Is the analogy so close that also *peccator* applies to the church in the same way as to the individual? Surely this is not possible. For in Luther's doctrine the one who in the believer is *peccator* is the *remaining* "Old Adam," the subject who *was* before Christ newly personalized the believer as one with himself, and who haunts the new Christ-subject until his death is final. The church, however, is not one person at all before it is made a community by Christ's identification with it. There is not, with the church, any one antecedent personhood to *remain* as the one *peccator;* there are only the antecedent persons who are made a community, to remain as *peccatores*.

VII

Where then do we go from here? We have been driven back from all attempts to describe the alleged basic difference as a difference about the church's mediation of salvation. Nor, indeed, does it turn out to be *quite* the case that we have simply circled back to the doctrine of justification at a new location. The pattern of the dialogues' history proves to be more like a spiral than a circle on a plane. It is, at long last, time to turn from the dialogues' immediate achievements and troubles to that quite different sort of question at which this study has always aimed.

Part 3

THE BASIS

§

Temporal Continuity

I

It was once proposed to Joseph Cardinal Ratzinger:

> Between Catholicism and Protestantism what is finally at issue is *being in time*. Catholicism sees that self-identical historical being means *institution*. And it sees that institutions of the gospel must share the gospel's mystery and cannot be mere human arrangements; as the latter, they would be frivolous. Protestantism sees that historical being means *freedom*. And it sees that the freedom of the gospel is God's own freedom, which humans cannot administer; our attempt to administer such freedom would be sin. What we are not in position to do, is to see both truths at once.[1]

The cardinal did not reject the construal.

With this chapter we leave the program initially laid before the dialogues and come to the defining project of my own enterprise, which has already shaped my tracing of the dialogues' progress. The dialogues have moved step by step down lists of traditionally divisive theological loci; their remarkable results, their sticking points, and some possible resolutions of the latter are the matter of the previous chapters. Both in the dialogues and in my analyses, something sustains division stubbornly and inventively, inducing logically strange and polemically circular behavior in the dialogical enterprise defined by the traditional list and in the history that produced the list; this is evidently neither a dispute on the list nor one located at the same conceptual level as are the items of the list. Hence the recent search for a *Grunddifferenz*.

If what sustains division is a problem not located in any of the theological loci officially in dispute, then two possible other sorts of location remain. The dynamic of separation may be located in some traditional locus that was not thought to harbor church-divisive controversy, such as Christology within the Western church. In this case, the greater conceptual depth of a basic problem will reflect differences in depth among theology's traditional topics as, for example, Christology is doubtless indeed conceptually basic to sacramentology. Or the problem may be located altogether elsewhere, in some region of reflection not thematised as one of theology's usual loci.

1. The exchange was by a letter of the author, 24 March 1988, and in personal conversation at Rome, 19 April 1988.

The chapters of this part bear titles two of which refer to standard loci of theology and one of which does not. A chapter on the doctrine of God follows the hypothesis to which the initial steps of my work led me. The present chapter results from aspects of the initial hypothesis, from indications that repeatedly appeared in the previous chapters, and from the whole sweep of the last three chapters on the church and its ministry; the present chapter begins directly where its immediate predecessor left off. A chapter of Christology exists both because the matter of Christology is a sort of bridge between the question of God and the question about time—though Christ himself is decidedly *not* a bridge between God and time—and because the profounder earlier proposals tended to look here.[2]

My first plan was to pursue the basic difference through Christology into the doctrine of God and thence into more abstract reflections about time. This order proved backwards to the matter. For in moving from God to time, one does *not* move deeper; there is no metaphysically or linguistically deeper level than the reality of God's identity. Our interpretation of time results from our interpretation of God and not vice versa; pervasive but uncircumcised reverence for abstractions enforces the more conventional opinion and shaped my first plan—indeed, this opinion is itself a form of the basic flaw I was looking for! Therefore, I will begin with the problem of temporal continuity; from it I will pursue the quarry sideways into Christology; and finally deeper into the doctrine of God.

At the *very* bottom of things I expect to find not a basic difference but a *shared* basic *flaw*. By my hypothesis a basic something indeed lies at the root of the theological disputes that divide the church, a perversion that can and does generate new divergences as fast as existing ones are resolved. This is not, however, a dissensus but an unthematic and disastrous consensus—or better, a much overdue common theological task.

II

In its response to the final report of international Anglican-Roman Catholic dialogue, the Roman Congregation for the Faith identified an explicitly so-called fundamental difference: "apostolic succession" in an inclusive sense that comprehends both the general continuity of the church with Christ and with the apostles, and the historically identifiable successions by which this occurs. This, they said, is the "heart of the entire ecumenical problem" that "conditions all questions."[3] Cardinal Ratzinger's personal comment on the same document identifies "the authority of the Tradition" as "the fundamental problem the resolution of which is the key to the problem of unity."[4] The Cardinal generalizes his diagnosis and

---

2. Perhaps most notably, Yves Congar, "Regards et réflexions sur la christologie de Luther," *Das Konzil von Chalkedon*, ed. Aloys Grillmeier and Hans Bacht (Würzburg: Echter Verlag, 1954), 482–86.
    3. Congregatione della fede, *Documentation Catholique*, 1830(1983): 511.
    4. Joseph Cardinal Ratzinger, *Église, oecuménisme et politique*, trans. P. Jordan, P.-E. Gudenus, and B. Müller (Paris: Fayard, 1987), 115. It is, by the way, interesting to note that the Cardinal uses Orthodoxy's language to make the point.

the congregation's, and moves one step deeper. "What is at issue . . . is the basic decision about how the mediation of then and now happens."[5]

We could hardly want a more august proposal for location of a *Grunddifferenz* than that constituted by the ensemble of these statements. We launch this chapter with the question How does the church remain itself through time? "In what sense can it be said that the Church has remained one from generation to generation?"[6] How does *any* historical entity remain itself through time? How indeed are then and now mediated?

Moreover, a pair of terms exists in which the discussion regularly casts the problem of churchly temporal continuity in partial coincidence and entirely parallel with the proposal set at the beginning of this chapter. The Catholic leader of the always diagnostic French dialogue formulated that the church "is an *event* of salvation, because it belongs to *the* event of salvation· in the church the event makes itself *Institution,* and by grace the institution continues as the place which 'guarantees' the present reality of the event."[7] (emphasis added)

To this primal Catholic insistence we may oppose its direct and authoritatively Protestant contradiction, from consensus in dialogue between the Reformed and Baptist world alliances. "The church is first and foremost an event, *rather* than an institution; the church 'exists' in that it continually 'happens,' namely where the Lord effectively exercises his rule and where it is recognized and accepted."[8] (emphasis added) We may recall a Lutheran outburst. "For us the church is decidedly not a mysterious reality, *given antecedently.* . . . For us, the church *occurs* in joint listening to God's Word."[9] (emphasis added)

Were we still seeking convergence between traditional teachings, we might find it in such a statement as this of the German church governments. "Thus the church is established institution and, by the power of the Spirit, ever new event. Both must be seen together. To emphasize always either the one or the other of these basic determinations could promote an institutionalist or an enthusiastic misunderstanding; both threats have repeatedly appeared in the history of the churches."[10] But at our present stage of reflection, such mere balancing can help little. It is

5. Joseph Cardinal Ratzinger, "Fragen zur Sukzession," *KNA—Kritischer Ökumenisches Informationsdienst,* 28/29:5: "Es geht . . . um die Grundentscheidung darüber, wie die Vermittlung von damals und heute geschieht."

6. International Reformed-Roman Catholic Dialogue, *Towards a Common Understanding of the Church* (1990), 114.

7. Bernard Sesboüé, "Analyse catholique," Comité mixte catholique-protestant en France, *Consensus oecuménique et différence fondamentale* (Paris: le Centurion, 1987), 53. "Elle est événement de salut, par-ce qu'elle appartient à l'événement du salut: en elle l'événement se fait institution et l'institution demeure par grâce le lieu qui 'garantit' la présence de l'événement."

8. *Report of Theological Conversations Sponsored by the World Alliance of Reformed Churches and the Baptist World Alliance* (1977), 36.

9. Kurt Aland, *Evangelium und Kirche,* ed. Kirchliches Aussenamt der Evangelischen Kirche im Deutschland (Frankfurt: Otto Lembeck, 1983), 82.

10. Arbeitsgruppe der deutschen Bischofskonferenz und der Kirchenleitung der Vereinigten Evangelisch-lutherischen Kirche Deutschlands, *Kirchengemeinschaft im Wort und Sakrament* (Paderborn: Bonifatius-Druckerei, 1984), 12.

precisely a standpoint from which to see "both truths at once"—or, perhaps equivalently, both errors at once—that we must now seek.

III

In the Catholic position before us, we may discern two presuppositions about temporal reality. The first: some events happen once and then belong to the past and are as punctual as the Baptists and Reformed would have the church-event to be, whereas other events remain available through subsequent time. The second: events that remain available do so because they are institutionalized and because the institution then carries them through time.

Also in the Protestant position, we see suppositions about temporal occurrence. A first: events and institutions are straightforwardly alternative forms of being, events do not themselves become institutions.[11] A second: events are intrinsically punctual; such a predicate as "exists" can be attached to them, as here to the church-event, only in an extended sense. A third: if an event that does repeatedly replicate itself, "continually 'happens'," so as in some extended manner of speaking to "exist," this may be due to institutionalization or to a quite different sort of factor, the intervention of a self-identical personal agent. Theology teaches that the continuing church belongs to the second of these latter classes and not to the first: when the Lord acts the church occurs, and when the same Lord acts again the same church occurs again.

Can we now discern suppositions that Catholics and Protestants *share*, even as they interpret temporal occurrence from such seemingly opposite viewpoints? I think we can.

First, both interpretations presume that time and personal being are mutually external. The Catholic interpretation can be stated entirely without mention of persons *as* persons. In the Protestant interpretation, time goes on and as it does isolating events in the past, unless some factor counters this antiquation; if the countering factor is a person, the picture of intervention is unmistakable.

Second, both interpretations work with what is popularly called a linear picture of time. In the Catholic interpretation, some events are left behind as time marches on and others are carried along by institutionalization. In the Protestant interpretation, time goes on with or without the repetition of any one event; repetition, if it occurs, is occasioned extrinsically.

Third, both interpretations seem to presuppose the mutual extrinsicality even of time and *events*. Events happen *in* time, by both interpretations, and may or may not be carried along *through* time.

Once we have noticed these three shared presumptions, we may perhaps also discern how they determine a kind of conceptual space within which the opposed

---

11. André Birmelé, "Trois documents recents à propos des ministères," *Positions Lutheriennes* 31(1983): 291, shows the problematic, as so often: "Du côté des Églises de la Réforme, la caractère visible de l'Église et son aspect institutionnel ne sont pas niér, mais l'accent est mis sur les signa externa de cette Église que sont l'annonce de la Parole et la célébration des Sacrements." Now, why that "mais"? Why are not these signs taken to be both visible and institutional? Clearly, because they are events, and the two classes are metaphysically presupposed exclusive.

Catholic and Protestant interpretations arise from a shared predicament. Time, events, and persons are for both interpretations independent scalar or polar coordinates of historical reality. Within the space thus defined, *institutional* reality is the indeterminate factor; different interpretations of historical continuity result depending on where institution then attaches itself. In the Catholic interpretation, institutions and *events* have a certain affinity: events can become institutions without losing their event-character. In the scheme of coordinates, institution thus becomes a possible *modification* of the event-coordinate. In the Protestant interpretation, the affinity of institutions is rather to *persons,* to which, however, they appear as rivals; in the scheme of coordinates, institution thus functions as a possible *replacement* of the person-coordinate.

I think all three shared suppositions about temporal reality, and the resultant sets of polar coordinates for the interpretation of historical reality, are simply false. Here is the most abstract version of that "basic" *false* "consensus" for which my study searches, an indicator for that point of *shared failure* that is the generator of the ever new dialectics of division.

Time and personal being are not mutually external. Whatever physical dimensions would obtain in a universe without persons, none would bear a resemblance to what we invariably intuit when we speak of time. Immanuel Kant correctly identified time as the horizon of consciousness, of personal being's inner sense. Nor does this convincing identification need to imply the subjectivity of time, for, as many in the history of philosophy have noted, one need only suppose an absolute Consciousness, to see how time can be as Kant described it and also be real independently of *our* consciousness and given to it from beyond it.

Moving on, time is not circular but need not therefore be linear. As entire schools of nineteenth- and twentieth-century theology excitedly proclaimed, Judaism and Christianity broke the circularity of mythically experienced time. But linearity is not the only alternative experience, nor is it the Jewish or Christian experience. In Jewish and Christian interpretation of time, the Exodus, for example, does not become farther away as time goes on from it. Time, in both the Hebrew Scriptures and the New Testament, is itself a sort of event; it is what happens when the Spirit "comes." To that gnomic proposition I will return in the final chapter.

Nor then can time and events be mutually external. If nothing ever happened, would there be time? As to ontological priority, it is by no means apparent, either in reflection on relativistic science or in the phenomenology of personal experience, that time is the possibility of events. The reverse is equally thinkable; we will see that Christian understanding of God shows it also to be the truth.

IV

The diagnosis just laid out covers all the sticking points found in my account of the dialogues. It was on the question about the *duration* of Christ's eucharistic presence, continuously after the event, that consensual affirmation of that presence proved after all fragile. One could even put it so: Does the event of the presence institutionalize itself? Again, in Tillard's clear formulation of contemporary Catholic teaching, there is a pause in the eventfulness of sacramental presence, *during* which Christ is just *there;* notably, the possibilities that emerge in that *pause* confront the dialogues with eucharistic sacrifice as the next matter of controversy.

Widespread implicit consensus about the *personal* and active character of Christ's eucharistic presence underlies much of the more formally achieved consensus about the presence itself. All the relevant dialogues shied away from identifying this presence with the fixed, thing-like presence of the bread and cup, and this shying was in turn the invariable occasion of Catholic restlessness with the dialogue results. In this context the notion of "thing" plays exactly the same role as does the notion of "institution" in dissensus about the church's historical presence. I asked earlier, Is not a person also a thing? Is a personal entity sheerly actual, there for others only in the very act of self-presentation? Does not a personal entity also have persistence, even a certain static givenness? We may ask, Is not personal being always also institutional being? Or, vice versa, is institution necessarily always so institutional?

The foundation of consensus about eucharistic sacrifice was the posit that some events occur in a sacramental mode of being. The characteristic of such events is that they are sacraments *of* other, nonsacramental events, and that they do not continue or repeat or complement the other events of which they are the sacraments, but simply *are* the present-tense occurring of those very events. "It was agreed that the unrepeatable sacrifice which was, now is in the Eucharist."[12] The concept of *anamnesis* is a key throughout such agreement. When an anamnetic event happens, the distance between a past event and a present event is mediated by the past event within the present event, so that the question of the new event repeating *or* relativizing the past event cannot arise. In some of the more profound dialogical uses of *anamnesis* this character of the eucharistic memorial is rooted in a personal agency. "The redemptive act of Christ on the cross . . . cannot be reiterated, but its power is eternally active in the perpetual intercession of the Son . . . before the Father."[13] Nothing of this can be true if time is simply linear, or again if events and things are mutually exclusive or if time and persons are mutually independent. It is the necessity of asserting sacramental *anamnesis*, within a conceptual framework in which it cannot be asserted, that generates dialectics of division.

Consensus about eucharistic sacrifice, built on new understandings of sacrament and *anamnesis*, reached a penultimate limit at its apparent implication that the church offers Christ's sacrifice. Those most consistent in rejecting this implication were also driven to reject the suppositions about time constitutive for ecumenical use of *anamnesis*, insisting that the word as used in the institution-texts does *not* assert the present actuality of Christ's death, but "only" of his person or efficacy.[14]

---

12. Kent S. Knutson, "Eucharist as Sacrifice," in *The Eucharist as Sacrifice*, vol. 3 of *Lutherans and Catholics in Dialogue*, ed. Paul Empie and T. Austin Murphy (Minneapolis: Augsburg, 1974), 13.
13. Groupe des Dombes, *L'acte sacerdotal du Christ dans l'activité sacerdotale de l'église* (1962), nrs. 3, 8.
14. See p. 8.

A German dialogue moved past this limit by making the concept of communion central; notably for our present interest, this dialogue attributed the polar positions of the past to *shared* lack of concepts by which to grasp the identity-in-difference of Christ's sacrifice then and the church's act now.[15] The communion-theology, in which new consensus was found, makes *personal* reality the context of the sacrifice's transcendence of time.

As the German dialogue suggested, both the Lutheran doctrine of "real presence" and the Catholic doctrine of "the sacrifice of the mass" were intended to "overcome the historical distance between the sacrifice on Golgotha and the celebration of Eucharist."[16] That is, both are intended as distinctively Christian doctrines about how "then and now are mediated." The polemics, I suggest, have been generated by a shared conception of historical distance that made that intention hopeless.

Finally, the chapters on ministry and episcopacy began the impetus that swept the dialogues and our discussion through to the question of churchly mediation, and so to the immediate occasion and conceptual starting-point of this chapter.

V

An article by Gerhard Forde, a long-term Lutheran member of the American Lutheran-Roman Catholic dialogue, summing up positions he espoused in the dialogue and that controlled much of its course, is perhaps the best available statement of the basic difference as so far laid bare, and of the Protestant tendency, given that grasp of the difference.[17] Forde's presentation can also serve to mitigate the abstraction of my analysis so far.

"There should be," Forde writes, "no disagreement over whether or not the gospel is mediated. . . . It is of the very essence of the catholic faith that it insists on the concrete mediation of God's saving gifts."[18] Precisely Luther's drastic insistence on the actual "word of the cross," the actual event of such person-to-person address as "I absolve you," as the locus of God's grace, makes it uniquely clear that "proclamation absolutely requires a proclaimer."[19]

The problem rather lies in the understanding of "*what* in fact is mediated"— that is, the proclamation-event—and in the way in which the conception of what is mediated "reflects back" on the conception and practice of "mediation . . . and the offices that carry it."[20] In Forde's presentation of the Reformation's understanding, what the proclamation as event *does*, since it is the word of the *cross*, is "the death of the old and the rebirth of the new," is freedom from continuing history and its necessities, over against the eschatologically new. "The mediation,

---

15. See pp. 8-9.

16. Ökumenisches Arbeitskreis evangelischer und katholischer Theologen, "Das Opfer Jesu Christi und der Kirche: Abschliessender Bericht," *Das Opfer Jesu Christi und seine Gegenwart in der Kirche,* ed. Karl Lehmann and Edmund Schlink (Freiburg: Herder, 1983), 3.3.1.

17. Gerhard O. Forde, "The Catholic Impasse: Reflections on Lutheran-Catholic Dialogue Today," *Promoting Unity,* ed. H. George Anderson and James R. Crumley, Jr. (Minneapolis: Augsburg, 1989).

18. Ibid., 75.

19. Ibid., 74.

20. Ibid., 75.

therefore, though absolutely necessary, is such that in the very act of mediation it limits itself . . . to this age, and ends itself precisely by its witness to the new age." What that means is that "The mediation is such that it seeks to remove itself once it has done the mediation." Forde is "tempted to use an image from the television show 'Mission Impossible' where the 'team' receives its instructions via a tape . . . that then announces that it will self-destruct in a number of seconds." What such offices and other structures obviously will *not* celebrate is their own "perpetuity."[21] The church will build no *monuments* to the "Prince of the Apostles."[22]

At work here is an understanding that sees the only authentic Christianity in the Christianity of the first generation of disciples, who indeed made no provision for institutional historical continuity, anticipating as they did the immediate coming of the kingdom.[23] But the Lord did not return as expected, and in the canonical documents from the generation that realized this, the Pastoral Epistles, we see the church arranging *offices* precisely for *perpetuity,* for historical continuity both with Christ and the apostles and with a now anticipated future history of the church. The heart of the usual Catholic position is that it does not regard this development as problematic but rather as in easy harmony with the Christianity of the apostolic age itself. *Both* Forde and the normal Catholic position are wrong.

Thus the Roman theological commission which produced a currently influential document on the priesthood, said that Catholic emphasis on succession in office "results . . . from the impossibility of conceiving a 'church of Christ' here below that was not connected to his Incarnation and to its whole historical efficacy."[24] It is here supposed that the incarnation, like any other event, has immanent historical effects and that it belongs to the authenticity of the church to maintain continuity with Christ *as* a continuity of such effects. Or again, Cardinal Ratzinger formulates the question between Catholicism and Protestantism so. "Can the authenticity of the word and of the church come forward in a break with the concrete continuity of the episcopally ordered . . . church? The problem . . . is the break with the catholic church's concrete continuity of tradition."[25]

Such Catholic positions suggest a particular understanding of the church and her historical self-identity as a total phenomenon that sees the church as at least *also* not unlike the self-identity of other historical communities. In this understanding, when one says that the church now is the same church as that of the apostles, one is at least *also* saying all the same sorts of things as when one says that the American nation now is the same nation as that of the founding constitutional fathers, and one is affirming all those multiple interweaving connections that constitute such a self-identity.

---

21. Ibid., 75–76.
22. The portal inscription of St. Peter's basilica in Rome.
23. Whether Martin Luther indeed understood matters the same way, i.e., whether Forde's Luther interpretation is right, is of course a separate question (Forde, "The Catholic Impasse," 70–72).
24. Internationale Theologenkommission (1970), *Priesterdienst,* trans. H. U. von Balthasar (Einsiedeln: Johannes Verlag, 1971), 94.
25. Sesboüé, "Analyse catholique," 54.

A certain amount of dialogical consensus has been built on what is in fact this Catholic understanding. Thus, early as always, the Groupe des Dombes agreed. Ministerial succession "should be taken within the context of the permanence of the church as a whole, which is founded by the apostles . . . and which, by virtue of the promise and command of the Lord and the help of the Spirit, carries through the continuity of history responsibility to proclaim the gospel."[26] Doubtless unsurprisingly, international Anglican-Roman Catholic consensus could go far in this direction. "Moreover, because they (bishops participating in an episcopal consecration) are representatives of their churches in fidelity to the teaching and mission of the apostles and are members of the episcopal college, their participation . . . insures the historical continuity of this church with the apostolic church."[27]

Therewith, of course, Catholic understanding of historical self-identity and consensus built on it involve all the antinomies and puzzles that plague every attempt to understand and cultivate the historical self-identity of nations, parties, and the like, including, for example, American constitutional interpretation. The doctrinal commission of the German Catholic bishops once restrained protestantizing tendencies in some Catholic ecumenists by laying it down. "For the catholic understanding of faith" only "the whole of the historically developed faith of the church" is the criterion of teaching, and not merely the historically first phase of that faith documented in Scripture.[28] Indeed, and the judges of the Supreme Court think this way about the American constitutional faith. But the justices do not solve the problem of "strict" versus actualizing interpretation; they merely state the truism that evokes it. It would not be altogether false to think of the Reformation as protest against the very same sort of finally uncontrollable lawmaking that has regularly outraged critics of the Court; nor may it be altogether from the point to note that the problem faced by the Court is apparently both ineradicable and insoluble.

VI

In these more concrete statements of dissensus we may discern a common supposition, which, in my judgment, is shared basic error. Both sides suppose that the life of the church—its interior eventfulness and missionary dynamism in the world—is temporally homogeneous with the life of this present age. Both assume that the church's time is a stretch of this world's time. Thus Forde's drastic and clarifying evocation of Protestant sensibility (that the proclamation confronts hearers with the immediacy of the kingdom and so terminates their *old* time) must also mean the termination of the *church's* time, must demand the ever-repeated dialectical cancellation of the church's structures of historical perpetuity. Catholic responses to such positions suppose that if the church's life indeed possesses perpetuity, that if it has time and in that time maintains self-identity through

26. Groupe des Dombes, *La succession apostolique* (1968), 1.

27. Anglican-Roman Catholic Conversations, *Ministry and Ordination* (1973), nr. 16.

28 "Das Ganze des gewordenen Glaubens der Kirche" "Glaubenskommission der Deutschen Bischofkonferenz zum 'Amtsmemorandum,' " *Herderkorrespondenz* 27:159.

identifiable historical structures, these continuities will be of the same general sort as those that anyway obtain in this world between a historical event and its communal consequences. To pick the analogy up again, both assume that a churchly magisterium, if there is to be one, will have the same sort of task and problem as does the U.S. Supreme Court. To avoid this, Protestantism tries to theorize away the temporal space in which such a magisterium could appear; Catholicism accepts the equally hopeless task and problem.

In the Pastoral Epistles we see the church arranging for its own historical continuity, by historically identifiable official successions. Catholicism has taken this development as unproblematic; Protestantism has on account of it perennially downgraded or exegetically evaded the Pastorals. Thereby both betray themselves. For surely it would be possible *both* to acknowledge how very problematic, over against the eschatologically immediate gospel, provisions for perpetuity are, and how outlandish historical provisions for such a gospel will be amid the normal historical continuities of this world, *and* to acknowledge them as God's gifts when in his providence the Lord delays. Surely it would be possible both to acknowledge that the development shown in the Pastorals is a kind of retreat and to say that God called it. It may be that the Lord's failure immediately to return refuted the gospel; but if it did not, if we are to go on with the church, a postapostolic church will necessarily be the church of the Pastorals, and this will be a very problematic phenomenon over against *both* the "pure" church of the apostolic age and the normal continuing communities of this age.

It is doubtful that either Catholics or Protestants will be happy with my characterizations or analyses of their positions. Neither tradition intends to affirm the lordship of this world's continuities, in the fashion I have just attributed to them. But that is the very point. What we together *do* intend, we do not grasp. Shared error poses false alternatives; those who embrace either alternative clearly perceive the error in the other. The irony is that the error thus perceived is basically the same on both sides.

Perhaps it may even be a symptom of avoidance that the question of "Scripture-and-tradition" has been so little explored in the modern Catholic-Protestant dialogues, despite the opinion of our fathers on both sides that here was a chief matter of division.[29] It may also be symptomatic that East-West dialogue, despite its relative infancy, has gone straight to the matter, and with surprising achievement.[30]

---

29. Such truisms as those of international Roman Catholic-Reformed dialogue are about as far as it goes. *The Presence of Christ in Church and World* (1977), nr. 28: "On the whole the Reformed sought a direct support for their doctrine in the apostolic witness of Scripture, whereas the Roman Catholic church perceived the apostolic witness more strongly in the life of faith of the whole Church, in the measure that it constantly strove in the course of the centuries to apprehend the fullness of the divine truth." This dialogue *did*, however, then put its finger on something. "This difference in attitude may rest on a difference in pneumatology: Catholic thought is primarily sustained by confidence in the continuing presence of the spirit." The best so far achieved, in my judgment, comes from multilateral dialogue, in "Towards a Confession of the Common Faith," *Apostolic Faith Today*, ed. H.-G. Link (Geneva: World Council of Churches, 1985), 2. "The essential elements of the Christian mystery are known to us through the witness of the apostolic community, transmitted in the Scriptures. These are

There is one Western ecumenist who has not avoided the question of Scripture and tradition but has instead pressed it as a primary ecumenical task and opportunity; thus Joseph Cardinal Ratzinger must appear as sage one last time in this book.[31] The following passage can show the parameters of his advocacy. "In the Catholic Church, the principle of 'tradition' does not . . . in the first instance refer to an inventory of doctrines or texts handed down from earlier epochs. It designates a particular way of relating the living word of the church and the primal word written in the Bible. What the term 'tradition' signifies is first of all the fact that the church which lives in the form of apostolic succession . . . is the place where the Bible is received and interpreted with authority."[32]

"Tradition," as understood in the cardinal's doctrine, is a location for biblical exegesis. Tradition by this understanding means that the church needs the Bible for purposes specific to it as an existing and continuing historical community, and so must read the Bible by hermeneutical principles appropriate to those purposes. In one way, that is so obvious that ecumenical discussion is hardly needed, consensus being antecedently given. But then what also has to be ecumenically granted without much discussion is that together we do not know how to do such specifically churchly exegesis. Here again is precisely a shared and just *so* divisive *lack* in the lives of the churches.

If Catholics and Protestants do not know how to do such exegesis, no more, I think, does Orthodoxy. Yet to get a glimpse of what an understanding of Scripture and of tradition could look like that might enable such exegesis or be enabled by it, I will make the first of several drafts on East-West dialogue.

An explicit consensual text on Scripture-and-tradition from international Orthodox-Lutheran dialogue reads: "This 'gospel' of salvation is the content of the Holy Tradition, preserved, confessed and transmitted by the Scriptures, by the lives of the saints of all times, and by the conciliar tradition of the church. . . . Holy Scripture, since it is the work of the Spirit within the Tradition, has as the criterion of its appropriate comprehension Jesus Christ himself in the life and teaching of the one church."[33] This is very much in the spirit of the *Reformation*,

---

the fruit of the Gospel and of the action of the Spirit in the primitive Church. On the one hand, they bear witness of the apostolic Church's understanding of the mystery of Christ. On the other hand, however, the truth they transmit could be fully grasped only in the context of the life of that early community faithful to the teaching of the apostles, to the fellowship of the brethren, to the breaking of bread and to prayer. . . . And so we can say that we exist as Christians through the apostolic tradition (the paradosis of the kerygma), attested in Scripture and transmitted in and through the Church by the power of the Holy Spirit. Tradition thus understood is made a present reality in the preaching of the Word, the administration of the sacraments, worship, Christian instruction, theology, mission, the witness given to Christ by the life of Christians."

30. So between Roman Catholicism and Orthodoxy in the so-called "Bari Document," *Episkepsis* 18(1987), 390:11; and between Lutheranism and Orthodoxy both internationally, *Ecriture et Tradition* (1987), *Episkepsis* 18(1987), 381:17–18; and in America, in the so-called "Allentown Document" (1985), *Episkepsis* 16(1985), 341:14–15.

31. See especially the one section of "Problèmes et espoirs du dialogue Anglicans-Catholiques," in Ratzinger, *Église*, 96–111.

32. Ibid., 110.

33. *Ecriture et Tradition* (Crete, 1987), *Episkepsis* 18(1987), 381:17.

yet at the same time any denial of tradition or opposition between Scripture and tradition is impossible in the terms used.

The relation of the Spirit with the church is the key to this consensus, a consensus that Western Catholics and Protestants among themselves have not been able to achieve in centuries of argument. Pentecost is the feast Western Christianity has never known how to celebrate. I will return to these matters at greater length in the final chapter.

VII

What then is the shared flaw, at this level of analysis? Catholics and Protestants alike think of time as outside God, a supposition that is plainly false. Time does not occur outside personal reality, so that if time is outside God then he is not its creator. Since the gospel affirms a Creator, we ought to know what person it is in whom time is located.

The time we inhabit, it is ecumenically taught, is indeed *created* and therefore radically other than God. It does not follow that God has no time of his own; therefore, it also does not follow that our time, given its contingent creation, is outside him.

If Christian teaching about events and persons and communities that appear both "then" and "now" is to be maintained, events and persons cannot be mutually extrinsic; nor can events and institutions, or persons and institutions. But only in the triune God are event and personhood fully one, or event and institution, or person and institution (I realize that these assertions are as yet unfounded). Only if our time is determined by God's time and embraced within it are these extrinsicalities indeed false; and only as we understand that our time is within God's time will we understand that and how they are false.

Our shared *false* construal of temporality also reflects a God. This is the God in whom there can be no time because timelessness is what makes he or she or it be God. Our shared false construal of temporality reflects the culture-diety of Western civilization, the Goddess once revealed to Parmenides of Elea. She revealed to him "the unshakable heart of . . . truth." That truth was that all that changes or can change, all for which time provides the horizon, is less than being. The difference between Catholic and Protestant construals of time is, finally, merely that the Catholic construal reflects the pre-Enlightenment avatar of this God and the Protestant construal reflects the Enlightenment version.

⑨
Christology

I

The church is driven into division because it has not completed its primary dogmatic task: the interpretation of God by what happened and will happen with Jesus. In consequence of a doctrine of God only partly bent to the gospel, there is a hidden contradiction in all the church's interpretation of its own source and purpose. Thus dialectics are generated within the church's practice and thinking that indefatigably pose alternatives each of which is dubious, and impel Christianity's division into polar communities that can neither be reconciled nor leave one another alone.

People do not first become religious when the gospel's messengers come to them. Christian proclamation of the triune God occurs always as mission and so as reinterpretation of some antecedent religious understanding. In the missionary history that led to the existing church and its divisions, the antecedent interpretation was that which came of Greece's experience within, and later theological domination of the religious world of Mediterranean antiquity.

Religion is the cultivation of some eternity, of whatever it is upon which a community relies to reconcile the discontinuities of time, to rescue our temporal tale from its threatening idiocy and give it plotted coherence, to make it indeed a tale. There are thus as many putative eternities as there are religions, or vice versa. To each putative eternity necessarily belongs a paired interpretation of time, and in the pairing of a particular eternity with its appropriate grasp of time, a particular apprehension of temporal continuity, of what eternity enables for time. If a putative eternity seems open to address and capable of response, if it is *personal*, the religion in question has a God or gods. Christian proclamation of the triune God is always reinterpretation of antecedent understanding of the relation of eternity to time and, if the antecedent religion knows one, of God.

The direct fruit of the gospel's confrontation with late Mediterranean antiquity's interpretation of God is the doctrine of Trinity. This doctrine is directly continuous in language with Hellenic reflection and accessing its sophistication, and is provoked by its questions and commitments. But then the doctrine affirms about God nearly everything that the Greeks denied. The Nicene and Constantinopolitan fathers said that a temporal figure, Jesus of Nazareth, is one identity of the eternal God; that this God's eternity is therefore constituted not in his abstraction from time but in the "infinity" of his liveliness, in creatures' inability to keep up with him; therefore, deity is not a predicate susceptible of degrees, so that there can be no mediating godlets between Creator and creatures.[1]

Naturally, antecedent religion does not meekly accept such violation, in general or in the present case, but attempts to maintain its understanding of eternity, even or especially within the church itself. When Christian thought must meet such resistance, the resulting reflection is Christology in the more specific sense. Christology is, or should be, the thinking involved in *getting over* the self-evidencies about God that antecedent religion will in each case of the gospel's missionary penetration have hidden in the minds of this new sort of believers. A christological proposition is adequate just insofar as it outrages something comprehensively and radically that everybody at a time and place supposes "of course" to be true of anything worthy to be called God.

Within the missionary strand that leads to the Christianity now divided, the great antecedently given self-evidency about God comes from the Greeks: God is eternal, so as to be God, by sheer immunity to time. The one maxim of all late Mediterranean theology was, "Of course, nothing can be true of God that would suggest that God can be affected by time's chances," can "suffer." One thing at least all cults and systems were sure they together knew about God, that God is "impassible."[2] Just so, the first technically christological propositions had to be such as these: "The Impassible suffers . . . the Deathless dies."[3]

II

It has been suggested before that the divided church's basic differences are christological.[4] It is a commonplace exchange, that Lutheran Christology is "monophysitic" or that Catholic and Reformed Christologies are "Nestorian." The decisive point about such trades, in my judgment, is that all sides are usually right. Traditional mutual christological disapprobations occur within a common tradition that itself harbors the flaw to be cured; so long as it is not, Antioch (the ancient academic home of Nestorian tendencies) and Alexandria (the ancient academic home of monophysitic tendencies) will again and again evoke and disapprove one another. This chapter must include more theological history-telling than was necessary in other chapters, since the analyses I propose depend upon a modestly innovative interpretation of the relevant history.

Through the great centuries of the ancient church's dogmatic conflict and creativity, Antioch was the intellectual reservoir within the church of fidelity to antecedent Greek religious common sense. The one constant concern of Antioch was to allow no thought to pass that might sully the deity of God; this deity was

1. Perhaps I may here be allowed to refer to my own study: Robert W. Jenson, *The Triune Identity* (Philadelphia: Fortress, 1982).

2. To this whole complex, see Jenson, *The Triune Identity*, 57–77, with copious notes. For a compendious version of the identical judgment, Jaroslav Pelikan, *The Emergence of the Catholic Tradition* (Chicago: University of Chicago, 1971), 52–54.

3. Melito of Sardis, *Antonius Caesar*, 13.

4. So most famously Yves Congar, "Regards et réflexions sur la christologie de Luther," *Das Konzil von Chalkedon*, ed. Aloys Grillmeier and Hans Bacht (Würzburg: Echter Verlag, 1954), 482–86.

self-evidently construed by the canons of late antique reflection, as constituted in "impassibility," in immunity to time's events. Therein Antioch but continued an established tradition; already Justin the Martyr had taken it as obvious that full-fledged God could not, for example, have lunched with Abraham; and as for emerging from a womb or hanging on a cross, a second-level deity must surely deal with such assignments.[5]

In the early fourth century, this commonsensical theology ceased (for reasons beyond this book's tracing) to be harmless and became virulent as Arianism. Since it was then still remembered that "the Logos" or "the Son" were titles of the concrete Jesus, the Arians' question was merely Antioch's inevitable question. "How can the Logos be God, since he sleeps like any other man, and weeps, and suffers?"[6] The outcome of the fourth century's confusions and struggles, the establishment of the doctrine of Trinity in 381 at the first Council of Constantinople, was a victory for the rival school of Alexandria, whose position may be crudely summarized: We have no idea how the suffering Jesus can be full-fledged God— who we too know must of course be immune to time's chances—but somehow he is or salvation is undone.

The Logos, said the councils at Nicea and Constantinople, is "of one being with the Father." Antioch bowed to the councils—and indeed quickly became super-Nicene—but in so doing, the Logos for Antioch became incapable of time's wombs and crosses. Thereupon the pressure of the axiom that God is immune to time simply shifted one notch, and where it had before divided Christ from God now divided Christ from himself. Antioch now asked, "How can Jesus be the Logos, since Jesus sleeps like other men, and weeps, and suffers?" Inevitably, the offense of Jesus' human temporality centered on those events of his life that, for him as for us, constitute it: birth and death.

This was the question that tore the Eastern church through the properly so-called christological controversies from 381 on;[7] it remains to this day the question that defines actual Christology. The historically actual christological question has merely been Arius's question in a new location.

Antioch's role in the christological controversy has had a good press from the great liberal historians of dogma for Antioch's alleged attention to the human Jesus. But what the texts actually show is a strange sort of attention, the same old anxiety that this humanity's temporality not contaminate God. Thus the great controversy was precipitated by Bishop Nestorius' sheer horror at his new congregation's liturgical delight in the Logos's occupancy of a womb.[8] To be sure, no more than in the trinitarian round could Alexandria provide explanations of *how* it could be true that Mary truly bore God, or, as it was insisted in the last decisive controversy, that "one of the Trinity suffered." But for the sake of salvation Alexandria had to insist that nevertheless such propositions are true.

---

5. Justin Martyr, *Dialogue with Trypho*, 126–28.
6. Arius as cited by (pseudo?) Athanasius, *Discourse against the Arians* III.
7. Also to this point, compendiously, Pelikan, *Emergence of the Catholic Tradition*, 229–32.
8. E.g., Nestorius, *Sermon* XIV, 286. Nestorius was in fact a perfect Zwinglian: "Who could think deity susceptible to beastly hands?" (*Sermon* X, 271).

The motive of all Antioch's christological proposals was to establish two agents of what happens with Christ. The one agent (for whom the titles "Logos" and "Son" tended now to be appropriated) must be divine, to do the empowering; to be divine, this agent must be "impassible." The other agent, the human Jesus, must be temporal and do the suffering. The terminology as such was never the point and could be negotiated. Conversely, the motive of Alexandria's formulations was to establish one sole agent of what happens with Christ. Alexandria insisted that only one subject is available for whatever we want to attribute to the Savior and that if time and timelessness become incomprehensibly affiliated in this subject, then the paradoxes must be swallowed. So Cyril, the one great theologian of Alexandrian Christology, wrote: "We teach that the one who is the Son begotten of the Father and is God only-begotten . . . did himself suffer in the flesh on our account."[9]

What was at issue in the ancient christological debates was the showdown between two irreconcilable versions of eternity, of time, and so of temporal continuity. It was a disaster for all subsequent Christianity in the territories to which the debates reached that the conflict was never fought directly on its true lines. Each party harbored *both* clashing systems within itself: Antiochenes alleviated the consequent dissonance by mitigating christological faith, and Alexandrians championed the faith by enduring desperate paradox.

The decrees of the Council of Chalcedon of 451 laid down the dogma of all subsequent orthodox Christianity, East or West. The council has been much praised for settling the issue between Antioch and Alexandria not by constructing new solutions to the disputed questions but by setting limits and within those limits declaring a truce. Doubtless Chalcedon's method was prudent in the circumstances, but the strategy also has its limitations—the same limitations that now plague the ecumenical movement's very similar search for convergence. It was perfectly possible for each party to proclaim a victory and thereafter approve the other as little as before.[10] Indeed, the frustration of ecumenical dialogue that is the occasion of this book may, insofar as we seek its pathology in Christology, be described as a continuation of the dialogue at Chalcedon and of that dialogue's frustration.

What appeared in the systematic vacuity of Chalcedon's formulas, besides ecumenical strategy was failure shared by all parties to overcome the old unbaptized *question.* "How can anyone be God, who suffers the slings and arrows of time?" Within the doctrine of Trinity itself a mighty spiritual and intellectual feat had been done: The gospel had successfully and fundamentally reinterpreted Mediterranean antiquity's antecedent understanding of deity, bending it to the gospel's definition of eternity by a death and resurrection. But the Greek question, successfully met within the doctrine of God proper—or at least within the more strictly trinitarian part of it—merely moved to take up residence in a new christological reflection which *should* have been precisely its critique. There it has not yet been overcome.

9. Cyril of Alexandria, *Third Letter to Nestorius,* 6.
10. James Moulder, "Is a Chalcedonian Christology Coherent?" *Modern Theology* 2(1986): 285–307.

Thus the paths of Antioch and Alexandria remained open, divergent, and exhaustive after Chalcedon. With great schematization the Western church took Antioch's way and Orthodoxy took Alexandria's. We must now quickly trace the path of the West. (I do not thereby suggest that Chalcedon's heritage has not been a mixed blessing also in the East.)

Key phrases of the Chalcedonian convergence-formulas were adopted at the insistence of the Western Pope, Leo; moreover, his so-called Tome, the long letter in which he did the insisting, was appended to Chalcedon's decrees as authorized commentary. And it has been Chalcedon read *as* an affirmation of Leo's Christology that has from Chalcedon on been the operative christological dogma of the West. The key passage of the Tome reads (in mildly disrespectful translation), "Each nature does its own thing, in cooperation with the other."[11]

Two great forces maintained the Leonine Christology through the history of Western Christianity. One was the great Augustine's uniquely uncritical and systematically dominating reception of the definition of God by impassibility.[12] From Augustine on, it was an unquestionable axiom that no theological proposition could be true from which it could follow that God is in any way different on account of his actual relations to temporal reality than he would have been without them. Applied to analysis of the hypostatic union of the Logos and Jesus, the axiom meant that no way of conceiving the union could be entertained from which anything would follow about the Logos himself.

The second force was the Anselmian doctrine of atonement, and its cognates of the same general pattern. According to Anselm, the atoning work of Christ was the work of the human nature since only humans owed the debt and only a human could pay it. Then Christ also had to be God in order that the merit of the human's work be infinite and so available to all the race. "Each nature does its own thing, in cooperation with the other" is the very summary of this soteriology.

Medieval scholasticism had thus to perform its brilliant analytical work on meager matter. The starting analysis is so undialectical a distinction between a "hypostasis" and the "nature(s)" hypostasized, that if several natures are hypostasized together, nothing is necessarily to follow about those natures. Thus that Christ's divine and human natures are of but one hypostasis is made to be a purely logical assertion in modern terms: that *somehow* propositions can be true that attribute acts or characteristics of either nature to the same real subject. Consideration of the "somehow" is postponed to another doctrine altogether, the doctrine of "communication of attributes," of the sharing of divine and human characteristics in the one Christ.[13]

11. Leo of Rome, *"Agit enim utraque forma cum alterius communione quod proprium est." Letter to Flavian of Antioch.* I am greatly tempted to translate: "Each nature does its own thing, so long as it doesn't hurt the other."
12. See Jenson, *The Triune Identity,* 114–31 and documentation.
13. So, for example, the doctrine of Duns Scotus: the Logos, as a purely "relative" hypostasis, has, as an hypostasis, no efficacy. Thus, since it is the Logos as hypostatically other than the Father or the Spirit that is incarnate, the Logos's union with a human nature has no effect on that nature. Nor, of course, is the Logos effected by the union, since as a divine hypostasis, the Logos cannot be effected

But this doctrine also turns out to be ruled by Leo. In propositions that state
such a communication, as "Jesus rules" or "The Logos is a child of Mary,"
"Jesus" and "the Logos" are analyzed as merely alternative phrases to denote
the same reality, the one hypostasis. About Jesus *as* a human person or about the
Logos *as* he is "one being with the Father," these propositions are held to say
nothing at all. Moreover, they are further to be analyzed as true—when they are—
only "in words" and not "in the matter":[14] though verified by facts, they do not
conform to the facts that verify them. To obtain a proposition conformed to the
fact stated, such a sentence as "The Logos was born of Mary" must be translated
into "The man Jesus (who is hypostatically one with the Logos) was born of
Mary."

Obviously, this pair of doctrines verges on vacuous circularity. The hypostatic
union is but permission to speak of Christ in the ways stipulated by the doctrine
of communication of attributes, but such speech, it turns out, can be true only by
way of a detour through the hypostatic union. Entire vacuity is avoided by use of
the doctrine of "created grace." The human Christ is said to be gifted with the
virtues and capacities needed for his role in salvation. These gifts are not different
in character from the graces otherwise given to saints but are unique as the particular
gifts appropriate to his unique hypostatic identity. Thus what finally is supposed
to make Christ savior is not *achieved in* the hypostatic union, but rather is given
to the human *picked out* by the hypostatic union.[15]

This common Christology of the Western church will not support the Christian
religion. Realities of faith and churchly communion that are in truth founded in
the fact of the risen Christ could not be founded in the Christ described by our
Christology. Thereupon we are driven either to seek other foundation for key
affirmations and experiences of the faith, and so to attribute elsewhere what belongs
to Christ, or to give up those affirmations and experiences. Catholicism, I suggest,
tends to do the first and Protestantism the second.[16] I must now look back over
the first two parts of this book, to show how this analysis also covers phenomena
there described and so discloses what it is that basically maintains dissensus.

---

by anything. That the Logos as hypostasis is the hypostasis of the human nature, therefore means only
that it is the "suppositum" of that nature, i.e., that it is what is denoted by the subject of true predications
appropriate to the nature. See, e.g., *The Oxford Manuscript,* III, I. To this whole subject, in the
presentation of one who thoroughly approves the scholastic doctrine, see R. P. Leon Seiller, *L'Activité
humaine du Christ selon Duns Scot* (Paris: Duchesne, 1944).

14. To this, let me this time instance Bonaventure. Re, e.g., the communication to Jesus of divine
ubiquity, *Four Books of Sentences,* III, XXII, 1,2. Or in the other direction, "the Son of God is said
to have died, because he was the man in whom occurred the suffering death" (ibid., III, XXI, 2,3).
In general, by the communion of attributes, nothing is communicated to the human nature "formally,
as a property . . . inhering substantially or accidentally" (ibid., III, XIV, 3,3.17). To the whole matter
in principle, ibid., III, XIV, 1.1–2.18.

15. Bonaventure again: the grace that as a "habitus" disposes Christ's soul for union with the Logos,
and his "personal grace," and the grace that equips him to move his members to sanctification and so
is "the grace of the (church's) head (gratia capitis)," are all the same grace (ibid., III, XIII, 2,2).

16. Thomas F. Torrance has the identical diagnosis, in of course very different terminology. "Karl
Barth and the Latin Heresy," *Scottish Journal of Theology* 39:461–82.

III

Ecumenists have noted a christological root of dissensus about the church's instrumentality. "The starting point of all reflections about the sacramentality of the church is the primal sacramentality of Christ. . . . Therefore the pivot of further ecumenical dialogue about (the church's) sacramentality must be the question about the soteriological meaning of Jesus' humanity."[17]

Indeed, the Protestant-French Roman Catholic dialogue could formulate their opposing ecclesiological tendencies—rubricized negatively as "Our Respective Temptations"—explicitly in terms of the ancient christological conflict. "The Catholic temptation is to 'ecclesiological monophysitism,' to an identification of the church with Christ, of the body with the head."[18] "The protestant temptation, oppositely, is to an ecclesial 'occasionalism' or 'Nestorianism.' The visible church remains a wholly human reality . . . exterior to the mystery to which it witnesses."[19] Nor were these christological categories chosen only as analogies. Catholic leader and official commentator Bernard Sesboüé notes regular Protestant use of strictly christological formulas as *criteria* of propositions about Christ's work and presence in the church, and then describes what he sees as a Protestant christological "monergism" that too much separates Christ's humanity from his divinity's saving work.[20] Had his Protestant counterpart picked up the line of analysis, he might doubtless have returned the compliment.

Sesboüé's analysis of the Protestant "temptation" is immediately convincing. But it is important to notice what suppositions he shares with the position he criticizes. He describes the Protestant christological flaw as "monergism," a tendency to slight the contribution of Christ's humanity to his divinity's saving work. The Catholic alternative is that Christ's humanity "cooperates"[21] with his divinity. Thus both the Protestant position Sesboüé criticizes and the Catholic position he holds depend upon a thoroughly Leonine posit of two agents in Christ; both think precisely of a possible *contribution* by the humanity to the divinity, the one to deny it and the other to affirm it. The two positions differ only in what they attribute to each nature within their "cooperation."

Let me suggest the following. The Protestant ecclesiological "temptation" is the direct *working out* of Western Christology's separation of God and humanity in Christ. The Catholic "temptation" is to try to *make up* for the separation at this point by mitigating separation at another, to make up for a too-feeble identification of the Logos with Jesus by a too-simple identification of Christ with the church.

---

17. Hans Jörg Urban, "Weiterführende Ansätze und Frage aus der Diskussion der Referate," *Die Sakramentalität der Kirche in der ökumenischen Diskussion*, ed. Johann-Adam-Möhler-Institut (Paderborn: Bonifatius-Drückerei, 1983), 222.

18. Comité mixte catholique-protestant en France, *Consensus oecuménique et différence fondamentale* (1987), nr. 14.

19. Ibid., nr. 15.

20. Bernard Sesboüé, "Analyse catholique," ibid., 68–71.

21. Ibid., 70.

The notion that Catholicism attributes an active role to the church in the mediation of salvation, Protestantism a passive role, and that this is a decisive difference between them, proved finally unintelligible. But perhaps we now know the real object of the fears that thus emerge on each side. Insofar as correct Catholic insistence on the active role of the church is betrayed by lacking Christology, it is tempted (despite all sincere protestations) to become in practice the assertion of the church's agency as a saving agency in its own right. Insofar as correct Protestant insistence that only God possesses saving agency is betrayed by the very same christological deficit, it becomes a denial of the salvific role that Bible and creed plainly attribute to the church.

But one-for-one paralleling of christological and ecclesiological factors can carry us only so far, and we must leave this schema. The church, as the French Catholics rightly remind themselves, is the body of Christ and not the head. The personal reality present through the church is neither Christ by himself or with an associated church, nor Christ undialectically *as* the church; it is Christ with the church precisely as his body.

A person's "body" is, in the usage of the New Testament and in theologically relevant usage, the person him- or herself, but insofar as the person is an *object* for other persons, and thereupon for her- or himself. A person's body is the person him- or herself, insofar as the person is *available*. Thus even in this age no one's body is merely the system of cells of which a mechanistic philosophy tempts us first to think, though its existence usually depends upon the existence of that system. For present purposes, we must be content with noting the fact while avoiding its analysis: a personal body is a personal availability constituted in a myriad of fundamentally *historical* factors, of perceptible familial, social, and national inclusions and manifestations, of interwoven personal narratives, even of such things as clothing and housing.

In "the days of his flesh," our Lord's availability to others of course involved an organism. What may be the place of the organism in his now risen embodiment is an ancient theological conundrum that may here be finessed. What is decisive for present concern is this: According to the New Testament, our Lord's present embodiment, his present availability to us, is the historically concrete body called the church.

Ecumenists proclaim that the church is real in this world as a living community. She is thus a body in the theologically relevant sense: she is the historical objectivity of some spirit, that spirit's availability to others and itself. The question about any body is, Whose is it? The New Testament astonishingly says that the church-body is that of an individual, the risen Christ.

A powerful tradition in Western theology, deriving finally from our incapable Christology, interprets the New Testament's assertion, "The church is the body of Christ," as in all uses a trope.[22] But the New Testament, quite inescapably, has

---

22. The current pitiable bowdlerization of this tradition is the "metaphor theology." Either this theology merely inflates a banality, that *all* language is metaphorically involved, producing a linguistic night in which all sorts of assertions are the same gray; or nearly all of its positions are childishly false.

two uses of "Christ's body" for the church, only one of which is a trope. Moreover, the trope appears exclusively in derivations from the ontologically straightforward use.[23] The Groupe des Dombes noted the necessity of this insight for ecumenical progress long ago.[24]

If neither the Catholic nor the Protestant temptations are to overwhelm us, our Christology must enable us to say straightforwardly that Christ now has the church as his body: this communal thing is now the object others may intend him as, that is, his availability to us and, indeed, to himself.[25] To do this, christological teaching must attribute to the human Christ God's own transcendence over created time and space, God's own ability to objectify himself, to make himself truly available when, where, and as he wills. Leonine Christology countenances no such attributions.

Next, our Christology must enable us to say that this ecclesial body of the *human Christ* is just so the own body of *God* the Logos. To enable this further step, we must cease to hesitate in the Cyrillian posit of a sole subject for what is said of Christ. We must drop the notion that those attributions to God in Christ that offend against abstract opposition of time and eternity are true only "in words."

For if we are to fall neither to the Catholic nor the Protestant temptation, what we must understand is that the church is God's own body. That is, neither is the church's agency an agency over against God's, nor is the church simply identical with God. The church is God the Logos himself, as he is our object, as he is available to us. That is, the church is Christ himself as we are allowed to find him, to intend him, to act reciprocally upon him, to be other free persons over against him.

Let me recall earlier distinctions and discussions. As a *community*, the church is God the Logos's body. It is not another agent than God, and *therefore* its agency is free and active over against the world and even over against the multitude of its members.[26] On the other hand, *as* that multitude of believers, as an association, the church is over against God as his bride. Its agency in this mode is other than

23. Foundational to New Testament usage is doubtless the progression from the ontological propositions of I Corinthians's 10th and 11th chapters to the tropes of chapter 12. In Ephesians, all instances are ontological; the work done by the trope in Corinthians is, most notably, done without one in 4:11ff. The situation in Colossians becomes, of course, yet more complicated, by the cosmic use of the language—most of this again is *not* tropological!

24. Groupe des Dombes, *L'Église, corps du Christ* (1958), nr. 2: "En effet, lorsque nous disons avec l'Écriture Sainte, que l'Église est le corps du Christ, cette affirmation ne doit pas être prise pour une simple métaphore; elle exprime le mystère de la relation vivante de Jésus Christ à son Église."

25. How far unreconstructed Protestantism will go to avoid this may be seen in a report of international Baptist-Reformed dialogue, *Report* (1977), nr. 13: "The concept of the body of Christ implies an understanding of the church as the community of those who are included in Christ, *i.e.*, those whose existence is determined by what has happened in and to the body of Jesus in the event of his cross and resurrection." (emphasis added)

26. J. M. R. Tillard, "Eglise et salut. Sur la sacramentalité de l'église," *Nouvelle Revue Théologique* 106(1984):664–65: Since Pentecost, Christ is inconceivable without his body, and "ce corps n'est pas purement passif. Animé par l'Esprit du Christ, il produit des actes qui sont, en lui et par lui, actes du Seigneur."

his, in that it is in response to his; and is the agency of the saved and not of the saving.

When the church is understood with ontological seriousness as the risen Christ's body, an appropriate dialectic of identity and difference between God and the church must result.[27] I *am* my body; yet I *have* my body. What my body does, I do; and yet I as subject must determine what my body shall do, and "in the flesh" have to struggle to make my body obey. Thus what the church does is done by Christ the Logos; and yet he is free over against his church and, indeed, so long as the church is in the flesh, must often reform his church. Here space opens in which Catholic theology may out of its own deepest insight share the Reformation's concern for the unmitigated lordship of Christ over the church, and in which that Reformation concern can be effective without separating the church's agency from God's or pretending it could be merely passive.

Let the following statement, by a Catholic ecumenist, display the truth for which Catholicism here stands and must stand, yet which in a context determined by Leonine Christology is too misleading for Protestantism to countenance. The statement also can display connections back to the matter of chapter 8.

> The church is not only a spiritual reality and the place of the proclamation of the gospel; the church is such a reality *as* an embodied salvific mystery, as incarnation formation in time and space—and that not merely punctually but in formed continuity, whose outward effective sign is . . . apostolic succession in the narrower sense. That is the offense of the sacramental church to all human thought, which can easily come to terms with a "spiritually" understood church: the church's structured reality, her tie to space and time in the continuity of patterned historical existence, her reference to her origin through the medium of her own structure.[28]

IV

The christological moves just demanded amount to the assertion that the unicity of hypostasis of God and humanity in Christ has material consequences for both God and humanity. They amount to a denial that God the Logos, God in Christ, is impassible. That is, they amount to the long-forgotten christological program of Luther and his more uninhibited followers.

Every confessional group supposes it is the exception to the scheme by which it classifies the other groups. I am Lutheran, at least in conviction that the Reformation was needed and that in the process Luther and a few of his coworkers achieved certain new theological insights. Perhaps I may this once allow this bias to appear. Luther and some of his followers were driven by the doctrine of justification to amend the standard Christology drastically, and in a hyper-Alexandrian direction.[29] They did not, any more than their predecessors, find the

27. This has been seen in dialogue, notably by the Groupe des Dombes, *L'Église, corps du Christ*, nrs. 15–16.

28. Johann Werden Mühlhammer, "Amtsfrage und Kirchenverständnis," *Catholica* 28:136.

29. The deed was done in two documents: the 1526 *Suevian Syntagma*, by the young Johannes Brenz and his friends, and Luther's 1528 *Confession of the Lord's Supper*.

fortitude to attack the maxim of divine impassibility directly, and since their intention was more radical even than that of Alexandria, they ended in even more intolerable paradox.[30] But their explorations constitute in my judgment a vital and so far unused ecumenical breakthrough. From the vantage they reached we may clearly see how flawed Christology maintains Catholic-Protestant dissensus.

The technical occasion of Luther's mature christological reflections was Zwingli's christological explanation for his denial of Christ's bodily presence as the elements, his doctrine of "alleosis." This doctrine was merely a simplistic statement of the standard Western understanding of the communication of attributes.[31] But Luther responded: "Beware! Beware, I tell you, of the 'Alleosis'! It is the devil's spawn. For in the end it sets up such a Christ that I wouldn't want to be called 'Christian' after him."

We quickly learn what Luther sees wrong with Zwingli's (and the tradition's!) Christ. In both directions, the "communication of attributes" is too puny. On the one hand, "For if I have to believe that only the human nature has suffered, Christ is too feeble a savior for me."[32] On the other hand, and centrally for the sacramental controversy: "Where you can say, 'Here is God,' you must also say, 'And so the man Christ is also here.' . . . If you could show me a place where God was and the man was not, the person would be neatly split, for I could promptly then say, 'Here is God who is not man.' . . . Don't give me any of *that* God!"[33] For Luther, the traditional doctrine that "Thus one must attribute to the whole person what happens to either part of the person"[34] has as its content that suffering is "really" communicated to the Logos, also as God, and God's infinite "energies" really communicated to the man Jesus.

We may use a very Eastern question to make clear Lutheranism's divergence from standard Western Christology. Is the "flesh" of Jesus "life-giving" by virtue of the "created graces" bestowed on the one united to the Logos, or by virtue of the union itself and the divine attributes thereby shared with this flesh? Does God save by the instrumentality of a specially equipped man, or by being a man? The Lutheran specificity was the monomaniacal energy with which it insisted on the second alternative.[35]

The Western church has been continuously torn by controversy about Christ's presence in the Eucharist. The question is indeed inevitable. How can the bodily

---

30. Thus Robert Bellarmine, *De controversiis Christianae fidei adversus temporis Haereticos*, III, II, xvii, x, demolishes the Lutheran teaching of ubiquity in a few sentences. "*Nam quod ubique est, impossibile est non ubique haberi*."

31. One may suggest that the flat-footed Zwingli related to the to the standard previous tradition in much the same way as had Arius. Both let a cat out of the bag.

32. Martin Luther, WA, 26:319.

33. Ibid., 321.

34. Ibid., 322.

35. This was clear very early. Johannes Brenz, *De personalis unione duarum naturarum in Christo,* 5b: "*si autem sermo est de gratia, profecto fieri non potest, quin filius Dei effundat omnem suam maiestatem in filium illum* hominis, *quem in unitatem personae unione hypostatica . . . gratuita clementia assumpsit.*"

risen man be present as loaf and cup? Strict conceptual limits have bounded all Western attempts to answer this question. It has been thought definitive for the reality of a body to have its own distinct place. Thereupon, Scripture and creed appear to tell us what that place is: the right hand of the Father, in heaven. It was always too mythological for the church to think of Christ moving spatially between heaven and the altars.[36] Leonine Christology does not allow that distinctions of place are transcended in the embodied Christ himself.

It is remarkable what Catholic-Protestant consensus is possible within the limits thus defined, until certain sensitive points set by the definition itself are touched. Thus international Reformed-Roman Catholic dialogue, on the basis of explicit affirmation of the traditional Western Christology, and specific if polite shared opposition to Lutheran innovations,[37] achieved an extensive common doctrine of Christ's presence. The mystery of the sacrifice of Christ's body is itself "dispensed to us in the eucharistic celebration." And "the realization of this presence of Christ . . . is the proper work of the Holy Spirit, which takes place . . . as the Church calls upon the Father to send down his Holy Spirit to sanctify." The presence, moreover, is "sacramental," meaning that "it is the concrete form which the mystery of Christ takes in the eucharistic communion of his body and blood."[38] Or we may note how international Anglican-Roman Catholic dialogue's remarkable achievements[39] are framed precisely by reassertion of the traditional metaphysical structure. "It is the Lord present at the right hand of the Father, and *therefore transcending* the sacramental order, who thus offers to his church, in the eucharistic signs, the special gift of himself."[40] (emphasis added)

But such agreement only poses the question the more urgently. How can it be *true* that such a presence occurs? Since Leonine Christology can provide no answer within itself, one will necessarily be sought elsewhere. Protestantism can still follow a further Catholic step: the fact of Christ's presence as bread and cup is "altogether supernatural, effected by the special power of God."[41] But if Christ's presence is in such fashion supernatural, the event must be, as it were, a reliable miracle, for we cannot be left wondering at each celebration if this time it is really happening. At this point mutual "fears" appear, with abundant justification on both sides.

Catholicism has guaranteed the supernatural event by reference to the supernatural church, by a *potestas* to consecrate, granted in ordination. Protestants are surely right in fearing that Catholicism must be tempted too strongly to understand this "power" as an *ability*, to do a marvel that others cannot.

---

36. John Calvin, *Institutes of the Christian Religion*, 1536, iv, 122: "For this is the hope for our own resurrection and ascension into heaven, that Christ rose and ascended. . . . And this is the eternal truth of any body, that it is contained in its place." Thomas Aquinas, *Summa theologiae*, iii,75,2: "*Manifestum est autem quod corpus Christi non incipit esse in hoc sacramento per motum localem.*"
37. *The Presence of Christ in Church and World* (1977), nr. 84.
38. Ibid., nrs. 82, 83.
39. *Eucharistic Doctrine* (1971), nrs. 3–11.
40. Ibid., nr. 7.
41. Aquinas, *Summa theologiae*, iii, 75, 1 and 3.

Protestantism therefore has always and rightly been concerned explicitly with denying that the church and its priesthood "make" the real presence happen. But Catholics are in turn surely right in noting that this denial has regularly turned out, in the practice and actual theology of Protestantism, to carry with it a mitigation of the supernatural event itself. How, after all, do we assert Christ's true bodily presence on the altar if Christ's body neither transcends space, *nor* travels to the altar, *nor* does anyone work a marvel?

The sensitive points earlier mentioned are, of course, those marked by reference to *eating*, to bread and cup as enduring *things*, and by the question about what unbelieving recipients of bread and cup receive. On these matters, the otherwise splendid Catholic-Protestant documents just cited are and had to be utterly silent. Indeed, no Catholic-Protestant reconciliation is possible until the Western Christology is transcended; until, if I may state it so, Luther's christological intentions are brought into ecumenical effect.

V

Roman Catholicism makes up for the vacuity of Western Christology by assigning great things to the church, and then making these assignments the church's contribution to "the full mystery of Christ." Protestantism avoids the pitfalls of this move by getting along without any very full mystery of Christ. But the more drastic Christology intended by both Alexandria and original Lutheranism obviates the need for churchly *contribution* to the full mystery of Christ, and just so enables acknowledgment of the church's full and constitutive participation in that mystery. The *totus Christus* does not need to be constituted by *addition* of the church to Christ; the *totus Christus* of Christ with his body is the one agent of salvation.

Christology has not yet become thematic in the modern dialogues between Orthodoxy and the West, but it was central in their medieval predecessors. Indeed, Gregory Palamas, the Aquinas of Orthodoxy, was moved to his great constructive work precisely by christological conflict with the West. Palamas taught that the hypostasis of the Logos, *in and with* the divine life that he lives with the Father in the Spirit, is present to us directly in our hypostatic individuality and plurality, in that one of us is hypostasized in him.[42] That, I think, is exactly what must be said and what the West has such difficulty in saying.[43] Such Christology in current dialogue enables Orthodox representatives to say against Catholic and Protestant alike: "Therefore Christ is himself the priest, who brings the offering celebrated in the church. It is in awareness that she is in her visible form the mystic body of Christ, that the church celebrates the Eucharist. The proper agent is Christ himself; the earthly priests, as his servants, are the sensible appearance of what is sacramentally done."[44]

---

42. E.g., Gregory Palamas, *Triads*, I,3,9-17: "The Son of God has united his own divine hypostasis (*ten heautou theiken hypostasin*) . . . not only to our nature (*te kath humas phusei*) . . . but . . . also to our human hypostases themselves (*kai autais tais anthropinais hypostasesin*) . . . associating himself with each believer by participation in his holy body." Or see *Homily* V.

43. Let it explicitly be noted that this does not mean that Palamitic theology does not have its own ways to mitigate the christological offense.

44. Bilateraler Dialog zwischen dem Ökumenischen Patriarchat und der Evangelischen Kirche in Deutschland, *Eucharistie und Priesteramt* (Frankfurt: Otto Lembeck, 1980), 105.

10

God

I

At long last it is time to develop my chief contention. It is the frustration of the dialogues that the repeated achievement of convergences never adds up to convergence, that something deep in the conceptual-spiritual structure of the church's life seems endlessly to pose and enforce choice between polar positions, each of which is compelled to and can justify itself over against the other. It is the long-announced thesis of this book that the "basic" perversion that does this is a shared incompletely christianized interpretation of God.

Targeted only against the Western church, the charge is far from new, having been deployed by the Eastern church since the ninth century. It will therefore be only just to take this Orthodox critique as my dialogical lead through parts of this chapter. Orthodoxy has claimed to discern a specifically Western doctrine of God and to find therein a fundamental error. This has its clearest symptom in the Western addition to the Nicene-Constantinopolitan Creed, according to which the Spirit proceeds "from the Father *and the Son,*" the notorious *"filioque."*[1] In this

---

1. For current ecumenical discussion of the problem itself, see Lukas Vischer, ed., *Le theologie du Saint-Esprit dans le dialogue entre l'Orient et l'Occident* (Paris: le Centurion, 1981). The group of theologians who produced this volume produced a consensus document, *Memorandum: La formule der Filioque, dans une perspective ecumènique,* ibid., 7–25. In this, it is agreed, II-III: "Il est un sens dans laquel il est correct de dire que le Saint Esprit procède du Père *seul.* . . . Le terme 'seul' se rapporte à la procession unique de l'Esprit venant du Père, et de l'être personnel particulier . . . qu'il reçoit du Père. D'une part, il faut distinguer la procession . . . de l'Esprit de l'engendrement du Fils; mais, d'autre part, il faut rapprocher cette procession de l'engendrement du Fils pars le Père seul. Et, alors que le Saint Esprit procède du Père seul, cette procession est néanmoins liée à la relation existant au sein de la Trinité entre le Père et le Fils, en virtu de laquelle le Père agit *comme Père.* L'engendrement du Fils par le Père parmet ainsi de dire que *le Saint Esprit procède du Père du Fils.*" But one may *not* say that the Spirit "procède 'du Père et du Fils.' " Articles in the same volume by Markos A. Orphanos, "La procession du Saint Esprit selon certains Pères grecs postérieurs au VIIIe siècles," and by Jean-Miguel Garrigues, "Point de vue catholique sur la situation actuelle du problème du Filioque," explore the technical possibilities. On the mere question of whether the interpolation belongs in the publicly recited creed, there is widespread consensus that it does not, though Roman Catholicism, having compelled its use in councils it deems ecumenical, has a special problem. Otherwise, we may take the statement of international Anglican-Orthodox Dialogue, "Athens Statement" (1978), 3, as typical: "Because the original form of the Creed referred to the origin of the Holy Spirit from the Father . . . because the *Filioque* clause was introduced into this creed without the authority of an Ecumenical Council and without due regard for Catholic consent, and because this Creed constitutes the public confession of faith by the People of God in the Eucharist, the *Filioque* clause should not be included in this Creed."

error Orthodoxy has found the source of an alleged general perversion of Western Christianity.[2] Orthodoxy has not, to be sure, seen any way in which its own interpretation of God could *share* any flaw with that of the West, nor has it found in such a flaw any explanation of its own ecumenical perplexities, which are extreme.[3] Since the present volume is largely restricted to the Western schism, I can give only passing attention to manifestations of unbaptized understanding of God also on the Orthodox side. But later in the chapter I must indeed give such passing attention, lest I be taken to think that in some part of the church the conversion of Mediterranean antiquity's interpretation of God has been completed.

In the context of contemporary contact between Orthodoxy and the Western church, Orthodoxy's polemic has become ecumenically specific.[4] Orthodox critics have turned their attention to those Western problems that have dominated Catholic-Protestant dialogue and this book, and have derived them from alleged Western misunderstanding of God the Spirit. Nikos Nissiotis, a great veteran of Orthodox ecumenism, once took up the very polarity in which the paradigmatic French dialogue cast basic Catholic-Protestant dissensus. In the West, "either the church as institution . . . is detached from the genuine event (of salvation) . . . or the institution is regarded as (in itself) sacral, as a direct result of Christ's commission . . . to the apostles. In this case, godly authority is attributed . . . to a human structure." This occurs, Nissiotis says, because the church is not understood in a fully trinitarian fashion, "because the institution is not seen as a charismatic work of the Spirit"[5]

In this line of criticism, Western teaching that the Spirit proceeds also "from the Son" is read as the expression of failure to acknowledge the saving work of

2. For an instance from the modern dialogue, and in blanket form, Georg Mantzaridis, "Betrachtungen über den Text von München," Centre Orthodoxe du Patriarchat Oecuménique, *Les dialogues oecuméniques hier et aujourd'hui* (Chembésy: Centre Orthodoxe, 1985), 251. "Das Filioque ist das charakteristische Symptom der Ideologisierung der westlichen Theologie. Während die orthodoxe Theologie in der göttlichen Ökonomie verankert ist, d.h. in der Anwesenheit Gottes in der Geschichte und der Erfahrung, die die Glieder der Kirche mit dieser Anwesenheit machen, wird durch das Filioque eine andere Art von Theologie eingeführt."

3. For a hint of the difficulties, stated from the Orthodox side, Thomas Hopko, "Tasks Facing the Orthodox in the 'Reception' Process of BEM," *Orthodox Perspectives on Baptism, Eucharist and Ministry*, ed. G. Limouris and N. M. Vaporis (Brookline: Holy Cross Orthodox Press, 1985).

4. This development undoubtedly derives in large part from the great influence of Vladimir Lossky and his followers within modern orthodoxy. See above all Vladimir Lossky, *A l'image et à la ressemblance de Dieu* (Paris: Aubres-Montaigne, 1967), 67–93. For a concise if unsympathetic description of the development by a Roman Catholic ecumenist, see André de Halleux, "Pour un accord oecuménique sur la procession de l'Esprit Saint et l'addition du Filioque au Symbole," in Vischer, ed., *Le theologie du Saint-Esprit*, 81–82.

5. Nikos Nissiotis, *Die Theologie der Ostkirche im ökumenischen Dialog* (Stuttgart: Evangelisches Verlagswerk, 1968), 71. In view of the last chapter, it may be worth footnote notice, though, in view of disputed exegesis of the texts, of no more, that Nissiotis exempts Martin Luther from the Orthodox critique; Nikos Nissiotis, "Is There a Church Ontology in Martin Luther's Ecclesiology?" *Luther et la réform Allemande dans une perspective oecumenique* (Chambesy: Editions du Centre Orthodoxe, 1983), 409. "There is no anthropocentric *ordo salutis pro me* in Luther's double opposition against subjectivist heretics and eady divino-human institutional identities. The one Spirit defeats both at the same time."

the Spirit as the Spirit's own, new, and particular initiative.[6] The Nicene-Constantinopolitan doctrine that the Spirit proceeds from the *Father*, that the Father is the "cause" or "source" of the Spirit's existence, does not attenuate the Spirit's personal reality over against the Father and the Son. For within the divine life the very particularity of the Father is the source from whom the Spirit and the Son receive their particularity in turn. But such is *not* the defining role of the Son, and therefore to say that the Son is also the source of the Spirit does indeed, according to this Orthodox critique, subordinate the Spirit, does deny his particular initiative in the triune life and so in the Trinity's saving action.[7] Those Orthodox theologians who have dependable knowledge of modern Western theology will often agree that its christocentrism is salutary,[8] but only if "we make pneumatology an integral part of Christology" itself.[9]

According to Orthodoxy, the Pentecostal coming of the Spirit is "a new intervention of the Holy Trinity in time," and on this occasion the intervention "issues from the third Person of the Trinity."[10] In the work of some Orthodox ecumenists, the point becomes theologically fundamental. "In so far as anything is merely historically given, it is the vehicle of 'nature' and so inimical to freedom. . . . Even Jesus has to be liberated from past history. To achieve that liberation is the work of the Spirit. . . . The Spirit . . . is God's eschatological otherness from the world, God freeing the created order for its true destiny."[11] When this specific role of the Spirit is not grasped, the Western pendulum between Catholic institutionalism and Protestant spiritualist individualism must, according to Orthodox polemic, necessarily ensue.

Institutions are the historical continuity of communities and, considered as institutions, constitute a purely inner-historical continuity. The inner-historical ground of the church's institutions must be their origin in the historical event of the incarnation, and, if the church's institutions have a historically verifiable authenticity, this authenticity must then be their inner-historical continuity with the historical incarnation. Thus "the institutional elements of the church . . . belong strictly speaking to Christology,"[12] that is, no specific reference to the Father or the Spirit is needed to account for the church being institutional or for the general pattern of its institutions. When one knows the circumstances of the

---

6. Ibid., 66–68. Whether in fact the *filioque* must or even can be read that way, particularly within the thinking of the major Western theologians who have expounded it, is a greatly disputed question that I will not undertake here. I believe that the error Orthodoxy sees in Western trinitarianism is indeed there, but one can think this without necessarily agreeing that the *filioque* is its one-to-one expression.

7. For a concise because sour statement of the argument, see again de Halleux, "Pour un accord . . . ," 81–82.

8. Nissiotis, *Luther et la réform Allemande,* 409.

9. John D. Zilioulas, "Die pneumatologische Dimension der Kirche," *Internationale katholische Zeitschrift* 2:139f.

10. Nissiotis, *Die Theologie der Ostkirche,* 74f.

11. The citation is from an excellent summary of the thought of John D. Zilioulas by Colin Gunton, *The Transcendent Lord: the Spirit and the Church in Calvinist and Cappadocian Theology* (London: The Congregational Memorial Hall Trust, 1988), 12–13.

12. John D. Zilioulas, "Die pneumatologische Dimension der Kirche," 2:139f.

church's historical origin, it is possible to predict what general sort of institution-alization the church will have, as it is possible to do this with any historically continuous community.

If the church is thought of as founded in the acts of Christ prior to the church's own post-Pentecost life, and not equally in the correlated continuing initiative of the historically free Spirit within that life, an inner-worldly institutionalism must result. From this institutionalism the only escape will be an opposite error of spiritualist individualism. If Christ and the Spirit are not experienced in the mu-tuality of their ecclesially founding activity, neither will the church's institutions and the church's charisms be seen in their proper mutual identity.[13] "In Western thought there is often a tendency to separate 'charism' and 'office' from one another, whereas Eastern theology always sees them together. . . . The church is at once charismatic and institutional."[14]

The church's fundamental institutionalization was the creation of the apostolate. The charismatic reality of this institution is described by Nissiotis. "As eyewit-nesses, (the apostles) represent the link between the historical event of the res-urrection and the abiding historical present reality of the risen Lord among his people. This linking function rests . . . neither on a power that the apostles possess 'de iure divino'—and that thereafter passes to the bishops—nor on the faith of the congregation or the proclamation of the kergyma alone." It took the new event of the coming of the Holy Spirit to "qualify them for the personal ministry of the proclamation of the kerygma in the . . . world."[15]

Thus the entire institutional life of the church is institutional divine *life*, charism. The Spirit unites the risen One with the church and does so by the way in which he structures the church in its reality as a historically actual community. The work of the Spirit is "the foundational structural work . . . that always unites the Head with the Body of Christ."[16] In Orthodox ecumenical initiatives, this charismatic origin and quality of church structure has been pressed in discussions of the church's *ministry* and *tradition*.

The church's ministry should, according to these proposals, be understood primarily from the ways in which the Scripture describes the work of the Spirit, of which "the most important for ecclesiology are 'Giver of life' and 'community.' " "The divine life which the Spirit gives is life in a community of persons. . . . Christ is the only Mediator . . . and every office and authority in the church is solely a participation in this one mediation. But this common participation is hierarchical, for we do not participate in Christ individually, but *in corpore*, in order and not in anarchy." Nor is it "sufficient to say, 'Thus the charismatic belongs to the nature of the church just as necessarily and permanently as Office and

13. Ibid.
14. Johannes Mabey, "Das Charisma des apostolischen Amtes im Denken und Beten der Ostkirchen," *Catholica* 27:263–79.
15. Nissiotis, *Die Theologie der Ostkirche*, 74f.
16. Ibid., 77.

Sacraments.' The office *is* charism, since the Spirit, the living Giver of life, is the source of the church's office."[17]

Such propositions have achieved some status in dialogue. An Orthodox-Roman Catholic group organized at Chambesy, Switzerland, considered "implications" of a postulated "pneumatological" Christology. A first implication must be that "such rapport between Christ and the Spirit prohibits seeing Christ as an isolated individual. Wherever . . . Christ is present in the Spirit, he is there with his body, the community of the saints."[18] Here "is rooted the ecclesial ministry. In that Christ is not present without his community, his ministry to the world is not performed within history except by the ministry of that community. Thus the ministry of the church is not parallel to that of Christ; it is within the ministry of Christ." "In that Christ is not present except in the Spirit . . . the ecclesial ministry is by nature charismatic."[19]

Obviously, we are again involved in Cardinal Ratzinger's question "about how the mediation of then and now happens." If the continuity of the church with its founder is in every moment the present work of the Spirit, and if this work is a genuinely community-creating work, that is, a work that consists in molding the institutions of common life, a specifically theological understanding of temporal continuity results. The Orthodox name for this continuity is the holy Tradition.

In the presentation of Orthodox ecumenists, Tradition is "a living actualization of the past, a true anamnesis, a synthesis between what is transmitted and present experience, brought about by the Invocation of the Spirit."[20] Tradition is "the constant action of the Holy Spirit . . . an unceasing presence of the revelation of the Word of God through the Holy Spirit, ever present, here and now."[21] Therefore it is not a "mere faithful memory" of what once was or was taught or done. To be sure "it is a deposit, but . . . a deposit that is always . . . rejuvenating the vessel . . . in which it is found."[22]

Thus these ecumenical interventions conceive the continuity of the church as founded in acts among persons of the Trinity: the Spirit, personally active and present, unites each moment of the church's life with the one person of the risen Son, and *so* mediates every churchly "now" with every churchly "then." It is the church's *life*, in its institutional actuality, whose moments are thus mediated. "By the term Holy Tradition we understand the entire life of the church in the Holy Spirit. This tradition expresses itself in dogmatic teaching, in liturgical worship, in canonical discipline, and in spiritual life. These elements together manifest the single and indivisible life of the church."[23]

17. Mabey, Das Charisma des apostolischen Amtes . . . ," 265.
18. *Reflexions de théologiens orthodoxes et catholiques sur les Ministères* (Chambésy: 1977) *Episkepsis* 183(1978), 7.
19. Ibid., 8.
20. Metro. Emilianos Timiadis, "The Trinitarian Structure of the Church and its Authority," *Theological Dialogue between Orthodox and Reformed Churches*, ed. Thomas F. Torrance (Edinburgh: Scottish Academic Press, 1985), 155.
21. International Anglican-Orthodox Dialogue, *Worship and Tradition*, 29.
22. Timiadis, "Trinitarian Structure," 155.
23. International Anglican-Orthodox Dialogue, *Moscow Statement* (1976), 10.

A report of international Anglican-Orthodox dialogue then displays the Father as the origin of this movement, thus making the conception fully trinitarian. "The tradition of the Church flows from the Father's gift of his Son 'for the life of the world,' through the sojourning of the Holy Spirit in the world. . . . The Church draws its life and being from this . . . movement of the Father's love; that is to say, the Church too lives 'for the life of the world.' Its tradition is the living force . . . of its mission to the world."[24]

To some extent, such themes of ecumenically directed Orthodox ecclesiology have become themes of ecumenical consensus. That the church is the continuing creation of the Spirit, that the life of the church can be simultaneously dynamic and self-identical through time because and only because the Spirit continuously creates it, and that it is the whole eucharistic and institutional and proclamatory and liturgical life of the church that is the substance of this continuity, have become almost commonplace in multilateral dialogue.[25]

Finally, in this section I must make more explicit a vital point that has so far appeared only at the margins. An Orthodox-Roman Catholic dialogue stated it. It is an implication of a "pneumatological" Christology that "by its own nature, the historical present of Christ is *eschatological*. Where the Spirit acts . . . he makes history enter into the last times . . . bringing to the world the foretaste of its final destiny. . . . It is this perspective which lets us comprehend the nature of the church."[26] (emphasis added)

If the church is understood as founded in the historical event of the incarnation, and if the place of the Spirit as the link between this founding and the church's present reality is not grasped, the continuity of the church will be understood and practiced as an inner-historical continuity with its own *past*. If, on the other hand, the Spirit's particular initiative is fully acknowledged, if it is acknowledged that the church is equally founded in what is not yet historical event, in a last *future*, then it will also be seen that the church's continuity with itself through history is mediated by its relation to the eschaton. The church is *eschatologically* self-identical through time, identical with itself in each present in that in each present it anticipates the one end.

II

The body of Orthodox critique and associated teaching just reported is in my judgment essentially true, whether or not the *filioque* is its direct expression. I have already begun to build on this teaching.

The great task of the theological and spiritual history that leads to the Christianity now divided is reinterpretation by the gospel of Hellenism's antecedent interpretation of God, as an analogous reinterpretation must be the heart of any strand of the gospel's history. And the heart of what needed reinterpreting in antecedent

24. International Anglican-Orthodox Dialogue, *Worship and Tradition*, 50.
25. Uppsala 1968, *The Holy Spirit and the Catholicity of the Church*, 14–16; Nairobi 1975, *Confessing Christ Today*, 33, 40.
26. *Reflexions* . . . , 7.

Hellenic theology is its posit of eternity as timelessness, as *immunity* to time's opportunities and threats, and so of being as *persistence*. The incomplete exorcism of the first cripples our Christology; the incomplete exorcism of the second imposes an understanding of time within which the historical self-identity of the church is finally incomprehensible.

If the church's liturgical and institutional life actually honored the Spirit as equal in deity with the Father, the experience and shaping self-understanding of the church would be very different than it is in the West. Eternity would be apprehended as the dramatic mutuality of Father and Spirit, of God as God's origin and God as God's goal, and therefore not as immunity to change but as *faithfulness* in action. Being would accordingly be apprehended not as persistence in what is but as *anticipation* of what is not yet. The church would know herself as the temporal mission not of resistance to time but of faithful change in time, and know her own continuity in that mission not as hanging on to what is already there but rather as receiving what must come.

Actually carrying out such understanding and practice, however, will push reinterpretation of Hellenism's antecedent identification of God beyond what Orthodoxy has also been willing to do. It will not do to say that the Spirit has his own initiative in God's saving work; it must be seen that God's triunity in itself demands and is this initiative. The contemporary explosion of trinitarian theology is a determination to carry out Karl Rahner's maxim that the "economic Trinity" *is* the "immanent Trinity" and vice versa, more drastically than even Rahner intended it.[27] Following that rule, if it is by *anticipation* that historical entities— or even just the one historical entity, the church—are through time each identical with itself, then God's anticipation of himself in the Spirit must belong to his very Creator-being, by which each created thing is itself.

It is standard teaching in East and West that the Father is the "source" of triune deity and the "cause" of the hypostatic reality of the Son and the Spirit, that he is "the fountain of the Trinity," *fons trinitatis*. To this standard teaching must now be paired another: that the Spirit is the *goal* of deity and the *liberator* by which the hypostatic reality of the Father or of the Son is set *free*, by which these "hypostases" are actual *persons*. This self-establishment of God from his own Future is as constitutive of deity as is his self-establishment from the Father as "fountain." Not only Jesus the Son must be liberated from mere historicality, God the Father is not God unless he is liberated from mere causality.

Insofar as the church does sometimes think of God as we go about our business, and insofar as it is the triune God of which we think, the mere fact that the church is indeed *going about* something means that our thought of God will envision God's *process*. We have, in fact, odd though it sounds to say it, a sort of flowchart of deity at the back of our minds, showing a circulation of derivation within God—

---

27. Karl Rahner, *The Trinity*, trans. J. Donceel (New York: Herder, 1970). Two treatises may perhaps be taken as now standard for this determination and for the questions raised in the following: Wolfhart Pannenberg, *Systematische Theologie*, vol. 1 (Göttingen: Vandenhoeck & Ruprecht, 1988), 283–364; and Robert W. Jenson, *The Triune Identity* (Philadelphia: Fortress, 1982), 103–84.

and indeed, actual such charts sometimes appear in treatises on the Trinity. This flowchart may be the single greatest shaper of the practical life of the church.

It is the chief residual paganism of the way in which the churches descended from the mission in Mediterranean antiquity have thought of God, that all the derivations run one way, from the Father through the Son to the Spirit: the Father begets the Son and the Son is begotten; the Father breathes the Spirit and the Spirit is breathed. All active-voice relations run from origin to goal; the relations from goal to origin are but their passive voice. Therein unbaptized Hellenism's celebration of beginning over ending, of persistence over openness, of security over freedom, maintains itself even within the doctrine of Trinity. The God whose eternity is immunity to time lurks even within the church's vision of the God whose eternity is faithful adventure in and through time.

When our interpretation of God shall have been wrenched into a next level of conformity with the gospel—that is to say, when our liturgy and preaching and church year shall have come to honor Pentecost and *epiclesis* equally with Easter and *anamnesis*—we will see the eschaton in God at least as clearly as we see in him the origin, experience in him freedom at least as potently as security, know ourselves in him by anticipation at least as definitively as by recall. On our implicit or explicit flowchart of deity, if the Father is in the language of the old theology marked as "unoriginate," the Spirit will be marked as something like "unsurpassed." If the Father is shown as "begetting" the Son and "breathing" the Spirit, the Spirit will be shown as "liberating" the Father and "achieving" the Son.

When our interpretation of God shall have been opened into and from this new depth of faith, our vision of the church in God will be temporally stereoptic. "Remembering" what the church must be to be herself, we will remember precisely the future.[28] We will ask not only what the church was, to know thereby what she must continue to be in order to hold on to herself, but what the church will be when she is devolved into the kingdom, to know thereby what she must anticipate in order to be open to herself. These two questions will be the *same* question.

To ask how these questions may be one and not two returns us to trinitarian speculation. How are we to look backward and forward to see one vision? If the Father is the fountainhead of Trinity *and* the Spirit is the liberation of Trinity, and if both of these self-establishments are intrinsic to God, how is this God *one?* Again I want to pick up suggestions from dialogue with Orthodoxy, though with final purposes that Orthodoxy will hardly recognize.

We should remember that the work of the Spirit in time is to unite the church with the risen Christ, to establish the church as the risen Christ's own body, as his own concretely historical availability to the world. From the other triune direction, we should remember that it is the Father on whose mission the Son, with his body, is in the world, and it is the Father who breathes forth the Spirit to rest on the Son.

---

28. Here again I may cite an Orthodox ecumenist, Nikos Nissiotis, "Towards Restoring Church Communion," *Mid-Stream* 26(1987): 526. "We remember with the offertory words . . . the past events of the incarnation, cross and resurrection . . . as well as the future of Christ's second coming."

Among official international dialogues between Orthodoxy and the West, the decisive discussions are those with Roman Catholicism. In such dialogue's most important report to date, there is a chain of agreed propositions that are theologically foundational. As the "one victor over sin and death," the risen Christ has now between Pentecost and his return a specific "mode" in which his "unique person and unique event exist and work." This mode is "sacramental," *in that* it is the possibility of tasting "the new creation . . . here and now."[29] Indeed, in that he is thus the present tense of both the past and the future, Christ himself "is the sacrament *par excellence*." For the same reason he can in this mode "exist only by the Spirit"; it is the Spirit who "prepared the event of Christ and . . . fulfilled it in the Resurrection."[30] Finally, again by the same Spirit,[31] "the sacrament of the event of Christ . . . becomes the sacrament of the Eucharist," which is in turn *our* "foretaste of life eternal."[32]

Thus the risen Son is, in his present-tense actuality, the identity within time of the Father's originating and the Spirit's liberating. Now a radical step is demanded by the logic of Christianity's identification of God but yet not taken by the church's teaching, East or West.[33] Again following the rule that the immanent Trinity *is* the economic Trinity, if it is in the Son's historical work that God's founding and perfecting are historically one, then also in God within himself it must be in the Son's history that God's unity is achieved.

The unity of the *triune* God cannot simply be given in advance as itself a timeless fact. The triune God is *identified* by events of his history with us: he is identified as the one who freed Israel from Egypt and Jesus from the tomb. Thus so his identity with himself must truly be *at risk* as Moses and the Pharaoh struggle or as Jesus dies. What if the Pharaoh had won? It will not do to say that such an outcome was ontologically impossible; either such a teaching is itself theologically empty or it empties the actual event of meaning. In the fate of Jesus, the existing world that is given by the Father, and the world that is not yet, to which the Spirit liberates, collided; in that collision the unity of the triune God was the very thing at issue. The resurrection of Jesus was the *executing* of the triune God's unity with himself.

Now, having drastically departed from anything existing Orthodoxy could recognize, I may nevertheless return again to draw on the positions it has maintained in dialogue with the West. As the risen incarnate Son is the "sacrament" of the present-tense reality in history of history's beginning and end, so the Eucharist is the sacrament of the Son in this very role. "The Eucharist is . . . the great mystery of our participation in the life of the Holy Trinity, the recapitulation of the entire

29. Roman Catholic-Orthodox Dialogue, *Le mystère de l'église et de l'eucharistie à la lumière du mystère de la Sainte Trinité* ("The Munich Statement") (1982), I, 1.

30. Ibid., 3.

31. Here we may turn to an earlier document of the same dialogue, *Foi, sacrements et unite de l'église* ("The Bari Document") (1987), 15-17.

32. Roman Catholic-Orthodox Dialogue, *Le mystère*, 2.

33. Among those, besides the author, who have seen the necessity of this step, the most prominent is Wolfhart Pannenberg, *Systematische Theologie*, 355–64.

history of salvation in Christ and the foretaste of the Kingdom to come. In the Eucharist, therefore, the church is placed in the very center of history, sanctifying . . . the world, by being a new creation, a new mode of life. At the same time she is placed at the end of history as a sign of the Kingdom."[34]

It is the final import of Orthodox proposals to the West that they suggest a revision of our understanding of how the entity of the church occupies *time*. "The past historical being of the church is ontologically the church's present. . . . We think of . . . the past not simply as realized events in sequence and continuity or discontinuity among themselves. We think of the past involving and being involved in all three time dimensions, ontologically and existentially." This is the metaphysical fact, "because the essence of the church is transcendental, transhistorical and eschatological. . . . The time concept appropriate for the church is a consequence of its own being as at once the Body of Christ and the issue of the charismatic operation of the Spirit. (The church) is therefore both at the same time: an historical past event as well as a future final reality . . . by anticipation."[35]

One more step of new construction is possible. We may at this point remember that the Son of God is also called the *Word* of God, the *Logos*. As origin and goal are reconciled in Jesus' death and resurrection, what occurs is God's utterance, God's speech to himself and to his creatures[36]—as indeed it is always in words that the future appears meaningfully in the present. And if origin and goal are one in the Son in that they are *reconciled,* then this Word spoken as the Son is a *story*, a *narrative* word. Jesus' death and resurrection are the turning event of God's own story; when the news of Jesus' death and resurrection is told, God tells himself and us the story of his life and, since in him we have our being, of ours.

Aristotle once said that a proper story is one in which each new event is genuinely unpredictable beforehand, yet afterward recognized as what had to happen.[37] Aristotle himself always fudged his use of this maxim; he thought that with sufficient insight one could see the oak in the acorn of even the most desperate tragedy. The story the triune God tells of himself is the one example of a story that satisfies Aristotle's criterion without fudging: the resurrection of Jesus could not be believed in advance but afterward is plainly the only thing that could have happened. God the Spirit is the Goal *of* the Father, his very identity is breathed by the Father; but the Spirit is also absolute freedom over against the Father.

The Eucharist is the sacrament of the Son, just as in him beginning and end are reconciled. Therefore, the Eucharist is the sacrament of the one good story,

---

34. "The Ecumenical Nature of the Orthodox Witness" ("The New Valamo Statement" (1977), now in *Apostolic Faith Today*, ed. H.-G. Link (Geneva: World Council of Churches, 1985), 176.
35. Nissiotis, "Towards Restoring Church Communion," 526.
36. When Tertullian struggled between translating *logos* as "sermo" or "verbum" and chose "sermo," he hit the theological truth dead on. That by and large the tradition took the opposite way is yet another mode of the error I am trying to unearth; a whole other chapter of this section might be written to it. See René Braun *"Deus Christianorum:" Recherches sur le vocabulaire doctrinal de Tertullien* (Paris: Presse Universitaire, 1962), 250–62.
37. Aristotle, *Peri Poietikes*, 1452a, 3.

the fully embodied telling of how beginning and end meet in time. The church is the community that lives this telling.

III

It is time to note that a chapter similar to this one would conclude a similar book on the split between East and West, in which Western critique of the East would find equal space. It is time for that passing attention.

It is difficult to believe such assertions as the following, laid down in dialogue not as a statement of what should be realized by East and West together but as a claim of what the East already has. "On the Orthodox side, there exists freedom and understanding of tradition as the constant action of the Holy Spirit in the church, an unceasing presence of the revelation of the Word . . . through the Holy Spirit. . . . Tradition is always open, ready to embrace the past and accept the future."[38] Such indeed should be the churchly consequence of right worship of the Spirit. But Orthodoxy's great demonstrated ecumenical disability is churchly immobility, a simple incapacity to acknowledge past historical change or to consider the possible necessity of future historical change.

Surely this disability, particularly in view of its blatant contradiction to what should be expected from Orthodoxy's doctrine of Trinity, demands explanation by some "basic" misinterpretation of God also on this side. I can quickly show that Orthodoxy also has its hiding place for an unbaptized Hellenic interpretation of God.

Renewing the theology of Gregory Palamas, a spokesman of Orthodox tendencies, underlies modern Orthodox critique of the West. Palamas taught Christology as in the previous chapter was demanded, including the most radical possible "communion of attributes" within the hypostatic union, between the Logos and Jesus and thereupon between the Logos and us.[39] But then we see that in the proper doctrine of God a peculiar exemption from this communion is posited. "God himself neither becomes nor suffers, so far as concerns his *ousia*."[40]

What is this "*ousia*"? Palamas has the doctrine of God neatly sorted out. "There are then three in God: *ousia*, energy, and the triune hypostases." These are distinguished according to the possibility or impossibility of creatures' participation in them. Because of the hypostatic union, we do indeed participate in God insofar as he is his own *life*, the dynamic complex of his "energies." The hypostatic union itself is reserved for the one creature only, Jesus who is one with the Son. "According to his *ousia* God cannot be participated in at all."[41]

Palamas's primary source for these distinctions was Gregory of Nyssa, who *can*, at least, be read as teaching that the divine *ousia* is sheerly the infinity-as-such of the divine life among Father, Son, and Spirit, which life is the only reality

---

38. International Anglican-Orthodox Dialogue, *Worship and Tradition*, 29–30.

39. Gregory Palamas, *Triads*, ed. John Meyendorff and published in *Défense des saints hésychastes*, 2 vols. (Louvain: Spicilegium Sacrum Lovaniense), I,3,9–17; *Homily* V, P.G., LCI:64d–65a; *Homily* XVI, P.G., LCA:193b.

40. Gregory Palamas, *Chapter* 133, P.G., CL:1213c.

41. Gregory Palamas, *Chapter* 75, P.G., CL:1173b–c.

called God. But with Palamas it is impossible to avoid the impression that the divine *ousia* is itself somehow entitive. Then it is impossible to avoid the impression that this *ousia* is to provide a refuge in which Hellenism's interpretation of God, as the one who is God because he "neither becomes nor suffers," can be maintained.

Thus ensconced, Hellenism's interpretation of deity is in place still to determine what it means to say someone "is God."[42] Therefore the results of Palamism's commitment to Alexandrian Christology may be deeply ironic. For now to identify Jesus' historical actuality as *God's* historical actuality may establish Jesus' history *itself* in immunity to becoming. The very story of Jesus, and of Jesus' church, may be frozen into an icon of timeless eternity. Orthodoxy's evocation of the church's Spirit-evoked temporal life may become the evocation of a sort of moving picture of God and his community rather than of an actual history of God and his community.

In voicing such suspicions, I am voicing nothing more than such "fears and concerns" as are typical in the dialogues. What would come of them in dialogue, or in a volume paired to this one, must remain to be seen.

IV

The ecumenical import of the evocation of God here demanded can best be displayed by reflection back over the immediately preceding questions about time, the church's location in time, and the church's salvific agency. I will not, however, do this by rehearsing them point by point.

Western reflection's standard interpretation of time is correlate to a thoroughly unitarian interpretation of God, lurking always at the back of our consciousness. In its specific Western version, this correlation is an inheritance from Augustine, who taught us that the past is *there* only *in* someone's memory, God's or thereupon ours, and that the future is analogously there only in someone's anticipatory consciousness, whereas the present is there not only *in* the mind but *for* the mind.[43] This Augustinian position has ruled unchallenged in the modern period, and most tyrannically of all in the "postmodern" period, supposing that there is such a thing. It is nonetheless an error.

The error might be disclosed by acknowledging that *all* things—past, present, or future—exist only as they are in the mind of God, so that the present is not in this respect privileged over against past or future. The difference between past, present, and future is not that the present is given both to and in mind, whereas past and future are given only in mind. The difference between past, present, and future is their difference *within* the mind of God and so within the created reality God posits.

But acknowledging this point revises our conception of the divine mind. Our basic fault is to think of God as a universal "transcendental unity of apperception"[44]

---

42. E.g., in Palamas, *Triads* III,1,10–13; 16–19; 3,26–27.
43. See, e.g., Jean McWilliam, "Augustine's Struggle with Time and History," *Atti del Congresso*, ed. G. Lawless (Rome: Augustinianum, 1987), 997–1012.
44. The conceptual lineage is, of course, the other way around.

and of time as the line seen from this point of unity. On this conception, God is eternal in that for the divine mind's eye all points on the line of time are equidistant.[45] For a created image of the divine unity of apperception, for a transcendental unity of apperception *on* the time line, the line flattens out. Then you have the situation supposed for creatures, in which the present becomes a geometrical present and as such is privileged as fully *there*, and in which past and future are *not* "present" but are "receding" or "approaching."

But the unity of the real God's mind is not that of a transcendental *point* at which lines of perception converge; nor, therefore, is anyone else's. God's cognition is the structured converse between Father, Spirit, and Son, in which the difference of source, goal, and mediation is antecedent.

Time is because the Spirit is not the Father, and because both meet in the Son. Time is because God is his own origin and *as* such is *not* his goal; because God is his own goal and *as* such is *not* the "natural" result of his own being as origin; because origin and goal in God are an irreversibly ordered pair; and because Father and Spirit meet and are reconciled in the Son. Time is what happens when the Holy Spirit comes, from the Father and to the Son.

Time and personal being are therefore very far from mutually external. Time is the inner horizon of the life of that one in whom all things live and move and have their being. Our time, we may even say, is the accommodation God makes for us in his own triune life. Time is therefore at once a communal phenomenon and the inner horizon of a personal consciousness: it occurs in that *meeting* occurs in God, between Father, Son, and Spirit; and it occurs in that Father, Son, and Spirit are the one God within whose creative subjectivity all things are posited.

Time is neither circular nor linear. God the Father is indeed the beginning of time and God the Spirit the goal of time, so that time is constituted by before and after, by the great irreversible arrow.[46] Time does not circle to make before and after relative. But neither is time simply the line on which before and after may be located. Father and Spirit are but one God; their oneness, moreover, is achieved by *reconciliation* and not in mere sequence. Time is the identity in difference of what is and what must be.

Time, one may rather say, is implosive. The Spirit's coming opens every established present reality for a future that does not simply result from it yet is its own true future. Thereby the Spirit sets each established present reality into the past of the next moment that does not bind that moment, yet is truly *its* past.

I have made few referenced drafts on particular theologians, but at this point one is unavoidable. In his treatise on God's eternity, Karl Barth specified the particular eternity of the triune God as "pure duration." What makes God's duration "pure" is that in it "beginning, succession and end . . . do not fall apart," that "between source, movement and goal there is no conflict but only peace." Source,

---

45. Which, of course, gives the famous Platonic circle of time, try to fudge this point as Christian Platonists may.

46. Relativity theory, by the way, does not challenge this. The slowing and accelerating of time relative to different inertial frames does not produce reversals of "causal" before-and-after.

movement, and goal "are not, however, distinguished because in eternity there are no such differences."[47]

If the infinity of God's time is rightly described by Barth, then what our finitude, our location *on* the time line, means is not that past and future are not *there* for us, but that they are not there in mutual peace. It is not that our grasp of temporal reality is not a grasp of past, present, and future in their mutual givenness, but that there are *disruptions* in it. The extent of the specious present is not in our control; pieces of temporal actuality do get away from us altogether, pending the eschaton; and most of the past is indeed *fixed* most of the time, though grace, which *forgives* what has been and turns its curse into blessing, even now can repair this disruption.

Finally, time and events are therefore not external to each other. Time is our accommodation within the event of the Father's and the Spirit's meeting in the life of the Son. If this event did not happen to the world, the world would be timeless. The relation of other events to this one is their location in time. Thus the mediation of past and present is not at all a mediation of something absent to something present. That is, it is not a matter of keeping the past moving up the line, of trying to keep the past in range of the present.

All these determinants come together, as God himself comes together, in the proposition: time is *narrative* in its own reality. The question has faced us at every step. How can *anticipation* be the great causal connection? How can the church know herself and in knowing herself guard her self-identity, *by* looking to what is yet to come of her? How can it be that the Exodus does not get further away as time "goes on"? The questions seem difficult because we assume that the story of the church is spread out on a line that is not itself a narrative. But this is a false assumption.

V

The church can and must discover and practice her temporal continuity as *dramatic* continuity, the kind of continuity that constitutes Aristotle's good stories. Looking forward at any time of historical challenge, the church cannot decide in advance what she must become; she cannot manipulate the Spirit's daily advent. She can neither faithfully wish thus to bind the future, nor hope to succeed if she attempts it. Yet after every large or small or partial step of change or resistance to change, she can look back and recognize that given the whole history of the church to this moment, this was what had to happen. Or she can look back and recognize that this is what had not to happen and must be repented.

So we may move to a final and most drastic key to all the questions of the dialogues: the church *is* the world's historical continuity. As the temporal community established in the Eucharist, and thereby in the death to which the Father gives the Son and in the resurrection of the Son by the Spirit, the church's own particular historical continuity is the creation's participation in the difference and

47. Karl Barth, *Kirchliche Dogmatik,* II/I (Zurich: Zollikon, 1940), 685–86, 690.

unity of the Father and the Spirit, in the difference and unity of all things' origin and goal. The church does not have to find continuity within the world's time, for apart from the world's participation in the church the world has no time. Rather, the church finds historical continuity for the world, as the church's members come from the world bringing worldly elements to be the body of the Son, and return as that body on the Father's mission to the world.

When the world exists simply apart from the church, it has no history. When the world has not yet encountered the church it lives in historical innocence; even the great Greek historians had no inkling of the abyss into which every new moment opens, into which all hope can vanish and from which alone hope can appear. When the world, once temporalized, then insists on living apart from the church, its history immediately deconstructs.

The church need not by its structures *establish* its own continuity within the world's time. In that the church occurs at all, it is a historical body, a structured before and after. Apart from the occurrence of the church, the world has no time in which the church might establish itself. Therefore, the church has no need to fear its essential historicality and its essentially institutional character; the church does not borrow institutionalization from the world, the world borrows it from the church. If the church confesses herself as "holy" she may freely acknowledge also her institutionalization as holy, as no mere contrivance for self-preservation.

We may finally ask why Protestantism so persistently finds it intolerable to say that the church is an active subject of God's saving work, despite repeated experience that on analysis the position melts into its opposite. A common supposition makes the Protestant position necessary: Catholics and Protestants alike think of the church and individual believers as inhabiting a temporality to which the risen Son is intrinsically alien.

If the succession of the individual's life is plotted on a sort of *neutral* time line, which would run as it runs whether or not the risen Lord were before the Father in the Spirit, and if the same is true of the succession of the church's history, then indeed the various interactions between the church-community and the individual are but "human works." When we apprehend reality so, we are ineluctably faced with the Protestant-Catholic dilemma. We can honor the uniquely salvific action of the risen Lord by placing no faith in the church's interactions with its members. Or we can honor what Scripture clearly says about the church by tortured formulations on the old Pelagian lines. "Of course only Christ saves—*but on the other hand* there must be some role for the church." The dilemma is false.

VI

Now it would be possible to work back through the problems from early chapters, showing how their resolutions may be illumined or enabled by deeper appropriation of the Christian God's specificity. But it would also be tedious, anticlimactic, and, I have come to think while writing, unauthentic. I cannot by this book create the "new depth of faith" for which such puzzles will not only be soluble—as they already are, I think, mostly solved in the previous chapters—but which will integrate the solutions spiritually. At the very best, I can hope to have performed a sort of intellectual evocation of that faith around its most decisive determinants. That I do hope.

A church that comes to look forward to God as clearly as it looks back to him, and that thus experiences the temporal unity of its own communal self as the personal unity of the risen Son, will know how its pastors can be authoritative teachers without being tyrannical, and will know how to counter clerical tyranny when it appears. It will know how things that come into being within its history can belong to the foundation of that history, and know how to tell the difference between such emergents and perversions or adiaphora. It will know how to offer sacrifice without claiming merit of its own. It will know how to honor holy things without making them into fetishes.

The task of interpreting our culture's antecedent God by the gospel will never be done, so long as our line of the gospel's history continues—as this, of course, must be true for *any* line of the gospel's history. Should we be so blessed as to become the church of the preceding paragraph, we will surely only discover some new and yet deeper task of understanding God and experience churchly disasters unpredictable now, if we lag in that task. Perhaps, however, we will be able to struggle with them around one table of the Lord. Or perhaps the Lord will come before any of these things happen. Then he will find us still divided, and surely our joy will be mixed with sheer embarrassment.

Indexes

Name Index

149

Subject Index

Index of Dialogues and Responses

DATE DUE

JAN 15 '95			
JAN 15 '96			
MAY 14 1996			
JUL 12 '97			
FEB 18 '99			